中国功能语言学研究会
CHINA ASSOCIATION OF FUNCTIONAL LINGUISTICS

中国英汉语篇分析研究会

U0865578

第 7 辑

功能语言学与语篇分析研究

Studies in Functional Linguistics and Discourse Analysis（VII）

主　编　黄国文

副主编　朱永生
　　　　张德禄
　　　　杨信彰

高等教育出版社·北京

图书在版编目（CIP）数据

功能语言学与语篇分析研究．第七辑 / 黄国文主编．-- 北京 ：高等教育出版社，2019.1
ISBN 978-7-04-050942-7

Ⅰ．①功… Ⅱ．①黄… Ⅲ．①功能（语言学）—文集 ②语言分析—文集 Ⅳ．①H0-53

中国版本图书馆CIP数据核字(2018)第294366号

GONGNENGYUYANXUE YU YUPIANFENXI YANJIU

策划编辑 贾巍巍　　责任编辑 王代军　　封面设计 杨立新
责任校对 张　凯　　版式设计 孙　伟　　责任印制 刘思涵

出版发行	高等教育出版社	网　址	http://www.hep.edu.cn
社　址	北京市西城区德外大街4号		http://www.hep.com.cn
邮政编码	100120	网上订购	http://www.hepmall.com.cn
印　刷	山东百润本色印刷有限公司		http://www.hepmall.com
开　本	787mm×1092mm 1/16		http://www.hepmall.cn
印　张	14.75	版　次	2019年1月第1版
字　数	311千字		
购书热线	010-58581118	印　次	2019年1月第1次印刷
咨询电话	400-810-0598	定　价	42.00元

物 料 号　50942-00

《功能语言学与语篇分析研究》编委会

此书献给系统功能语言学创始人
韩礼德（1925年4月13日—2018年4月15日）

纪念韩礼德

In Memory of M. A. K. Halliday

韩礼德（Michael Alexander Kirkwood Halliday）1925年4月13日生于英国里兹，2018年4月15日在澳大利亚悉尼逝世，享年93岁。这是语言学界的重大损失。

韩礼德教授曾经为中国的抗日战争事业做出过积极贡献，其语言学研究又开始于中国，他的大半生始终对中国怀有特殊的感情；我国改革开放以后，他不仅培养了一批中国系统功能语言学研究的先行者，还多次前来中国为年轻后学授课、讲学，并一贯给予积极提携和激励；晚年，他和夫人韩茹凯（Ruqaiya Hasan）教授以出资人的身份，支持在中国成立了“韩礼德—韩茹凯语言学国际基金”。他对当代中国语言学事业的发展与繁荣做出了卓越贡献。

我们怀着深深的敬意和无限悲痛的心情，惟愿韩礼德教授在天之灵安息！

中国英汉语比较研究会功能语言学专业委员会

中国英汉语比较研究会英汉语篇分析专业委员会

韩礼德—韩茹凯语言学国际基金

2018年4月15日

目录

语篇分析与教学研究

四十不惑：第40届国际系统功能语言学大会（代前言）

黄国文

华南农业大学

1. 引言

“四十不惑”的说法来自孔子的“吾十有五而志于学，三十而立，四十而不惑，五十而知天命，六十而耳顺，七十而从心所欲不逾矩。”（《论语·为政篇》）。四十不惑有多种解释，其一是：一个人活到四十岁，有了很多经历，也有了自己的判断力，明了过去的所作所为，也知道以后该怎样做；“惑”是被迷惑的意思。四十不惑是指：人到了40岁以后，应该明白自己要做的事。

做个类比：国际系统功能语言学大会（International Systemic Functional Congress，ISFC）经历了40个春秋，也到了“不惑”之年。第40届大会于2013年7月15—19日在广州召开，由中山大学承办，意义深远。对于我个人来说，它了却了一个多年的心愿。自从1996年1月我从英国回到中山大学工作，就一直盼望着有机会在广州召开一次国际系统功能语言学大会。多年的愿望得以实现，现在我也就不在乎举办此次会议所经历的酸甜苦辣和个人的得失了。当年从英国返回，正好四十岁，也是不惑之年。

在这次大会上，Robin P. Fawcett教授做了一个题为“Forty Years Back, Forty Years Forward: A Brief History of the Major Concepts and the Social Structures of Systemic Functional Linguistics, with a Look Ahead to the Future”（过去四十年，未来四十年——系统功能语言学的主要概念发展简史及其社交结构）的大会报告，这大概也是系统功能语言学的“四十不惑”吧。

2. 关于ISFC40

国际系统功能语言学大会的前身是Robin P. Fawcett于1974年在英国（Walsall, England）组织的“系统语言学工作坊”（Systemic Workshop）。为了适应学科发展的需要和扩大学术影响，几十年中前辈学者几易其名：1974—1981：系统语言学工作坊；1982—1987：国际系统语言学工作坊（International Systemic Workshop）；1988—1991：国际系统语言学大会（International Systemic Congress）；1992至今：国际系统功能语言学大会（International Systemic Functional Congress）。

第一至第八届会议在英国召开（West Midlands College; University of Essex; University of Nottingham; Hatfield Polytechnic; University of East Anglia; UWIST, Cardiff; University of Sheffield; University of Birmingham）；1982年走出英国，先后在各大洲和地区举办：1982年：York University, Toronto；1983年和1984年回到英国（University of Nottingham; University of Stirling）。以后的情况如下：1985年：University of Michigan, Ann Abor；1986年：University of Kent, Canterbury；1987年：Sydney University；1988年：Michigan State University, East Lansing；1989年：Helsinki University；1990年：University of Stirling；1991年：Christian University, Tokyo；1992年：Macquarie University；1993年：Victoria University, BC；1994年：Ghent University；1995年：北京大学；1996年：University of Technology Sydney；1997年：York University, Toronto；1998年：University of Wales, Cardiff；1999年：National University of Singapore；2000年：Melbourne University；2001年：Ottawa University；2002年：Liverpool University；2003年：University of Lucknow；2004年：Doshisha University, Kyoto；2005年：Sydney University；2006：São Paolo University；2007年：Southern University of Denmark；2008年：Macquarie University；2009年：清华大学（北京）；2010年：University of British Columbia；2011年：Lisbon University；2012年：University of Technology Sydney；2013年：中山大学（广州）；2014年：Universidad Nacional de Cuyo, Mendoza；2015年： RWTH Aachen University。中国承办过三届大会：1995，北京大学（召集人：胡壮麟）；2009，清华大学（召集人：方琰）；2013：中山大学（召集人：黄国文、常晨光）。

按照过去10多年来的约定，会议轮流在欧洲、大洋洲、亚洲、美洲召开。2009年在亚洲的会议由中国清华大学承办。按照常规，2013年的会议应该由另一个亚洲国家承办。但正如我在“人生处处皆选择”中所说，“由于中国在国际上的地位和影响力的不断提高，中国学者的国际活动参与意识不断增强，也由于中山大学这些年在系统功能语言学研究与应用方面所做出的成绩和贡献，国际影响越来越高，所以中山大学破例获得了2013年的ISFC40承办权。当然，由于这次的申办多少有些特殊，所以结果公布后，有个别知名学者对这个决定公开表达了不同意见。”当时我们申请这个会议，有很多“高大上”的理由，我个人也有个“自私”的想法：如果2013年的会议不在中山大学召开，那我在中山大学做教授期间就应该不会有承办大会的机会了。在我看来，承办这个会议是对系统功能语言学发展的重大贡献的一种表现。承办这个会议，要提前三年向执行委员会提出申请，然后由该委员会决定是否给予举办权，这与体育界申办奥运会的性质一样，都要提出申办报告和对申办情况进行说明。此次会议对中国、对中山大学和对我个人都有非常重要的意义。现在回想起来，我们努力争取这次机会的确获得了执行理事会的理解和支持。至于会议的有关情况，陈瑜敏、严小庆在“系统功能语言学研究路径的拓宽和互补——第40届国际系统功能语言学大会综述”已有介绍，这里不再赘述。

3. 中国功能语言学研究会

关于中国功能语言学研究会的成立背景，我曾多次提到过。在1995年7月北京大学召开的第四届全国功能语言学研讨会暨第22届国际系统功能语言学大会之前，经当时的国家教委高教司和季羡林先生领导的中国外语教学研究会的批准，成立“中国高校功能语法教学研究会”，选举了理事会，胡壮麟任会长，朱永生、任绍曾、方琰三人任副会长。这个研究会是挂靠在“中国英语教学研究会”的下属机构，而中国英语教学研究会隶属于“中国外语教学研究会”。

自1995年至2003年，研究会会长由胡壮麟教授担任，2003年在秦皇岛燕山大学召开的第八届全国功能语言学会议的研究会理事会上，胡壮麟教授考虑到他本人年事已高，事务繁忙，加之国内已形成一支强大的研究队伍，提议我接任会长，得到了理事会的支持。

研究会成立之初，使用了“中国高校功能语法教学研究会”名称，后来经理事会讨论，参照别的研究会的做法，最后使用了“中国功能语言学研究会”这个称谓。

中国高校功能语法教学研究会成立以后，一直主办着两年一次的全国功能语言学研讨会。据胡壮麟教授回忆，研究会成立之后，发起召开第一届“全国话语分析研讨会”的任绍曾教授与胡壮麟教授商定，把两年一次的全国话语（语篇）分析研讨会交给该研究会“托管”。这样，两个隔年召开的全国性的学术研讨会基本上是轮流召开。就最近几年的情况看，2013年7月在中山大学召开第13届功能语言学研讨会（与第40届国际系统功能语言学大会合并），2014年9月在长安大学（西安）召开第14届语篇分析研讨会，2015年4月在北京师范大学召开第14届功能语言学研讨会，2016年10月在宁波大学召开第15届语篇分析研讨会。

4. 英汉语篇分析专业委员会

10年前，尽管全国性的话语（语篇）分析研讨会基本上是隔年召开一次，但活动的主办单位是中国功能语言学研究会。

2006年11月在山东烟台鲁东大学召开的中国英汉语比较研究会（国家民政部注册和主管的一级学会）的常务理事会上，我带头申请设立二级学会（专业委员会）“中国英汉语比较研究会英汉语篇分析专业委员会”，得到杨自俭老会长和潘文国新会长等学会主要人物的大力支持，得以批准。在2007年4月的第十届全国功能语言学研讨会（江西师范大学，南昌）开幕式（2007年4月12日）上，时任中国英汉语比较研究会会长的潘文国教授向媒体宣布了这一振奋人心的消息。

考虑到中国功能语言学和语篇分析的教学和研究团队的教育背景与研究兴趣等实际情况，英汉语篇分析专业委员会与中国功能语言学研究会在实际操作中是一帮人马“两顶帽子”，每年举办一次会议：要么是“功能语言学”，要么是“语篇分析”，讨论的主要是功能语言学与语篇（话语）分析方面的各种问题；对于很多人来说，不会特别去区分某一年是功能语言学研讨会还是语篇（话语）分析研讨会。当然，对于会议组织者来说，是哪一种、哪一届会议，他们是非常清楚的。

5. 功能语言学专业委员会

大概是2013年，有一个来自官方的说法：国家要求正式的学术团体机构认真做好自我检查工作，并清理一些不规范的学术团体；一级学会下面的二级学会只能称“专业委员会”，下面不再设立三级“研究会”或其他机构。按照这一精神，中国功能语言学研究会这个团体就必须重新注册找个“婆家”。这件事涉及很多问题，我和研究会的有关人员经过多次讨论、商量和沟通，决定由彭宣维教授带头寻找合适的挂靠机构，最终确定申请挂靠中国英汉语比较研究会。中国英汉语比较研究会于2015年4月18—19日在杭州浙江财经大学召开的第6届理事会上接受了中国功能语言学研究会作为该会二级学会的申请，同时更名为“中国英汉语比较研究会功能语言学专业委员会”。

在2015年4月23—26日第14届全国功能语言学研讨会期间，原中国功能语言学研究会（现中国英汉语比较研究会功能语言学专业委员会）和中国英汉语比较研究会英汉语篇分析专业委员会召开理事会，正式公布原中国功能语言学研究会领导的“分流”情况：

中国英汉语比较研究会功能语言学专业委员会
名誉会长：胡壮麟、方琰
会长：彭宣维
副会长：朱永生、张德禄、杨信彰、王振华、严世清
秘书长：于晖
副秘书长：刘承宇

中国英汉语比较研究会英汉语篇分析专业委员会
名誉会长：任绍曾、杨忠
会长：黄国文

副会长：常晨光、李战子、刘世生、苗兴伟
秘书长：何伟

之所以要“分流”，是因为原先的中国功能语言学研究会不存在了，取而代之的是两个专业委员会，而按照有关规定，专业委员会的会长人数不能太多，并且不宜在别的专业委员会中重复任职。这次“分流”前有关人员的讨论和商量，充分体现了中国政治中的“协商民主”，一切决定都是在民主协商的基础上做出的。

在2015年4月23日晚上的理事会上，中国高校功能语法教学研究会创会会长胡壮麟教授出席会议并做了重要讲话；大家都表示，尽管“一分为二”了，但大家还会团结一致、同心同德，要把功能语言学和语篇分析的研究做得更好。“分流”的工作是在友好、轻松的氛围中完成的。我个人也颇感欣慰：当年胡壮麟教授把充满活力、团结友好的中国功能语言学研究会交给我，今天我把同样充满活力、团结友好的团体成功“分流”了，把“功能语言学”机构的“椅子”完好地交给了彭宣维教授。

6. 结语

我于2003年接任中国功能语言学研究会会长后，尽了最大的努力做了一些有益的工作，也记录了中国功能语言学研究者的一些工作和成绩，有关情况可参见我为《功能语言学与语篇分析研究》（第1—6辑）写的“代前言”以及“中国的系统功能语言学研究：发展与展望”（黄国文，2009）、“Challenges of Developing SFL in China”（黄国文，2011）、“Foreword：Systemic Functional Linguistics Studies in China”（黄国文，2016）、Zhang, McDonald, Fang & Huang（张德禄等，2005）和Huang & Wang（黄国文、王红阳，2010）等文章中的有关描述。

《功能语言学与语篇分析研究》丛刊的出版，得到了高等教育出版社的大力支持，尤其要特别感谢的是贾巍先生，是他主动跟我说到要为中国功能语言学的教学与研究出版这个丛刊的。

我想借此机会，感谢这些年在不同方面帮助我为中国功能语言学的发展而做出努力的所有学者和朋友：是你们的关心、鼓励、支持、帮助，让我做成了一件又一件有意义的事情。

“忘记过去就意味着背叛”这句人们常引的话，是谁首先说出来的已经不重要了；重要的是我们要记住过去，尊重过去，总结经验教训，以此审视现在、展望未来。在过去10多年里，我一直通过各种文集书刊的“前言”和“后语”记录着中国功能语言学的教学与研究的发展状况。我希望，今后有其他人来续上这项工作；毕竟，总结和梳理学术研究历程也是一个事业，也需要薪火相传。

参考文献

陈瑜敏、严小庆，2014，系统功能语言学研究路径的拓宽和互补——第 40 届国际系统功能语言学大会综述，《中国外语》第 1 期。

黄国文，2009，中国的系统功能语言学研究：发展与展望，载庄智象主编《中国外语教育发展战略论坛》。上海：上海外语教育出版社。

黄国文，2011，Challenges of Developing SFL in China。《当代外语研究》第 12 期。

黄国文，2016，人生处处皆选择，《当代外语研究》第 1 期。

黄国文（Huang Guowen），2016，Foreword: Systemic Functional Linguistics Studies in China, In J. J. Webster and X.W. Peng (eds.), *Applying Systemic Functional Linguistics in China*. London: Bloomsbury Academic.

黄国文、王红阳（Huang Guowen & Wang Hongyang），2010，SFL Studies in the Chinese Context. In C. Wu, C.M.I.M. Matthiessen and M. Herke (eds.) *Proceedings of ISFC 35: Voices Around the World, Volume 2*.

张德禄、马爱德、方琰、黄国文（Zhang Delu, Edward McDonald, Fang Yan & Huang Guowen），2005，The Development of Systemic Functional Linguistics in China, In Ruqaiya Hasan, Christian Matthiessen and Jonathan Webster (eds.), *Continuing Discourse on Language: A Functional Perspective*. London: Equinox.

后记

上面这个“代前言”是2015年末写的，距今已经有三年了。这三年，发生了很多变化，我也于2016年调离中山大学，到华南农业大学开拓生态语言学研究。

有很多事情可以在这里补充，但我想就补充两点：

（一）中国英汉语比较研究会英汉语篇分析专业委员会和中国英汉语比较研究会功能语言学专业委员会的班子成员有了变动。（1）2016年10月在宁波大学召开的第15届全国语篇分析研讨会期间召开的理事会上，补选何伟教授为英汉语篇分析专业委员会副会长，该会的秘书长改为杨炳钧教授担任，同时增补陈旸教授为副秘书长。（2）2017年6月底7月初在贵州师范大学召开的第15届全国功能语言学研讨会期间，功能语言学专业委员会同意朱永生教授因年龄关系提出辞去副会长的要求，增补于晖教授为副会长，该会的秘书长改为刘承宇教授，增补杨延宁教授为副秘书长。

（二）国际系统功能语言学2014—2018年的召开情况（地点和召集人）是：第41届（2014年）：National University of Cuyo, Mendoza, Argentina (Cristina Boccia et al.)，第42届（2015年）：Aachen University, Aachen, Germany (Stella Neumann et al.)，第43届（2016年）：Indonesia University of Education, Bandung, Indonesia (Emi Emila)，第44届（2017年）：University of Wollongong, Wollongong, Australia (Pauline Jones)，第45届（2018年）：Boston College, Boston, USA (Maria Brisk)。

黄国文

2018年4月5日于华南农业大学外国语学院

第40届国际系统功能语言学大会开幕式致辞

胡壮麟

北京大学

Dear Professor Michael Halliday,
Dear Professor Guowen Huang, Chairman of ISFC,
Distinguished guests, scholars and participants,
Ladies and Gentlemen,

On this great occasion of the opening of the 40th ISFC, together with the launch of Sun Yat-sen University's Michael Halliday Library and the publication of the journal *Functional Linguistics*, you can't imagine how excited I am, especially to come to this campus where Halliday had been studying about 60 years ago. And now with all these activities I witness the return of Michael Halliday to this campus.

First, I will talk about my participation in ISFC's congresses. I had chances to attend the 14th ISFC held in Sydney in 1987, the 16th ISFC held in Helsinki in 1988, the 20th ISFC held in Victoria Canada in 1993, and the 26th ISFC held in Singapore in 1999.

So far as China is concerned, I was honored to host the 22nd ISFC held at Peking University in 1995, to cooperate with Professor Fang Yan to sponsor the 36th ISFC with held at Tsinghua University in 2009, and now attend the 40th ISFC sponsored by Professor Huang Guowen in Sun Yat-sen University. I sincerely hope when China is luckily enough to sponsor the conference several years later, I would be still healthy enough to follow the step of Professor Halliday and be present to meet all of you again.

At this point, I can't help mentioning that I am here with my teacher Prof. Halliday again this morning. It is Michael who brought me to this big family of ISFC. I still remember when I first talked to Michael Halliday in his office in January 1979, I told him friendly and naively that I planned to do Chomsky's TG Grammar. Michael answered me frankly that he did not know much about it. I simply knew nothing about the academic confrontation between the two approaches! Then I said I wanted to do London School. At that time, I also had no knowledge about the historic and theoretical connection among London School, Neo-Firthian Linguistics and Systemic Functional Linguistics. After all these were turned down, I started to do Systemic Functional Linguistics.

Anyway, I have witnessed the development of Systemic Functional Linguistics since then. Today, Michael would be happy to find that, apart from his work, the systemicists in China are also quite familiar with Hasan's generic structure potential, Fawcett's Cardiff School, Martin's Sydney School, Matthiessen's Cartography and other contributions made by systemicists in Australia, Britain, Canada, the United States and elsewhere. Today Systemic Functional Linguistics research has developed in various directions and made contributions to various fields from the end of last century to the present day.

Now, allow me to skip over the well-known concepts of transitivity, the three metafunctions, contexts and texts, etc. I would like to mention some new developments in SFL. Halliday remarked as early as 1973 "the internal organization of language is not arbitrary but embodies a positive reflection of the functions that the language has evolved to serve in the life of social man." This helps us understand that it is Michael who has on the one hand realized Saussure's founding insights: that semiotics is "the science of the life of science in society", and, on the other hand, further remarked creatively that meanings and semiotics are shaped by the relations of power. Following Halliday's unyielding work, we now have social semiotics by Robert Hodge, Gunther Kress, van Leuween and others as well. At the turn of the new century, we have been amazed by the work done by Jay Lemke, Paul Thibault and others that we have begun to see the study of meaning from social ecological perspective, the system of which conveys not only the traditional link between concept and sound image, but also the role of social man, object, context, time, culture, etc. in reflecting the world from various perspectives. This finally leads to the development of social ecological semiotics today.

In the development of text linguistics and discourse analysis, it was Fowler, Hodge and Fairclough who managed to apply Michael's views in appraisal theory and critical discourse analysis at the ideological level. This has pushed forward the work of discourse analysis, text linguistics, varieties of language, stylistics, etc. Here, I would mention the work of James Martin on PDA (1999, 2004). As emphasized by Martin, in communication, we should also learn how to use language properly to get problems solved in our life and live harmoniously.

Linguistics, although a branch of semiotics, dominated the semiotic scholarship in the last century, as represented by structuralism, generativism, functionalism, and cognitivism. Today we have come to see that meaning can be communicated by multiple modes, such as sound, image, picture, touch, smell, etc., and now we have multimodal linguistics and multimodal semiotics. It goes without saying Michael's insights have played an active and influential role in this new domain of knowledge pursuit.

Michael Halliday is one of the early pioneers of transdisciplinary research. In 1990 Michael Halliday explored the nature of theme-based research as well as complexity in the history of intelligence. According to his illustration,

— academic work in the early period of Europe was marked by the study of mathematics;

— the study of the natural law was the theme of knowledge research in the 18th century, which put the dynamic perspective within the synoptic perspective;

— the theme of 19th century was shown by historical transition, which took the form of "evolution" or "change", and was seen as the adoption of dynamic perspective;

— the theme of the 20th century in academic research is structuralism, which studied the law of any phenomenon autonomously, and thus returned to the synoptic perspective.

From the end of the 20th century to the present, Halliday further argued that the study of knowledge structure should be theme-based, which covers both how things are organized and how things have been changing. Thus we need both the synoptic perspective and the dynamic perspective. Halliday also noticed the complementarity between transdisciplinarity and the 3 metafunctions of systemic functional theory. Halliday knows quite well to apply his theme-based notion of transdiciplinarity to the study of educational linguistics, which deals with grammar, language planning, language strategies, the difference between FLT and ESP, etc. Following Michael's guidance, we also have Ruqaiya Hasan's comparative study of code and consciousness as well as her elaboration of synoptic and dynamic approaches. Jim Martin, Francis Christie, Eija Ventola, Claire Painter and many others have been doing well on the study of the relation among language, knowledge and education, which is a wonderful illustration of how SFL's Sydney School has made contribution to language education by means of transdisciplinary research.

In face of all the new orientations as well as problems or complexities in our research, it was Halliday again, at the turn of this century, stood out and introduced the notion of "appliable linguistics", which summarizes the work of systemicists in the past decades and informs us of what is the guiding principle of judging the value of our work and points out the right direction of our work in the new century.

Now allow me to shift to the work of Chinese systemicists. Apart from the many Chinese scholars attending the ISFCs held in different years and in different parts of the world, the Chinese systemicists have kept running the national conferences, systemic weeks and high-level forums biannually. I'd like particularly to mention some latest developments.

With an increase in returned scholars trained abroad as well as new PhD and MA graduates in China every year, we can find more universities well known for their teaching and research in Systemic Functional Linguistics, such as Sun Yat-sen University, Beijing Normal University, Xiamen University, China University of Science and Technology, Tongji University, Tsinghua University, Peking University, Shanghai Jiaotong University, Nanjing University of International Relations, Northeast Normal University, etc.

In the past decade, in addition to the increasing papers of SF linguists in Chinese academic journals, more SFL publications can be found in China. Peking University Press has published Michael Halliday's ten-volume collected works edited by Jonathan Webster in 2007. Shanghai Jiaotong University Press has published Martin's eight-volume collected works in 2012. Beijing Foreign Language Teaching and Research Press has published Ruqaiya Hasan's *Selected Works on Applied Linguistics* in 2011.

As for the work of Chinese systemicists, apart from the biannual proceedings of the selected collections of papers from each conference, I would like first to mention Prof. Yang Xueyan's publication *Modelling Text as Process: A Dynamic Approach to EFL Classroom Discourse* published by Continuum in 2010. In mainland China, the textbook *Introduction to Systemic Functional Grammar*, and later the second version *Introduction to Systemic Functional Linguistics* co-authored by myself, Zhu Yongsheng, Zhang Delu and Li Zhanzi was published by Peking University Press in 2005. Peking University Press also published *Systemic Functional Grammar: The Cardiff School*, co-authored by Huang Guowen, He Wei, Liao Chuyan in 2008. Under the co-editorship of Huang Guowen and Xin Zhiying, *The Study of Systemic Functional Linguistics: Present and Past* was published by Foreign Language Teaching and Research Press in May, 2012. This collection of papers is a comprehensive review of the work done not only by Halliday but also by his students and systemicists elsewhere. I would like to point out that the Chinese contributors of these books are of different ages, old, middle and young. This guarantees the continuation and constancy of Systemic Functional Linguistics research in China. Accompanying these books, I am glad to learn that Jonathan Webster and Peng Xuanwei are working together on a new book, which will focus on the creative work done by Chinese systemicists.

Finally, if we open our eyes wide, we will find Chinese systemicists have also been playing an active role in the study of language education and FLT, semiotics, stylistics, discourse analysis, cognitive linguistics, computational linguistics, multimodal linguistics, etc. In a word, Halliday's call on appliable linguistics will no doubt serve as the guiding principle of the future world of SFL in China.

Wish the 40th ISFC a great success.

定型表述的功能句法分析

李战子

解放军国际关系学院

1. 引言

文化定型的研究由来已久，文化定型话语在当今的社会政治话语甚至日常文化话语中此消彼长，这是由定型的认知特征决定的。定型化的过程亟待研究，由于定型主要涉及对“他者”的看法，对定型重新评价有助于我们发掘当代社会歧视和偏见的根源，但由于它是一个跨越社会学、社会心理学、文化史、心理分析和后殖民理论的跨学科领域（Pickering, 2001），在语言学研究中反而不多见了。本文认为从功能句法考察文化定性，有助于我们对其保持觉察，并且对跨文化交际话语中的文化定型有更为清晰的认知。

2. 有关文化定型表述的代表性理论

定型的词典定义比较简单，指的是简化的或标准化的某个概念，通常是一个人群拥有的对另一个人群的看法，定型可以是约定俗成的，或者简化的，出发点就是假设另一群人具有一些共同的特质。定型可以是肯定或否定的，通常是我们对于自己不属于的那个群体所做的概述，我们将人群根据种族、民族、宗教、性别、年龄等等各种范畴进行分群分类。

研究者会把定型和意识形态联系起来。例如，Scollon & Scollon（2000：155）指出，“定型只是过度概括的另外一种说法，但和过度概括不同的是，定型还带有意识形态的定位。一个群体的特征不仅被过度概括到群体中每一个成员的身上，而且这些特征还被夸张地赋予了肯定或否定的价值。这些价值接着又被当做论据来支持各群体中的成员们之间的社会或政治关系。”他们还指出，“定型大体来说是意识形态的，在定型后面通常有一些精确的文化观察所得的东西，这些观察的结论本身是否正确并不是问题，问题在于：定型使我们对一个个体的性格或行为中其他同样重要的方面视而不见了，之所以说定型局限了我们对人类行为和跨文化话语的理解，是因为它们让我们满足于把人类行为中几个突出的方面当成是整个图景。此外，它们在意识形态上允许那些拥有更大的政治权势的人对一些个体和群体采取歧视的对待。”（ibid：156）

定型还可以从评价语义上加以区分，简单地分为肯定和否定。例如Scollon & Scollon就区分了肯定和否定的定型（ibid：158-159），它们的由来和问题是不同的，否定的定型步骤更为复杂。首先，在单一的维度上对比两个文化或两群人。例如：在引入论题时，所有的亚洲人都是归纳型的，所有的西方人都是推理型的。实际考察一下亚洲人和西方人，这个论断是有一定依据的，但它忽略了一个事实，即在很多情况下，亚洲人也会用推理的策略，而西方人也常用归纳的策略。

接着把这个人工的和意识形态上的不同当作交际上的问题。

第三步是为一个策略或群体赋予一个肯定的价值，而为另一个策略或群体赋予一个否定的价值。这时候，一个西方人可能就会说：亚洲人和西方人的跨文化交际问题在于“他们”拒绝以我们能理解的方式引入论题。这个本来纯粹是描述上的区别导致人们认为另一个群体的人是有意为之的，使理解成为困难。

第四步也是最后一步，重新概述这个过程并运用到整个群体，这些特征被认为是种属的（generic）或者种族的特征。

肯定的定型问题出在把各个群体的所有成员看成是等同的。无论肯定还是否定，定型化的问题出在把对比建立在单一的、两分的（非此即彼的）分析维度上。

本文从5部学术著作[1]中采集文化定型表述，并运用功能句法的范畴进行区分描述，以讨论其种类和复杂性。

3. 定型表述的功能句法分类

3.1 定型与名词化

名词词组有比较稳定的逻辑结构，表示逻辑语义关系，其中心概念是修饰和被修饰的关系。名词词组具有复杂的经验结构，即指示语、数量语、修饰语、类别语和事物（胡壮麟等, 2005：235）。出现在定型表述中的名词短语大多为“事物”本身，或者“类别和事物”，如：南方（中国）人、北方人、亚裔美国人等等；如果再带上修饰语，则名词短语本身就可能蕴含了一个定型表述，如：丑陋的中国人、勤劳勇敢的中国人等。

1 即 Ting-Toomey, Stella & Chung, Leeva. 2004. *Understanding Intercultural Communication*. Oxford：Oxford University Press.Tregidgo, P.S. 1972. *A Background to English*. London：Longman. 杜正艾，2007，《俄罗斯外交传统研究》。上海：上海人民出版社。郭常义，2005，《日本语言与传统文化》。广西：广西师范大学出版社。塞缪尔·亨廷顿著，程克雄译，2005，《我们是谁？美国国家特性面临的挑战》。北京：新华出版社。

文化定型形成的过程，就是逐渐形成归于一个特定的群体成员的特征的一系列夸张的信念和期待。例如：加州人、纽约人、律师、医生（职业定型）、小孩子、老人（代的定型）等等。就文化定型而言，民族、种族、国家和文化在名词化的主体中被混为一谈，即使在一个相对单一的主体中，例如“上海人”，也是有这几重维度的交织，以及个体间的差异。可以说，任何以这样的主体展开的在关系过程或心理过程中的句子，即构成了文化定型的重要句法特征。下文将分别论述关系过程和心理过程。

如我们所知，大多数国家在民族或种族方面都不是单一的。例如，根据BSA反种族主义纲领（1997），亚洲人通常被认为指亚洲次大陆的人，即印度、巴基斯坦、孟加拉和克什米尔人。然而在某些情况下可能有人会反对把各种不同的文化和种族的群体，而且和英国社会的关系也各不相同的群体归拢到一个名字下，此外，有些特定群体的成员还反对用他们原来的国家的名字称呼他们，因为他们已经在英国生活了好几代人（Baldwin et al., 2005：70）。从这个例子可以看出，名词化的过程在文化定型的表述中极为复杂，可以说让每一个定型表述从主语来看就构成了质疑和挑战的前提，但我们的认知和日常交际的需求又让我们不得不混杂地谈论各种种族、民族、文化和人群，这就是文化定型表述的张力所在。

名词化的另外一层含义是将特征名词化，从而使文化定型话语更加连贯流畅，也更加隐蔽，这是我们在分析文化定型时要加以注意的。例如：

俄罗斯民族性格上的矛盾性和易偏激性这一奇怪现象引起俄罗斯的思想家们的极大关注。

首先将名词化的短语予以拆开，即：俄罗斯民族在性格上是矛盾和偏激的；或者俄罗斯民族具有矛盾性和偏激性。关系过程将定型彰显，有助于我们在阅读时对原来的论述加以质疑。同样：

俄罗斯人这种强烈的民族优越心理的进一步发展，则表现为俄罗斯人的使命意识。

这同样可以拆分为“俄罗斯人具有强烈的民族优越心理；俄罗斯人具有使命意识。”又例如：

> To other Europeans, the best known quality of the British, and in particular of the English, is **'reserve'**. Closely related to English **reserve** is **English modesty**. Within their hearts, the English are perhaps no less conceited than anybody else, but in their relations with others they value at least **a show of modesty**. This reluctance to communicate with others is an unfortunate quality in some ways, since it tends to give the impression of coldness, and it is true that the English (except perhaps in the North) are not noted for their **generosity and hospitality**. This **self-deprecation** is typically English, and, mixed with **their reserve**, it often produces a sort of general air of indifference which appears to a foreigners as a pose, difficult to understand and even irritating.

这里黑色部分的抽象名词有“英式保留”“英式谦虚”，作为固定概念，进而到典型的英式“自我贬低”，相互强化，使定型更加固定。

3.2 关系过程

关系过程指事物之间归属、识别等关系，归属类指的是某个实体具有哪些属性，或者归于哪种类型，可以表述为：a是x的一种，主语就是属性的载体，动词可以有表示内包的系动词以及表示所有关系的“有”动词等，还有一个表述属性的成分。

在识别类中，内包式指一个实体确定另一个实体的具体身份，两个主要参与者是识别者和被识别者。可以有主动语态和被动语态。

系统功能语法对识别类的关系过程做了精辟的区分，在识别类小句中，有一个实体是标记（token），另一个是价值（value）。标记指的是外表、符号、形式和名称，价值指的是实质、意义、职能和身份。在我们关注的文化类型中，无疑标记就是各类表示文化、民族身份的群体的名称，而价值则是对他们的定型化的描述。

关系过程作为最简单的认知过程，其中含有很多复杂性，如主动的和被动的区别，就有所有和唯一的区别，强化归属性（intensive attributive）动词有成为、变成、依然是、似乎是、看起来、听起来等等，这是不可以倒置的，即主语和表示属性的表语不可互换位置。

以下两例是典型的关系过程：

俄罗斯是世界上最具民族主义情绪的国家。

正如别尔嘉耶夫所说的：“极权主义是古老的俄国传统”。

另外的复杂性表现在关系过程中的“拥有”过程，即“有”：例如：

恰达耶夫曾经指出：“在俄国人民中，有一种注定的静止，有一种无望的恒定，这就是——人民对统治他们的权利之性质完完全全的漠不关心。”

3.3 蕴含在心理过程中的文化定型

心理过程是表示感觉、反应和认知等心理活动的过程，有两个参与者，一个是心理活动的主体，也叫感知者，通常是人，一个是客体，即感知的对象。在定型中出现的心理过程主要是认知性的，即以believe等为动词的句式，感知者是各种文化类型的群体，而感知对象则是各种信念、思想等。

心理过程的句法特点是感知者和感知对象都可以做主语，可以出现成对的句子，例如：

I believe this is true.

This convinced me.

在这些学术著作中，我们发现较多的蕴含在心理过程中的文化定型。例如：

俄国认为只有它才是世界上最正宗的而且也是世界上唯一的基督教国家。

俄罗斯人认为，俄罗斯民族有拯救其他民族，拯救世界的使命。

正如别尔嘉耶夫所说的："极权主义是古老的俄国传统"，"极权主义始终融化在俄国的血液中"。

其实心理过程在这里可以扩展为态度的表达，而态度的表达可以是文化定型，也可以是某些特定态度的表达，这之间的边界是宽松的，例如以下三例即可看作文化定型，表达了特定人群特定的价值观。

美国人很少或完全没有欧洲人所特有的那种地方依附感。

对于美国人来说，意识形态重于疆域。

在日本，放弃小我，追随大我是作为一种美德而被人们称道的。

3.4 文化定型中的评价

关于文化定型中的评价，最著名的研究就是Katz和Braly 1933年在美国普林斯顿大学的学生中所做的问卷调查。研究目的是调查美国人对其他民族的文化定型的看法。他们发现学生们拥有清晰地、否定的定型，他们几乎毫不困难地回答了问卷中的问题。大多数学生是美国白人，其他种族的定型包括：犹太人很精明、善于理财，日本人精明、狡猾，黑人懒惰、得过且过，美国人勤奋、有智慧。问卷表上有84种个性特征，要求选5—6项，作为某个群体的典型特征。调查结果表明选项有很大的一致性，美国白人都被选作勤奋的、进步的、有雄心大志的，非裔美国人都被看做是懒惰的、无知的、有音乐天赋的。大多数学生对他们毫无个人接触的种族或民族也选择了典型特征。研究的结论是：种族文化定型是广泛传播的，并且有特定的社会群体的成员共同拥有的。他们在1951年和1967年重复了这项研究，发现了一些变化，人们拥有这些定型的范围也有所变化，后来的定型变得更加肯定了，但某些特定的种族群体拥有某些特定的特征，这样的信念依旧存在。当然，值得注意的是这项研究完全依据言辞上的报告，因此在生态效度上是非常低的，参与调查者选了几个特征，并不是说他们就会在实际的交际中按照这样的定型认识去做。此外还有问卷研究本身所蕴含的问题，如人们可能撒谎或者迎合调查者等等。

Spencer & Franklin（2010：145）在讨论定型时问道：谈论一个特定群体的特征有用吗、可行吗或者有害吗？如果有用的话，这些特征怎样才能被最好地识别？我们更加关注的是第二个问题，即在评价的话语语义系统中，哪些评价语义在用于文化定型时是被接受的，哪些是容易造成歧视和偏见的。这并不仅仅是说肯定的评价是易于被接受的，因为即使在肯定的评价中，有一些也是约定俗成地用于某些群体的。例如：

日本文化体系可以说是非常富有包容性的。日本人既有着执着传统的精神，对自己的传统感到自豪；又有包容外来文化的特殊心理，大胆吸收外来文化，不以为耻……

To this day Jewish people are sometimes stereotyped in media as being *intellectually gifted, nit-picky, and focused on money*.（wikipedia）

第一例是肯定的评价，第二例中，既有肯定的——intellectually gifted，也有否定的——nit-picky，还有中性偏否定的——focused on money。

我们要做的是对评价的语义领域做一梳理，得出哪些评价领域是适用于文化定型的，可接受的，哪些是会带来负面效应的，哪些是模棱两可的，等等。同时预测文化定型话语在某些语类中的作用（如在外交语类中作为寒暄和开场白、在笑话中作为结盟手段等等）。

“根据定型所涉指的对象的不同，民族文化定型又可分为自定型和他定型”（宋洪英，2012：71），顾名思义，前者是特定群体对自我的认知和评价，后者则是对其他群体的认知和评价。这在评价的研究中也构成了饶有意味的研究领域。如，我们经常说，“中华民族是勤劳勇敢的民族”，这是自定型，而搜索文献则会发现各种各样的他定型。

自定型对于自我认同有重要作用，这是因为个体在社会化过程中通过认同并采取该社会文化价值取向的观念，这是社会化的一部分，Scollon & Scollon（2000）中也有论及。他定型通过他人或各种语类的大众话语包括文学作品等获得，同时进行传播和扩散，并横向传播。我们关注的是自定型和他定型语义领域的交替、更迭、重复以及变迁。这将是评价理论可以大大施展的研究领域，也有助于语言和跨文化交际研究的深入和细化。

从评价的分级来看，文化定型可以被大大地合法化，例如使用many等限定主体，使用tend to等限定动词部分，以下的文字来自Ting-Toomey主编的《跨文化交流学》，鉴于这是一部较有影响的跨文化交际教材，它的语言在此类话语中很有代表性（Ting-Toomey, 2004：61-62）。

Asian immigrants（e.g. Vietnamese Americans）and Native Americans *tend to* revere the past. African Americans *tend to* have a strong sense of both past and present references. Latino/a Americans *tend to* have a strong response to the present experience. European Americans *tend to* emphasize concern for the immediate future. More specifically, for example, *many* Vietnamese Americans believe in the Buddhist precepts of karma in rebirth. They believe that “an individual life cycle is predetermined by good and bad deeds from a previous life. The goal is eventually to achieve spiritual liberation ... Ancestors are worshiped for four generations after death”. Thus, for *many* Vietnamese American immigrants, their past profoundly influences their present identities.

Many Mexican Americans, in contrast, prefer to experience life and people around them fully in the present...

Furthermore, *many* Africans and African Americans *tend to* embrace a combination of past–present focus...

Human Nature Orientation While middle-class European Americans and African Americans *tend to* perceive human nature as neutral, *many* Native American groups *tend to* emphasize the inherent goodness of human nature（Sue & Sue, 1990）. *Many*

European Americans *tend to* believe in the individual's personal will power to shape the development of human nature, whereas *many* African Americans *tend to* believe in the importance of the environment in shaping the nature of a person. (Ting-Toomey, 2004: 63)

几乎整部教材的叙述都是通过限定主语或限定动词部分，使原本可能是过度概括的描述变得合法，虽然教材的语言因此变得臃肿一些，但有效地避免了在这样一部跨文化对比教材中最不应该出现的定型表述，这也从反面证明了文化定型表述其实是无所不在，很难被彻底消除的。此外，通过增加感知对象、通过比较等，定型也可大大获得合法性。以下分别是一个例子：

To other Europeans, the best known quality of the British, and in particular of the English, is 'reserve'. (*Tregidgo, 1972: 33*)（增加感知对象）

We may also mention at this point that the people of the North and West, especially the Welsh, are much less reserved than those of the South and East. (*Tregidgo, 1972: 33*)（比较）

4. 结论

作为结语和进一步的思考，本文作者认为文化定型有三个特点：即（缺乏）精确性、评价性和语境性。

精确性：从以上分析的限定表述可以看到，文化定型总是不精确的，虽然在表述上想要尽可能贴近事实，但这些限定表述的存在恰恰从反面说明定型表达在本质上是一种近似，而无法做到精确。

评价性：与精确性相比，我们的研究更关注的是定型的评价性，这可以从关系过程和心理过程以及名词化的分析看到，定型的评价既有约定俗成的一面，又有细微的难以区分的描述加评价，同时评价还可分为自评价和它评价，肯定的和否定的评价，通常在表达歧视和偏见时，人们就会采用否定的定型表述；而对一个群体的肯定评价也可能蕴含对其他群体的否定评价。

语境性：我们在本文中对定型的分析着重讨论句法结构的几个因素，定型的形成和使用常常是特定语境的结果，同时也构建了特定的语境，结合语境和话语研究定型表述是极为必要的。

本文通过考察几部文化论著中的文化定型表述，从功能句法的几个方面对文化定型表述的功能句法特征进行了粗略的描述，并提出了进一步研究可以展开的维度。其实文化定型的传播不仅仅在文化的学术论著中，更多的是在影视媒体、新媒体以及人们的日常互动中，我们不仅应全面考察定型的句法特点，包括句法语义特点，更应研究它在形成过程中的变形和各种变体，在研究手段上结合语料库等工具，在这方面还有广阔的空间。

参考文献

Baldwin, E. et al. 2005. *Introducing Cultural Studies*. Beijing: Peking University Press.

John, A. A. 1968. The Ethic Scene in the Soviet Union: The View of the Dictatorship. In E. Goldhagen (ed.) *Ethnic Minorities in the Soviet Union*. New York: Praeger, 14-21.

Kottak, C.P. 2008. *Anthropology*. Beijing: China People's University Press.

Mcleod, S. A. 2008. *Simply: Psychology: Stereotypes*. Retrieved from http://www.Simplypsychology.org/kats-braly.html.

Pickering, M. 2001. *The Politics of Representation*. London: Macmillan.

Scollon, R. & S.W. Scollon. 2000. *Intercultural Communication: A Discourse Approach*. Beijing: Foreign Language Teaching and Research Press.

Spencer-Oatey, H. & P. Franklin. 2010. *Intercultural Interaction: A Multidisciplinary Approach to Intercultural Communication*. Beijing: Foreign Language Teaching and Research Press.

Timer, D. (ed.) 1989. *Contemporary Critical Theory*. New York: Brace Jovanovish.

Ting-Toomey, S. & L. Chung. 2004. *Understanding Intercultural Communication*. Oxford: Oxford University Press.

Tregidgo, P. S. 1972. *A Background to English*. London: Longman.

Wierzbicka, A. 2010. *English: Meaning and Culture*. Beijing: Foreign Language Teaching and Research Press.

杜正艾，2007,《俄罗斯外交传统研究》。上海：上海人民出版社。

郭常义，2005,《日本语言与传统文化》。广西：广西师范大学出版社。

胡壮麟、朱永生、张德禄、李战子，2005,《系统功能语言学概论》。北京：北京大学出版社。

塞缪尔·亨廷顿著，程克雄译，2005,《我们是谁？美国国家特性面临的挑战》。北京：新华出版社。

宋洪英，2012, 从模因论看民族文化定型，《外语学刊》(1): 69-73。

文卫平，2002, 跨文化交际中的定型观念，《外语教学》(3): 12-17。

Structure and Function of Measure Nominals in English and Chinese

杨炳钧
上海交通大学

1. Introduction

"Describing a sentence as a construction of words is rather like describing a house as a construction of bricks, without recognizing the walls and the rooms as intermediate structural units" (Halliday & Matthiessen, 2014: 362). Similarly, describing a group as a construction of words makes the description too simple, not being able to reveal the internal structure and function of the group. This is particularly true with nominal group that functions as measuring in both English and Chinese, i.e. measure nominals under the category of Numeratives.

There are two types of Numerative: quantifying Numerative which specifies either an exact number (e.g. *three books*) or an inexact number (e.g. *many books*); and ordering Numerative which specifies either an exact place in order (e.g. *the second game*) or an inexact place (e.g. *a forthcoming game*). In theories other than SFL, quantifying Numeratives are discussed under the category of count/mass nouns. It is generally believed that the count/mass distinction applies to most languages but differences are obvious, so those languages in which classifiers are not obligatory for nouns are called non-classifier languages and those in which classifiers are obligatory are called classifier languages (Allan, 1977; Wu & Bodomo, 2009). Following such distinction, Chinese is treated by many as a typical classifier language and English a typical non-classifier language.

In this article, I will argue against this distinction by revealing the similarities in structure and function of measure nominals in English and Chinese. First, I will provide a sketch of measure nominals in English and Chinese and then discuss their structure and function from the perspective of SFL, through which one will see the reason why such a distinction is not well-grounded for Chinese and English.

2. A Sketch of measure nominals

2.1 Measure nominals in English

In English grammar books, nouns are divided into count nouns and mass nouns. Count nouns refer to entities which present themselves naturally in discrete and countable units, while mass nouns refer to substances which do not present themselves in such units. In order to be counted, mass nouns have to be preceded by measure words: *three bottles of milk*. Such groups of English for mass nouns are called measure nominals. Measure nominals may include those groups formed for count nouns, but in this article we focus mainly on the construction "numeral + measure word + noun".

Measure nominals include both measure partitives and general partitives. The former relates to precise quantities denoting length, area, volume and weight (e.g. *a mile of cable*), and the latter relates to other quantities (e.g. *a crowd of people*) (Quirk et al., 1985: 251). Measure words, when they include both measure partitives and general partitives, equal classifiers by other linguists (Allan, 1977; Lehrer, 1986). According to Lehrer (1986), classifiers in English can be put into the following categories by combining Keith Allan's taxonomies with Eloise Jelinek's proposal:

(1) Unit counters: *two heads of cattle*
(2) Fractional classifiers: *three quarters of the cake*
(3) Number set classifiers: *dozens of birds*
(4) Collective classifiers: *two clumps of grass*
(5) Varietal classifiers: *two species of wheat*
(6) Measure classifiers: *one liter of wine*
(7) Arrangement classifiers: *two rows of beans*
(8) Metaphorical comparison classifiers: *a bear of a man*

This taxonomy is illuminating in understanding measure nominals, which usually denote a part of a whole. The structure of these nominals is basically the same, except that metaphorical comparison classifier is special and needs to be treated separately. However, a very important issue is what is the status of "of noun" in these nominals. "In most cases of cannot be replaced by another preposition, nor can it be paraphrased as a compound which reverses the order of the two nouns" (Lehrer, 1986: 110). But is "of noun" a Postmodifier of the measure word? If so, is it a downranked prepositional phrase?

2.2 Measure Nominals in Chinese

Wang (1985: 260-75) proposed that measure nominals in Chinese can be put into six types: natural units; collective units; units of length, volume, weight and monetary units; container; units about writing; event units out of actions. A different categorization was then put forward by Lu Jianming (Lu, 1987), who classified measure words in modern Chinese into four categories: action (e.g. cì次, tàng趟, zhèn阵); time (e.g. tiān天, nián年, miǎo秒); unit (e.g. jīn斤, chǐ尺); nominal (e.g. gè个, zhāng张, zhī支, tiáo条, wǎn碗, bēi杯). Lu's categorization avoids overlapping and simplicity in Wang's categories, but the action type and the nominal type are still too general. Some measure words serve as typical cases in both the action type and the nominal type, e.g. "zhāng" in yī zhāng gōng (一张弓, "a bow", action) and yī zhāng zhuōzi (一张桌子, "a table", nominal).

A more comprehensive categorization was later put forward by Shi Xiyao. Shi (1992: 38-46) divided measure nominals in Chinese into two general categories: individual and collective. Those for individual things were further classified into six types:

(9) Shape measure nominal: yī piàn xuě huā (一片雪花, a flake of snow)
(10) Activity measure nominal: liǎng tiāo shuǐ (两挑水, two shoulders of water)
(11) Component measure nominal: sān tóu niú (三头牛, three head of cow)
(12) Container measure nominal: sì píng jiǔ (四瓶酒, four bottles of liquor)
(13) Unit measure nominal: wǔ dūn mǐ (五吨米, five tons of rice)
(14) Other measure nominal: liù wèi yào (六味药, six tastes of medicine)

For shape measure nominals, the size of shape or the shape itself may be perceived differently: so such expressions as yī piàn yún (一片云, a piece of cloud) and yī piàn shù yè (一片树叶, a piece of leaf) are all acceptable. For activity measure nominals, some measure words which originally describe activity may collocate with nouns which are not directly related to activity. For example, in liǎng tiāo shuǐ the measure word tiāo originates from the activity of shouldering water and in wǔ zhāng zuǐ (五张嘴, five mouths) the measure word zhāng originates from the activity of opening mouth. For container measure nominals, the choice of the measure word sometimes depends on the actual container in context. So yī bēi jiǔ (一杯酒, one glass of liquor), yī píng jiǔ (一瓶酒, one bottle of liquor), yī wǎn jiǔ (一碗酒, one bowl of liquor), yī tongjiǔ (一桶酒, one barrel of liquor) are all good collocations. The measure words may extend to any container that can hold the thing:

(15) yī dài jiǔ (一袋酒, one bag of liquor); yī hé jiǔ (一盒酒, one box of liquor); yī xiāng jiǔ (一箱酒, one case of liquor); yī tán jiǔ (一坛酒, one jar of liquor); yī chē jiǔ (一车酒, one wagon of liquor)

Measure nominals for collective things are further classified into two categories: those for pairs and those for groups.

(16) Pair measure nominals: liǎng shuāng xiézi (两双鞋子, two pairs of shoes)
(17) Group measure nominals: liǎngpái liǔ shù (两排柳树, two rows of willow)

Pair measure nominals are restricted to nouns in which two components of things always appear together, and the measure words for them include duì (对, pair), shuāng (双, pair), fù (副, pair or set), and others. For Group measure nominals, the measure words vary with the nouns and there are a large number of such measure words in Chinese: sān tào jiā jù (三套家具, three sets of furniture), sānqún rén (三群人, three crowds of people), among others.

So far we have briefly reviewed the principal studies of measure nominals in Chinese. Yet a question arises: a measure word to measure nominals is mandatory or not in Chinese? Before answering this question, it is helpful to turn to the distinction between classifier language and non-classifier language.

2.3 Classifier or Non-classifier?

The languages of the world can be divided into two groups with regard to numeral classifiers: those that have classifiers, such as the majority of languages in East and Southeast Asia, and those that do not, such as most European languages, including English (Allan, 1977; Greenberg, 1990). It is thus widely believed that English is a non-classifier language while Chinese is a classifier language, for in Chinese all nouns are like mass nouns in the sense that, for a noun to be counted, a measure word is mandatory.

Upon discussing measuring words in Chinese, some scholars identified two categories: classifier and massifier (e.g. Cheng & Sybesma, 1998), one for a closed class and the other for a non-closed class. Soon after, Cheng & Sybesma (1999) argued that classifiers in Chinese are equivalent to a definite article. But Wu & Bodomo (2009) argued against this position on empirical grounds and proposed that Chinese classifiers are not on the same footing as definite determiners. Some other scholars even distinguished between classifiers and "true measure words", though they structurally both follow immediately after a numeral and appear before a noun (Lyons, 1977; Li,

2000). They held this view for two reasons: true measure words usually occur with uncountable mass nouns but classifiers usually occur with count nouns. Whatever argument it is, the general viewpoint is that Chinese is a classifier language.

For my understanding, however, to label Chinese as "classifier language" and English as "non-classifier language" is not well-grounded for the following reasons: both languages contain numerous classifiers but some are covert and some others are overt, and the choice of a classifier (the measure word) is entirely context-dependent; the structure and function of measure nominals where classifiers locate are basically similar between English and Chinese.

3. Context-dependency in using measure words

The choice of a classifier (the measure word) entirely depends on contexts. First, if one takes all possible contexts into consideration, both English and Chinese contain countless things that are mass and numerous things that are countable. The cognitive foundation for countability is basically similar although cultural diversity may result in differences. It is already well-known that English and Chinese regard things that cannot be individuated as uncountable, and things that can be individuated as countable. Consequently, we have many uncountable nouns such as "water, sand, grass, warmth" in English and their counterparts in Chinese.

Second, in contexts where the units can be inferred, the measure word is not necessary for Chinese, not for uncountable nouns in English either. Such contexts include idiomatic expressions and expressions to which measure words are redundant. See (18).

(18a) wǔ fēng shí yǔ (五风十雨, five wind and ten rain, "timely wind and rain")
wǔ hú sì hǎi (五湖四海, five lakes and four seas, "all corners of the country")
(18b) six waters a cart (COCA)
40,000 soaps each day (COCA)

Third, the omission of measure words in Chinese and English results in various usages for different contexts rather than improper collocations. Count nouns in Chinese can be directly put after numerals without measure words while mass nouns in English can be used directly after numerals without measure words. This brings forth usages of different kinds, particularly true to spoken forms of the two languages. See (19).

(19a) sān fáng (三房, "three houses")
(19b) three coffees

The instances in (19) may have a lot of meanings in different contexts. First of all, (19a) may mean: sān gè fang jiān (三个房间, three rooms) or sān gè qīzǐ (三个妻子, three wives). Similar colloquial nominals can be found in Chinese where measure words are redundant. It is even abnormal to use measure words together with some nominals, for example, wǔ xíng (五行, five elements, i.e. metal, wood, water, fire and earth), sān shēng (三生, the three births, or reincarnations, past, present, future). Likewise, the meaning of (19b) in English depends on context. It may mean: *three cups of coffee; three packs of coffee; three cans of coffee*. In certain contexts, these nominals may sound rather strange to ordinary people. To stevedores, (19b) may mean three ships of coffee; and to real estate staff, (19a) may mean sān dòng zhù fáng (三栋住房, three buildings of houses). In other words, the presence of the measure word is not mandatory here.

To sum up, the presence of measure word is necessary for mass nouns in both English and Chinese, but mandatory only to cases where things need to be referred to as units. Mass things, if put into certain containers or divided into certain units, will be used in the same way as count nouns do. The presence of the measure word is redundant for count nouns in English, but count nouns can be used as measure words in other expressions (e.g. *a book of words*). Measure word is necessary for mass nouns in English, but mass nouns can be used as measure words in other expressions (e.g. *a cloud of words/smoke*). Clearly, it is not fixed but context-dependent in using measure words for nouns both in English and in Chinese. It is, therefore, not appropriate to say that measure words are mandatory for nouns in Chinese and mass nouns in English.

This view gains support from Allan (1980), who proposed eight levels of countability argued for the degree of uncountableness. He found that nouns in English "can be used both countably and uncountably in different NP environments" (Allan, 1980: 541). The issue of countability of nouns was not taken into account in Halliday (1994), but "cline of countability" was suggested for considering nouns in Halliday & Matthiessen (2004: 326; 2014: 385), which ranges "from those nouns (and pronouns) which construe things as fully itemized, at one end, to those which treat them as totally unbounded at the other". Being countable or uncountable just reflects certain usages in certain typical contexts. When the elements of the context change, the degree of countability will alter and will the necessity of using measure words.

After getting aware of context-dependency, I shall move back to the question raised in Section 2.1 above: Whether *of noun* constitutes a downranked prepositional phrase to modify the measure word in English measure nominals? I will seek for answers to this question by analyzing the structure and function of measure nominals from the perspective of SFL.

4. Analyzing metafunctional meanings of measure nominals

4.1 Experiential meaning of measure mominals

Structure and function, in general operation, go hand in hand and cannot be separated in SFL analysis. According to Halliday & Matthiessen (2014: 392), the internal structure of the measure expression (or other embedded numerative) in English can be drawn as follows:

a	cup	Of	tea
Numerative			Thing
Premodifier	Head	Postmodifier	
β	α		

Figure. 1 Internal structure of the measure expression

(Halliday & Matthiessen, 2014: 392)

It is known that linguistic analysis by means of SFL should be carried out for the purpose of locating or revealing "meaning". However, when we take "cup" in "a cup of tea" as Head (see Figure 1), it will be odd to locate a meaning of this nominal which focuses not on "tea". If "of tea" is Postmodifier, it is secondary in status to "cup". But in fact, it is not difficult to locate "tea" as the most important information in this nominal expression.

The problem becomes more apparent if we follow the analysis in Figure 1 to analyze the internal structure of the measure expression in Chinese, which is typical both for count nouns and mass nouns. See Figure 2 below.

yī 一 a/one	bēi 杯 cup	chá 茶 tea
Numerative		Thing
Premodifier	Head?	Postmodifier?
β	α ?	

Figure. 2 Potential internal structure of the typical measure expression in Chinese

Closer examination of yī bēi chá reveals that it is unreasonable to take bēi (cup) as Head and chá (tea) as Postmodifier, for chá should be the word which carries the most important information. The group may be well-understood if bēi is omitted but difficult to get across if chá is absent. One may argue that the two languages are different in measure nominals and should be analyzed differently. This sounds rational, but since all would agree that both "a cup of" and "yī bēi" function as Numeratives, why it seems all right to take "cup" as Head while it is quite unreasonable to take "bēi" as Head. When "of tea" is taken as Postmodifier, it is downranked in status, lower than "cup". Likewise, when "chá" is treated as Postmodifier, it is downranked in status, lower than "bēi". This is contradictory to the fundamental meaning of the nominal group, in which those function as Thing should be higher in status. See an improved analysis for such expressions in Chinese in Figure 3.

yī 一 a/one	bēi 杯 cup	chá 茶 tea
Numerative		Thing
Premodifier		Head
β		α

Figure. 3 Improved internal structure of the typical measure expression in Chinese

In this analysis, Head is conflated with Thing and the measure word comes together with the Numeral, functioning as Numerative and Premodifier. In other words, the measure word "bei" is part of the Premodifier and it should not be treated as Head. The Head and the Premodifier can be further modified by other modifiers respectively. In the same manner, "cup" in "a cup of tea" shall not be taken as Head.

The Numerative denotes the number while the Thing is always the most important information. In cases where the Thing is the default information known to language users, the Numerative may become more prominent. This applies to measure nominals both in Chinese and in English. Therefore, we may provide an improved analysis of "a cup of tea" in Figure 4.

a	cup	of	tea
Numerative			Thing
Premodifier			Head
β			α

Figure. 4 Improved internal structure of the measure expression in English

Here we treat "a cup of" as an adjectival group, functioning as Numerative and Premodifier in the experiential meaning. In the default use of a measure nominal, the Thing ("tea" in this example) is what to be modified. All those that denote the measuring of a Thing should be treated as modifiers. For example, "cup" and "tea" can be further modified (e.g. two full cups of green tea), but all these modifiers are eventually used to modify "tea".

Such treatment finds supports from the history of English in the use of preposition "of". According to *Oxford English Dictionary* (OED), "of" displays about 63 distinct usages in the history of English. One of these usages is to indicate "quantity, age, extent, price, etc." See the following instance which was used in 1523:

(20) syxe foote of lengthe (six foot of length)

Can we say that "of lengthe" is a Postmodifier of "foote"? This is redundant both in meaning and structure, for "six foot" is already the exact length. Another explanation is to follow the usage illustrated by OED and say that "of" here functions as the indicator of "quantity", so "foote of" should be treated as a whole, functioning as Epithet. The modern measuring construction (e.g. *a cup of tea*) most probably inherits this usage, and one may consider "of" in "a cup of tea" as an indicator of quantity.

Such measuring constructions are quite different from other types of "of nominals" in English. For example, *the legs of three compasses*. In these instances, "of nominals" functions as Postmodifiers of "legs". The most important information conveyed in these instances is "legs", which functions as Head, conflating with Thing. Chinese counterparts of these nominals may further help explain the status of "of nominals" here (e.g. zhǐ nán zhēn de zhǐ zhēn, 指南针的指针). In the counterparts, the most important information loads on "zhǐ zhēn" (指针, legs).

4.2 Logical meaning of measure nominals

In the section above, we have already noted the logical structure of measure nominals in the four figures. Logical meaning, however, is more complicated than that. According to Halliday & Matthiessen (2014: 390), "What the logical analysis does is to bring out the hypotactic basis of premodification in the nominal group, which then also explains its penchant for generating long strings of nouns." Univariate and multivariate structures are identified in logical analysis. When each element in a structure has a distinct function with respect to the whole, the structure is multivariate. For example:

(21) those two splendid old electric trains (Halliday & Matthiessen, 2014: 364)

The functions of the elements in (21) are as follows: Deictic + Numerative + Epithet1 + Epithet2 + Classifier + Thing. The logical structure, therefore, is multivariate, with "trains" as the anchoring element.

The nominal group is unusual for we have to interpret its structure in both ways simultaneously "to understand how it functions as a resource for construing complex things" (Halliday & Matthiessen, 2014: 390). As to the measure nominal, the logical analysis in Figure 1 shows that the measure word is regarded as the central element in the logical structure (α). This measure nominal is a multivariate structure. The problem is, then, how to determine the status of "of noun" in the logical analysis of measure nominals. One can see no answer to this in Figure 1 and the discussions related.

If one views measure nominals from a different perspective and take "a cup of" in "a cup of tea" as an adjectival group, the logical analysis will be without contradictions. See Figure 5 for an improved analysis of the logical meaning.

a	cup	of	tea
Premodifier			Head
β			α
β β	β α		

Figure. 5 Improved logical analysis of the measure expression in English

In this analysis, the only element that has not been explained is "of". Since we treat "a cup of" as a whole and "of" is only meaningful in association with "a cup" and the noun that follows, we may label it as "Relator". By contrast, in Chinese measure nominals, no relator is needed (See Figure 6).

yī 一 a/one	bēi 杯 cup	chá 茶 tea
Premodifier		Head
β		α
β β	β α	

Figure. 6 Logical analysis of the measure expression in Chinese

4.3 Interpersonal Meaning of Measure Nominals

Expressions which contain typical measure words may not be used to measure. Such expressions carry strong interpersonal meaning and they are frequently used in English and Chinese. See (22) for some English expressions and their Chinese counterparts:

(22a) hundreds of, rows and rows of, first/last of
(22b) chéng qiān shàng wàn (成千上万), yī pái pái (一排排), shǒu gè (首个)

The interpersonal meaning of these expressions includes probability (hundreds of, chéng qiān shàng wàn), intensity (rows and rows of, yī pái pái) and temporality (first, shǒu gè). They are not measure nominals, for they do not measure anything but just describe degrees of probability, intensity or temporality.

Typical measure nominals such as "a cup of tea" do not carry much interpersonal meaning, except when "cup" is used out of expectation. For example, if the speaker/writer finds "tea" in a huge mug but uses "a cup of tea" to express that, he/she already conveys some comments.

When some modifiers which usually appear together with measure nominals are taken into consideration, the interpersonal meaning is obvious. We input "cup of" in the advanced search box of OEDon CD-ROM (v. 4.0) published in 2009, and the following expressions pop up as part of the hundreds of instances. Chinese counterparts are also provided in brackets for comparison.

(23) a cup of hot wine (一杯热茶, yī bēi rè chá)
a cup of very peculiar-tasting tea (一杯味道特别的茶, yī bēi wèi dào tè bié de chá)
a cup of pure water (一杯纯净水, yī bēi chún jìng shuǐ)
a cup of her ale (一杯她的啤酒, yī bēi tā de pí jiǔ)
a cup of such coffee (一杯这种咖啡, yī bēi zhè zhǒng kā fēi)

These instances show that modifiers can be naturally used before the Thing, conveying modality in them. The Epithet "hot" (rè) in "a cup of hot tea" (yī bēirè chá) indicates some degree of intensity in typical context. In some particular context (e.g. in outdoor places), it may function interpersonally in the same way as "good" (hǎo) do. The Epithet "pure" (chún jìng) in (23) carries some degree of judgement concerning morality, and "very peculiar-tasting" (wèi dào tè bié) conveys some degree of appreciation concerning desirability. As to the last two instances, "her" (tā de) and "such" (zhè zhǒng) show some degree of deicticity. Modifiers can be put before the measure word as well. See (24) from OED for example. Their Chinese counterparts are also provided for comparison.

(24) a comforting cup of bovril (一杯舒适的牛肉汁, yī bēi shū shì de niú ròu zhī)
an excellent cup of coffee (一杯上乘的咖啡, yī bēi shàng chéng dekā fēi)
a refreshing cup of tea (一杯提神的茶, yī bēi tí shén de chá)

a silent and thoughtful cup of tea (一杯默默而体贴的茶, yī bēi mò mò ér tǐ tiē de chá)

In (24), the Epithets "comforting, excellent, refreshing" (shū shì, shàng chéng, tí shén) convey some degree of judgement concerning morality. What is special here is that the last two measure nominals in (24) are not simple. The Epithets "silent and thoughtful" (mò mò ér tǐ tiē) imply that the expressions are metaphorical. It is not easy to decide what element the Epithet in each of (24) modify. Traditional grammar treats these Epithets as modifiers of "cup" but the Chinese counterparts already give us hints for a different interpretation. These Epithets modify the whole nominal group rather than "cup", for the focus is on the Thing in each of them. The interpersonal meaning of judgement therefore falls on the entire nominal. Besides modification shown in (23) and (24), measure word and Thing can be simultaneously modified by Epithets. See (25) and their Chinese counterparts in brackets.

(25) a giant cup of Irish breakfast tea (一大杯爱尔兰早茶, yī dà bēi ài ěr lán zǎochá)
a whole cup of hot coffee (一整杯热咖啡, yī zhěng bēi rè kā fēi)
a second cup of hot tea (第二杯热茶, dì èr bēi rè chá)
the small cup of iced coffee (这小杯冰咖啡, zhè xiǎo bēi bingkā fēi)

From the instances in (25), we may find that Epithets, Identifiers, Ordinatives, Deictics can all be used in the measure nominals, either before the measure word or before the Thing. Such uses carry interpersonal meanings of different degrees. The interpersonal meanings of these may become more apparent if we follow Martin and White (2005) and consider Judgement and Appreciation. To save space, we are not going to discuss that here.

5. Conclusion

Whether to use or not to use a classifier may not be grammatically determined (Li, 2000), but it could be discourse and/or pragmatically sensitive (Hopper, 1986). Since countability is a matter of degree (Allan, 1980) which varies with contextual elements, it is not constructive to look into measure nominals from the perspective of mass / count distinction. From what we have observed, transference of countability needs to be carefully considered. A typical uncountable noun can be transferred to be countable, and vice versa (e.g. *two coffees, a cloud of smoke*).

Functional analysis of measure nominals in English and Chinese further reveals that such a distinction as classifier language and non-classifier language should be withdrawn in discussing measure nominals. The distinction may be useful in certain context, but the choice of measure words is a matter of context. Both English and Chinese contain numerous count nouns and mass nouns, and both languages may or may not use measure words in expressing measuration. The group "of noun" that follows the measure word in a measure nominal does not modify the measure word as Postmodifier, and it is not a downranked phrase. The word "of" after the measure word can be taken as Relator in measure nominals and "measure word + of" functions as an adjectival group. Context dependence should be highly respected before typicality is considered in specific contexts. A more constructive and meaningful way of studying measure nominals is to categorize the potential contexts and principles of identification via such theories as SFL.

References

Allan, K. 1977. Classifiers. *Language*, 53: 281-311.

Allan, K. 1980. Nouns and Countability. *Language*, 56: 541-67.

Cheng, L. L.-S. & R. Sybesma. 1998. *Yi-wan Tang*, *Yi-ge Tang*: Classifiers and massifiers. *Tsing Hua Journal of Chinese Studies*, 3: 385-412.

Cheng, L. L.-S. & R. Sybesma. 1999. Bare and Not-so-bare Nouns and the Structure of NP. *Linguistic Inquiry*, 30: 509-42.

Greenberg, J. H. 1990. Dynamic Aspects of Word Order in the Numeral Classifier. In K.M. Denning & S. Kemmer (eds.) *On Language: Selected Writings of Joseph H. Greenberg*. Stanford: Stanford University Press, 227-40.

Halliday, M. A. K. 1994. *An Introduction to Functional Grammar* (2nd editionn). London: Arnold.

Halliday, M. A. K. & C. M. I. M. Matthiessen. 2004. *An Introduction to Functional Grammar* (3rd edition). London: Arnold.

Halliday, M. A. K. & C. M. I. M. Matthiessen. 2014. *Halliday's Introduction to Functional Grammar* (4th edition). London: Routledge.

Hopper, P. 1986. Some Discourse Functions of Classifiers in Malay. In C. Craig (ed.) *Noun Classes and Categorization*. Amsterdam: Benjamins, 309-25.

Lehrer, A. 1986. English Classifier Constructions. *Lingua*, 68: 109-48.

Li, W. 2000. The Pragmatic Function of Numeral-Classifiers in Mandarin Chinese. *Journal of Pragmatics*, 32: 1113-1133.

Lu, J. 1987. On Numeral-classifier with Adjectives Inserted Between. *Language*

Teaching and Research, 4: 53-73.

Lyons, J. 1977. *Semantics*. Cambridge: Cambridge University Press.

Martin, J. R. & P. R. R. White. 2005. *The Language of Evaluation: Appraisal in English*. London: Macmillan.

Quirk, R., S. Greenbaum, G. Leech & J. Svartvik. 1985. *A Comprehensive Grammar of the English Language*. London: Longman.

Shi, X. 1992. Origin and Use of Measure Words for Thing. *Language Teaching and Research*, 2: 38-46.

Wang, L. 1985. *Modern Chinese Grammar*. Beijing: The Commercial Press.

Wu, Y. & A. Bodomo. 2009. Classifiers Determiners. *Linguistic Inquiry*, 40: 487-503.

《说文解字》词汇语义范畴的及物性分析

彭宣维

广东外语外贸大学

1. 引言

本文以系统功能语法的“及物性”为描写框架，对《说文解字》（简称《说文》）中有关词汇语义的范畴化过程做系统分析。

系统概念语法的“及物性”是通过小句对外部和内部经验流进行结构性识解（construal）、从而把这些经验片段加工成为“过程”类别（“process”types）的语法模型（Halliday, 1994：106-107），包括物质、心理、关系、行为、言语和存在六个次类（同上, 107-109）。其中“物质”过程分为“及物”（transitive）和“不及物”（intransitive）两个次类，即一个参与者（即“动作者”Actor）的过程是否延伸到另一个参与者（“目标”Goal），如the lion chased the tourist（及物）和the lion sprang（不及物），其中the lion为动作者，chased和sprang为过程，the tourist为过程chased的目标（同上, 109-112）（另见胡壮麟等, 2005）。

笔者发现，《说文》中大量语义范畴的构成可以通过系统功能语法的及物性过程框架来加以合理描述。

（1）摯 zhì 握持也。从手从執。脂利切

按《说文》，“摯”的构件“執”意为“捕罪人也，从丮从幸”，和甲骨文（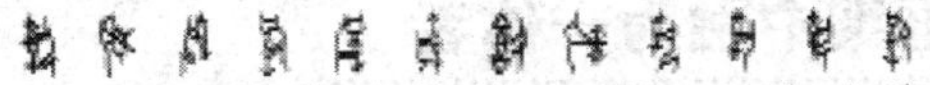；对比孟世凯，2009：515）表达的“以手铐将人铐住之形”一致（董莲池, 2005：409-410）；其中“丮”（），《说文》解释为“持也，象手有所丮据也”（双手拿着），含有“人”的信息（，即跽坐的人形）；“幸”（）“取象于手铐”（同上）。据此，我们把“摯”涉及的词汇语义过程通过下面的方式来加以描述：【人$_{动作者}$ · 丮$_{过程}$ · 幸$_{目标}$ · 手$_{手段方式环境}$】= 摯。其中，“【 】”在这里为及物性框架标示符；“·”可以理解为各输入成分“人”“丮”“幸”和“手”在及物性框架内导入的加工符（在数学上的意义为“乘积”）。“【 】”和“·”协同表达一种及物性过程。我们把各语义成分理解为乘积关系，是因为它们之间不是简单的加减关系，而是有机的逻辑-语义关系：四

个局部的语义特征之和不等于而是小于整体范畴“摯”。这显然是一种带有典型词汇语法特点的“过程”：整体范畴关注的是经验流本身，但同时包含了相关参与者信息“人”和“幸”以及过程的运作手段方式环境“手”。

当有关范畴在及物性框架内出现成分空缺时，这里采用的描写方法的优势就体现得尤其充分。

（2）亂 luàn 治也。幺子相亂，受治之也。讀若亂同。一曰理也。郎段切

（3）插 chā 刺肉也。从手从臿。楚洽切

例（2）“𤔔”与“亂”的金文同为，以手治丝之象：丝不顺而“𤔔”之（事件/动词）；后以“𤔔”转喻，指代丝不顺之状（品质/形容词）。其框架为：【（$X_{\text{动作者}}$）·$受_{\text{过程}}$·$幺_{\text{目标}}$ ≡ 治也】= 𤔔。“（）”内的成分是通过及物性框架补足的特征。

例（3）中“臿”（chā，舂去麥皮也。从臼，干所以臿之）的显性成分只有环境“臼”和“干”，隐没了动作者（人）和目标（麦）；过程（舂）属于半隐半现，即包含在“臼”和“干”的合体关系中，但整个范畴“臿”可直接作为显性过程看待，因为“干”是一个动词，其所指是从工具“干”（“圆盾”）转喻来的。这里涉及处所环境“臼”和手段方式环境“干”。所以，“插”的及物性框架为：【（$X_{\text{动作者}}$）·$臿_{\text{过程·处所环境}}$·（$X_{\text{目标}}$）·$手_{\text{手段方式环境}}$】= 插。

我们发现，《说文》中不少范畴并不只涉及单一及物性框架，有的有两个或以上。例如，

（4）製 zhì 裁也。从衣从制。征例切

“製”中的“制”，裘锡圭解释为“以刀截割木材”（转引自董莲池，2005：170）。据此，在“製”这个范畴中“制”是隐喻性的。“製”的及物性框架应为：【（$[X]_{\text{动作者}}$）·制（裁/截割）$_{\text{过程}}$·衣/（木材）$_{\text{目标}}$】= 製。其中[]”为两个框架的共享成分；“/”为角色叠加，包括词汇隐喻（但在拼音标注时表“或”，如mài/mò）。

本文拟主要从成分隐没的角度组织相关分析结果，包括（1）各构成成分融为一体的范畴；（2）有单一成分隐没者；（3）有两个或两个以上成分隐没者。分析对象以象形、指事和会意合体字为主，旁及形声字和合体假借字，后二者构成方式单一，不宜广泛引用。

2. 构成成分在及物性框架中融为一体者

例（1）“摯”为主要构成成分完备，这样的情况不多，不少范畴的构成成分均相同。先看构成成分不同的情况。

（4）作 zuò 起也。从人从乍。則洛切

其中“乍”在甲骨文中为，曾宪通（1992）认为其中的主体部分取像于耒字，上部v字形像是被耕起来的土块，意思是“以耒起土”，“引申为耕作、農作之‘作’”（引自董莲池，2005：503）；“人”旁是后加的。如此，“作”的及物性框架则是：【$人_{\text{动作者}}$·$乍_{\text{过程·目标}}$】= 作，即过程和目标均由“乍”体现（对比过程和环境融为一体的“畀”和“咎”）。类

似情况有：“巹”（jǐn，謹身有所承也；从己、丞）：【己$_{动作者}$·丞$_{过程·目标}$】= 巹；

“丞”的甲骨文写作，意思是拯救——两手拉掉入坎陷中的人。和“作”一样，都是动词性的事件范畴。

（5）伊 yī 殷聖人阿衡，尹治天下者。从人从尹。於脂切

“尹”早期写作，像手持“筆”或执杖之形，过程是通过手（“又”）和目标“丨”的接触关系体现出来的。“尹”字加上“人擎”作，使动作者前景化。所不同的是，“尹”是一个动词性的事件范畴，语义侧重点在治理上；而“伊”是一个名词性的事物范畴（有权之人），语义重心是主体“人”。“伊”的及物性框架为：【人$_{动作者}$·尹$_{过程·目标}$】。

（6）瀕 pín/bīn 水厓。人所賓附，頻蹙不前而止。从頁从涉。符眞切

这是一个处所范畴；其中“涉”的甲骨文写法有，意为徒步过河段注将“頁”分析为：“顰戚，各本作顙戚，今正。此以顰戚釋从頁之意也。將涉者，或因水深，顰眉蹙頞而止。故字从涉頁。”据此，其构成应为：渡河者意欲涉河因水厓而停止【（渡河者$_{动作者1+2}$）·〖涉$_{过程1}$+[頁]$_{过程2}$〗·[水厓]$_{空间处所环境1+原因环境2}$）】= 瀕。

以下范畴构成成分相同。

（7）冓 gòu/gōu 交積材也。象對交之形。

【魚魚$_{动作者·目标}$·（相遇$_{过程}$）】= 冓

字在甲骨文中为诸形，表示“二魚相遇之形，从彳从止有相进行之意……许说与甲骨文字形‘交積材也’非是”（马如森, 2008：101）。

（8）覞yào 竝視也。从二見。弋笑切

【儿儿$_{动作者·目标}$·見$_{过程}$】= 覞（饶炯：“两人相对而视”）

（9）虤yán 虎怒也。从二虎。五閑切

【虎虎$_{动作者·目标}$·（鬥$_{过程}$）】=虤。

朱俊声认为此字表“两虎斗也”（甲骨文：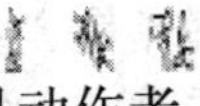）。

例（4—9）在表征上都是部分融合；下面是动作者、过程、目标三者完全融合的例子。

（10）㹜yín两犬相齧也。从二犬。語斤切

【㹜$_{动作者·过程·目标}$】（小篆適：“两犬相咬”）；也可处理为【犬$_{动作者}$+（咬$_{过程}$）+犬$_{目标}$】。

（11）競 jīng 競也。从二兄。二兄，競意；一曰：競，敬也。居陵切

【競$_{动作者·过程·目标}$】

（“强劲貌”或“小心谨慎”；甲骨文作：“竞逐”；马如森 2008：59）

（12）尼 ní 從後近之。从尸匕聲。女夷切

【尼$_{动作者·过程·目标}$】

（甲骨文作；“昵也”，像二人亲昵之态）

以下二例，范畴的“过程”和“目标”融为一体。

（13）兼 jiān 并也。从又持秝。兼持二禾，秉持一禾。古甜切

【（$\text{X}_{\text{动作者}}$）·$\text{秝}_{\text{过程·目标}}$·$\text{又}_{\text{手段方式环境}}$】= 兼

“兼”在金文中作，小篆顺势作“䄬”，确为一手（“𦥑”）持二禾之像。

（14）曟 chén 日月合宿从辰。从會从辰。植鄰切

【（$\text{日}\cup\text{月}_{\text{载体1}}$）·$\text{辰}_{\text{处所环境属性1}}$】+【（$\text{日}\cup\text{月}_{\text{动作者2·目标2}}$）·$\text{會}_{\text{过程2}}$·$\text{辰}_{\text{环境2}}$】=

【（$[\text{日}\cup\text{月}]_{\text{载体1/〖动作者2·目标2〗}}$）·$\text{會}_{\text{过程2}}$·$[\text{辰}]_{\text{处所环境属性1/空间处所环境2}}$】= 曟

这里存在延伸关系（“+”）；其中“辰”表从地球视角确立的“日月交会点”：“即夏历一年十二个月的月朔时，太阳所在的位置”；此范畴预设了交会过程（见徐中舒, 1996：1502-1503）。

范畴中也有涉及部分假借现象的。例如，

（15）卸 xiè 舍車解馬也。从卩、止、午。司夜切

【$\text{卩}_{\text{动作者}}$·$\text{止}_{\text{过程}}$·$\text{午}_{\text{目标}}$】= 卸

（止：舍，停止，隐喻；午：馬，假借；整个字为部分假借）

其实，绝大多数都存在成分隐含的情况，如（2）和（3）。接下来我们逐一分析及物过程框架内主要成分隐没的情况；主要成分指过程、动作者和目标；如果一个范畴不提供环境成分，分析不便操作，所以不单独谈环境成分隐没的情况，除非有其他主要成分同时隐没。但需要明确的是，任何一个范畴在情景中都可能涉及环境因素，我们也可以根据百科知识予以补充；但这样做会永无止境。下面的叙述以成分隐含为主体，分别关注单一和复合视角。

3. 及物过程框架下有一个主要成分隐没的范畴

典型情况是动作者、过程和目标之一隐没。先看“动作者”隐没的实例。

（16）糴 dí 市穀也。从入从糴。徒歷切

《说文》对“入”的解释是“内也；象从上俱下也”，是一个及物事件；从对“糴”的释义“市穀也”看，“入”应是“买入”的意思。“糴”（dí）是一种谷物。所以，“糴”的语义框架是：【（$\text{X}_{\text{动作者}}$）·$\text{入}_{\text{过程}}$·$\text{糴}_{\text{目标}}$】= 糴。

有趣的是，《说文》中同时存在一个意义相反的范畴“糶”（tiáo）：“出穀也”（其他特征相同，只是过程“出”相对）。这两个范畴的立足点在相关事件上。

（17）逐 zhú 追也。从辵，从豚省。直六切

【（$\text{X}_{\text{动作者}}$）·$\text{辵}_{\text{过程}}$·$\text{豚}_{\text{目标}}$】= 逐

这是一个使役性范畴，即X使“豚”（豕）“辵”（但对比董莲池, 2005：68）。与此相似的是它的训释范畴“追”（zhuī 逐也；从辵𠂤聲；陟隹切）：【（$\text{X}_{\text{动作者}}$）·$\text{辵}_{\text{过程}}$·$\text{𠂤}_{\text{目标}}$】= 追。“𠂤”本指“土丘”，卜辞借用为“師”（军队）（马如森, 2008：148-149；也见董莲池, 2005：68）。于是释义的出发点是假借义，不再关注本义。与此相似，“絞”也是一个使役性范畴：使“糸”“交”，只是这里的

“交”是隐喻性的。所以“絞”的图示可表示为：【（$X_{\text{动作者}}$）·交$_{\text{过程}}$·糸$_{\text{目标}}$】。但“絞”这个复合范畴涉及一个隐含对象（Y）（人或物）。结合上面的模式，其对象当为原因环境。于是，絞＝【（$X_{\text{动作者}}$）·交$_{\text{过程}}$·糸$_{\text{目标}}$·（$Y_{\text{目的原因环境}}$）】。

（18）鼓 gǔ 擊鼓也。从支从壴，壴亦聲。公戶切

“鼓”中“支”的事件特征是“手持木杖以击物”（马如森，2008：79），“壴”是“鼓”的独体象形字，两个部首放在一起的目的是要表明击鼓动作：【（$X_{\text{动作者}}$）·支$_{\text{过程}}$·壴$_{\text{目标}}$】＝鼓。“支”除了核心义“击打”，还包含工具“丨”和“用手持拿”的手段方式两个环境特征。

（19）寇 kòu 暴也。从支从完。苦候切

“寇”字，金文写作等形，容庚（1985：219）分析为“从人从支在宀下會意”。这里“人”（或：见金文字内左侧部首）有两种可能的理解：“支”的动作者或目标。董莲池解为“像以手持器入室擊人状”（2005：125），这样，“人”当为目标。于是，“寇”的及物性构成框架可表述为：【（$X_{\text{动作者}}$）·支$_{\text{过程}}$·人$_{\text{目标}}$·宀$_{\text{空间处所环境}}$】＝寇。

（20）陟 zhì 登也。从𨸏从步。竹力切

【（$X_{\text{动作者}}$）·步$_{\text{过程}}$·𨸏$_{\text{目标}}$】＝陟

甲骨文作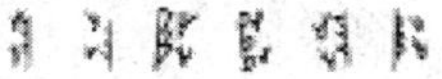（𨸏：ēù，大陸，山無石者；对比“降”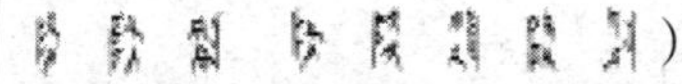）

（21）媛 yuàn 美女也。人所援也。从女从爰。爰，引也。玉眷切

【（$X_{\text{动作者}}$）·爰$_{\text{过程}}$·女$_{\text{目标}}$＝事物∪品质】＝媛

“媛”，甲骨文作，马如森（2008：103）解释为“从两手、从丨，象两手引取物器之形”；李孝定认为“象二人相引之行”（转引自徐中舒，1996：852）。

其他类似情况包括：“男”（“丈夫也；从田从力；言男用力於田也”）、“娩”（“生子免身也；从子从免”）、“畋”（“平田也；从支、田”）、“牧”（“養牛人也；从支从牛”）。注意，“牧”是事物（名词），指人，其他为事件（动词）。

（22）屋 wū 居也。从尸。尸，所主也。一曰尸，象屋形。从至。至，所至止。室、屋皆从至。烏谷切

【（$X_{\text{动作者}}$）·至$_{\text{过程}}$·尸$_{\text{目标}}$】＝屋

如果“尸”作“主体”解，“屋”的及物性框架结构就该是：【尸$_{\text{动作者}}$·至$_{\text{过程}}$·（$Y_{\text{目标}}$）】。

这是后面要讨论的目标缺失的例子。此外，“室”的构成跟“屋”一样。所以，“屋”和“室”的及物性结构可以合写在一起：【（$X_{\text{动作者1}}$/矢$_{\text{动作者2}}$·[到]$_{\text{过程1/2}}$）·〖尸或宀〗$_{\text{目标1}}$】。当然，如果“屋”中“尸”作“主”解，其词汇语义过程就应该是：【尸$_{\text{动作者}}$·至$_{\text{过程·目标}}$】。

（23）聿 yù 所以書也。楚謂之聿，吳謂之不律，燕謂之弗。从𦘒一聲。余律切

此字在甲骨文中为以手执筆之状：，因此显性部分包含了三个成

分：过程是通过“又”和“丨”的交叉关系协同体现的：【（X动作者）·聿过程·目标·手段方式环境＝所以書也】。

（24）鄉 xiāng 國離邑，民所封鄉也。从𨛜皀聲。許良切

董莲池认为，“鄉”在甲骨文中有 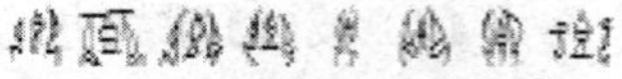 诸形，表二人相对跽跪（和）面簋（）而食：【动作者·（吃过程·食物目标）·簋手段方式环境】= 鄉。

“配”也属于这种情况（：配享；董莲池, 2005：261, 589-590）。

（25）娶 qǔ 取婦也。从女从取，取亦聲。七句切

此与（4）相类；“取”也是隐喻性的，字在甲骨文中写作 ，灭敌后取耳计数。所以，“娶”包含一个隐喻性的复合框架：【（[X]动作者）·〖取：：迎娶回家/割取回朝〗过程·女/耳目标】= 娶。其他涉及复合框架的范畴如下。

（26）𡵨 cén 入山之深也。从山从入。鉏箴切

【（[X]动作者1/载体2）·〖入过程1·山目标1 +（深结果属性2）〗】= 𡵨。

类似情况有“貧”和“甏”。

（27）貧 pín 財分少也。从貝从分，分亦聲。符巾切

【（[X]动作者1/载体2）·〖分过程1·貝目标1 +（少结果属性2）〗】= 貧。

“分”的构成成分“刀”和“八”不再是动词事件，所以不宜再做进一步拆解；“汲”中的“及”（从人从又：捕人）和“𠬝”（；ēú，治也。从又从“卩”。“卩”，“事之節也”。形如以手按人跪伏之状，表降服、制服意）同此，因为这些部件跟“聿”（）、“尹”（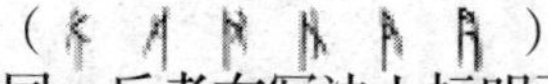）、“史”（）、“支”（）等不同，后者在写法上标明了过程特点，均有持握之像。

（28）甏 ruǎn 柔韋也。从北，从皮省，从夐省。而兖切

其中的“夐”字，读作xuàn/xiòng，《说文》的解释是：“營求也；从夏，从人在穴上”。徐铉认为“北”系“反覆柔治之也”（引自段玉裁, 2006：122）。所以，它在“甏”的词义化过程中应为鞣制（“北”）目的原因环境：为“營求”“柔韋”的目的而“反覆”加工。注意该字在《说文》中的写法：古文作“𤿭”，籀文作“𤿯”，小篆作“𤿰”。前二形均有“人”和“穴”字：古文在右下（左当为“皮”之意象），籀文分别在顶上和中间（皮在下）；而小篆变为二人（顶上；“穴”居中；“皮”在下），“相背以治皮”之意，其下不应为“瓬”（瓦）字，而是“皮”和“又”（手）的组合（严可均；见董莲池, 2007：74）。“[皮]”为两个过程套叠的共享成分。如果上述理解可基本接受的话，则“甏”的词义化过程为：【（X动作者1）·北过程1·夐目的原因环境1·[皮]目标1/载体2·（柔属性2）】= 甏（鞣制皮革）。

（29）佼 jiāo/jiǎo/xiào 交也。从人从交。下巧切

“交”在甲骨文中作或：“交脛也”，即“骹”初文，字像一人形，两

条小腿做交叉状，是一个事件范畴：【（脛$_{\text{载体}}$）·交$_{\text{属性}}$】= 骹。

但在及物性过程中，“交”的意义已经脱离了上述初始意义而进入人际之间的交往范围。如果说“交”的一致式特征是生理性质的话，它在“佼”这个范畴中则被映射到社会域：

【（脛$_{\text{载体}}$）·交$_{\text{属性}}$】×【〖F$_{\text{双方}}$〗$_{\text{动作者}}$=｛个体$_1$，个体$_2$，个体$_3$，……｝】=

【人〖F$_{\text{双方动作者1}}$〗/（脛$_{\text{载体2}}$）·[交]$_{\text{过程1/属性2}}$】= 佼。

显然，这里出现的新特征明显，即“人”为转喻：由个体指代非个体。

我们再看“过程”缺失的例子。对比前面提到的“保”和“朢”。

（30）伐 Fá 擊也。从人持戈。一曰敗也。房越切

【人$_{\text{动作者}}$·（持$_{\text{过程}}$）·戈$_{\text{目标}}$】= 伐

（31）后 hòu 繼體君也。象人之形。施令以告四方，故厂之。从一、口。發號者，君后也。胡口切

此为“毓”异体；“后”在甲骨文作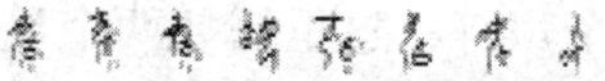（马如森, 2008：208；对比“孕”字）。这里的“子”更准确地说是过程涉及的范围：【女$_{\text{动作者}}$·（生娩$_{\text{过程}}$）·子$_{\text{目标}}$】= 后。

（32）孕 yùn 裹子也。从子从几。以證切

从甲骨文“鋅”可见，这里的动作者和过程应为一体，由“几”体现；“子”和“几”分开只是权宜之计。其结构为：【人$_{\text{动作者}}$·（裹$_{\text{过程}}$）·子$_{\text{目标}}$】= 孕。

（33）件 jiàn 分也。从人从牛。牛大物，故可分。其輦切

【人$_{\text{动作者}}$·（分$_{\text{过程}}$）·牛$_{\text{目标}}$·（Y$_{\text{成品角色环境}}$）】= 件

角色环境指由过程发生导致的成果性背景信息，如“她转眼就长成大人了”中的“大人”，由名词词组承担。下面是带复合过程的范畴。

（34）舝 xiá 車軸耑鍵也。兩穿相背，从舛；䇧省聲。䇧，古文偰字。胡戛切

【虫$_{\text{动作者}}$·（咬$_{\text{过程}}$）·[止]$_{\text{目标}}$】+【止$_{\text{载体}}$·（被害$_{\text{结果属性}}$）】=

【虫$_{\text{动作者1}}$·（咬$_{\text{过程1}}$）·[止]$_{\text{目标1/载体2}}$·（被害$_{\text{结果属性2}}$）】= 舝

裘锡圭认为，“舝”的甲骨文为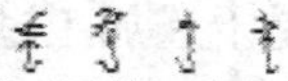，意为“足趾被虫所咬，伤害之害”（见董莲池 2005：217）。“朙”同此：因“照”而“朙”；注意“朙”中有“从月到月光”的转喻修辞：

（35）贙 xuàn 分别也。从虤對爭貝。讀若迴。胡畎切

【[虤]$_{\text{动作者1/属有者2}}$·（争$_{\text{过程1}}$）·[貝]$_{\text{目标1/被属有者2/载体3}}$·（分别$_{\text{结果属性3}}$）】= 贙

这里提供了“争”的过程和原因：“争”的起因是“貝”，从而达到“分别”的会意目的。

（36）順 shùn 理也。从頁从巛。食閏切

【（X$_{\text{载体=属有者1}}$）·頁$_{\text{属性=被属有者1}}$】×【頁$_{\text{动作者2}}$·（循$_{\text{过程2}}$）·理$_{\text{目标2}}$】×

【巛$_{\text{动作者3}}$·（流$_{\text{过程3}}$）】=【（X$_{\text{载体=属有者1}}$）·[頁]$_{\text{属性=被属有者1/动作者2/动作者3}}$

·（循$_{\text{过程2}}$·理$_{\text{目标2}}$）/巛$_{\text{动作者3}}$·（流$_{\text{过程3}}$）】= 順（遵循，仿效）

最后是“目标”缺失的例子。这种情况不多：一般说来，如果目标显现，动作者和过程相对容易恢复；如果目标隐没，可能的范围广，不容易具体化，范畴的针

对性会受到影响。

（37）係 xì 絜束也。从人从系，系亦聲。胡計切

【人$_{\text{动作者}}$ · 系$_{\text{过程}}$ ·（Y$_{\text{目标}}$）】= 係

（38）晝 zhòu 日之出入，與夜爲界。从畫省，从日。陟救切

【日/（人$_{\text{动作者}}$）· 晝/刻畫$_{\text{过程}}$ ·（时间/玉$_{\text{目标}}$）】= 晝

指白天的时间，为隐喻；“晝”金文作，从聿从周；周即琱，治玉也，故晝本义为“刻畫”（董莲池, 2005：118）。

下面的范畴带复合框架。

（39）嬔 fàn 生子齊均也。从女从生，免聲。芳萬切

【女$_{\text{动作者1}}$ · 生$_{\text{过程1}}$ ·（[子]$_{\text{目标1/载体2}}$）·（齊均也$_{\text{结果属性2}}$】= 嬔

（“嬔”的意思是“生子多而素质均匀”；复合框架）

显然，本小节讨论的现象不可能涉及形声字体现的范畴，因为典型的形声字都是一个意符和一个声符；这里需要两个显性意符；但这种情况并不排除合体假借字，如（15）“卸”。

4. 及物过程框架下有两个或以上主要成分隐没的范畴

这个类别的例子占及物类的绝大多数，我们分为四个次类逐一讨论：（1）动作者和目标隐没；（2）过程和目标隐没；（3）动作者和过程隐没；（4）动作者、过程和目标同时隐没；以第1、3者居多，故前二者一起讨论。先看只有过程和环境出现、动作者和目标隐没的实例。这样的情况大都比较复杂。

（40）授 shòu 予也。从手从受，受亦聲。殖酉切

【（X$_{\text{动作者}}$）· 受$_{\text{过程}}$ ·（Y$_{\text{目标}}$）· 手$_{\text{手段方式环境}}$】= 授

（41）仝 quán 完也。从入从工。疾緣切

即“全”：纯玉。其中“工”为曲尺，“入”表进入（杨树达；见徐中舒, 1996：47）。鉴于“仝”关注的是上述加工过程的促动因素“完也”：“纯玉”，在符号的表征上是隐性的。所以，“仝”的模式应为：【（X$_{\text{动作者}}$）·（使）入$_{\text{过程}}$ ·（玉$_{\text{目标}}$）·〖工$_{\text{手段方式环境}}$ +（完$_{\text{目的原因环境}}$）〗】。

这种使动特征在“連”中也存在：

（42）連 lián 員連也。从辵从車。力延切

即使“車”“辵”；但段玉裁的解释是人拉车，这样就涉及两个过程：【（X$_{\text{动作者}}$ · 拉$_{\text{过程}}$）· 車$_{\text{目标}}$】+【（車$_{\text{动作者}}$）· 辵$_{\text{过程}}$】。注意“辵”的甲骨文写法：。据此，“連”的及物性框架可以合写为：【（X$_{\text{动作者1}}$ · 拉$_{\text{过程1}}$）· [車]$_{\text{目标1/动作者2}}$ · 辵$_{\text{过程2}}$】= 連。

（43）灋 fǎ 刑也。平之如水，从水；廌，所㠯觸不直者；去之，从去。方乏切

字中“水”是一个标准性成分：像“水”一样（公）平；“去”是事件：去除违法者；“廌”当为“去”的促动因素：要像“廌”那样“觸不直”，于是整个范畴就带上了隐喻。“灋”的及物性框架为：【（执法者$_{\text{动作者}}$）· 去$_{\text{过程}}$ ·（罪犯$_{\text{目}}$

标）·〖水$_{手段方式环境}$ + 鹰$_{目的原因环境}$〗】。

下面是复合过程；这一现象（4）“揫”已经涉及了。

（44）醉 zuì 卒也。卒其度量，不至於亂也。一曰潰也。从酉从卒。將遂切

许慎提供了两种解释。就“卒也”的解释看，我们有理由把“卒”看作终止“饮酒”的行为，据此“醉”可初步描述为：【（X$_{动作者}$）·卒$_{过程}$·（酒$_{目标}$）·酉$_{手段方式环境}$】。但这个框架没能把事件“止酉”前的过程表达出来。我们对上面的模式做如下修正：【（[X]$_{动作者1+2}$）·〖卒$_{过程1}$ +（[饮]$_{目标1/过程2}$）·（酒$_{目标2}$）〗·[酉]$_{手段方式环境1+2}$】。这里的动作者和环境为两个过程共享；“饮”既是目标（事物），也是过程（事件）。而就后一种解释“溃也”看，其模式应为：【（[X]$_{动作者1+2}$）·卒$_{过程1}$·（酒$_{目标1}$）·酉$_{手段方式环境1}$·（溃也$_{结果属性2}$）】。

下面是一个形声字的例子。其中声符“古”也可作“表义”。

（45）故 gù 使爲之也。从攴古聲。古慕切

【（X$_{动作者}$）·攴$_{过程}$·（Y$_{目标}$）·|古s ≡ 使爲之也】= 故

此类现象在以部首为及物类事件的范畴中比较常见，如这里涉及的“攴”，其他如“殳”等。

过程和目标同时隐没的情况不多，下面是有关实例。

（46）歊 xiāo 歊歊，气出皃。从欠、高，高亦聲。許嬌切

【卩$_{动作者1}$·（吐$_{过程1}$·气$_{目标1}$）·口$_{手段方式环境1}$】+【（气$_{载体2}$）·高$_{属性2}$】=

【卩$_{动作者1}$·（吐$_{过程1}$·口$_{手段方式环境1}$·[气]$_{目标1/载体2}$）·高$_{属性2}$】= 歊

（“欠”：鸦鸭丫芽；“欠”在这里被拆解成“卩”和“口”两部分）

现在看动作者和过程成分同时隐没的范畴。这些范畴同样复杂，实例较多。

（47）飤 sì 糧也。从人、食。祥吏切

这是后来的“飼”字，表达一个使役性事件：【（X$_{动作者}$·过程$_{过程}$）·Y$_{目标}$·食物$_{手段方式环境}$】= 飤。具有相同结构的有餽（guì/kuì，“吳人謂祭曰餽；从食从鬼，鬼亦聲”）。但对比祭（“祭祀也；从示，以手持肉”）：【（X$_{动作者}$·持$_{过程}$）·肉$_{目标}$·〖示$_{原因环境}$ + 又$_{手段方式环境}$〗】。

（48）便 pián /biàn 安也。人有不便，更之。从人、更。房連切

【（X$_{动作者}$·鞭打$_{过程}$）·人$_{目标}$·手$_{手段方式环境1}$·更$_{手段方式环境2}$】= 便

唐兰认为，这是鞭的原始字，在金文中写作：用手（右下角）持鞭鞭人之背（徐中舒 1996：66）；‘环境$_2$’（右边的中间部分）表工具，在及物性框架中为手段方式环境。

（49）冥 míng 幽也。从日从六，冖聲。日數十。十六日而月始虧幽也。莫經切

【（X$_{动作者}$·持$_{过程}$）·巾$_{目标}$·又$_{方式环境}$】×【（幽$_{载体·结果属性}$）】= 冥

（“冥”甲骨文作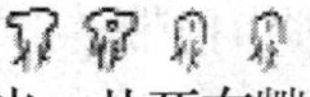，唐兰认为“像两手以巾覆物之形”）

（50）葬 zàng 藏也。从死在茻中；一其中，所以薦之。則浪切

【（X$_{动作者}$·掩埋$_{过程}$）·〖死：：死者：：尸体〗$_{目标}$·茻$_{空间处所环境}$】= 葬

其中的转喻涉及下面的及物性框架：【（人$_{动作者}$）·死$_{过程}$·（尸体$_{成品角色环境}$）】。

（51）反 fǎn 覆也。从又，厂反形。府遠切

【（X$_{\text{动作者}}$·攀$_{\text{过程}}$）·厂$_{\text{目标}}$·又$_{\text{手段方式环境}}$】= 反

（“反”甲骨文作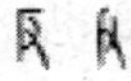，其中“厂”意为“山石厓巌”，字“谓人以手攀厓也”）

（52）尿 niào 人小便也。从尾从水。奴弔切

【（X$_{\text{动作者}}$·撒$_{\text{过程}}$）·水$_{\text{目标}}$·尾$_{\text{空间处所环境}}$】= 尿

这里的目标更确切地说是“范围”，即过程延伸的内容，包括“泅水”“爬山”“走关东”“吃食堂”“吃苦头”“唱歌”“跳舞”“打针”“踢球”“开飞机”“骑自行车”“打游击”“看戏”等，即传统语法说的同源宾语（见龙日金、彭宣维，2012）。

（53）祓 fú 除惡祭也。从示犮聲。敷勿切

【（X$_{\text{动作者}}$·祭$_{\text{过程}}$）·示$_{\text{目标}}$·|犮s（目的：除惡）≡ 除惡祭也】= 祓（形声字）

以下范畴均涉及复合框架。

（54）罷 bǎ/bà/pí 遣有辠也。从网、能。言有賢能而入网，而貫遣之。薄蟹切

【（X$_{\text{动作者}}$·遣$_{\text{过程}}$）·能$_{\text{目标}}$】+【（Y$_{\text{载体}}$）·能$_{\text{属性}}$】=

【（X$_{\text{动作者1}}$·遣$_{\text{过程1}}$）·能$_{\text{目标1/属性2}}$·[Y]$_{\text{载体2}}$】= 罷

（55）俄 é 行頃也。从人我聲。五何切

【（X$_{\text{动作者1}}$·砍$_{\text{过程1}}$）·人$_{\text{目标1}}$·戈$_{\text{手段方式环境1}}$】×【人$_{\text{载体2}}$·（顷$_{\text{属性2}}$）】=

【（X$_{\text{动作者1}}$·砍$_{\text{过程1}}$）·[人]$_{\text{目标1/载体2}}$·戈$_{\text{手段方式环境1}}$·（顷$_{\text{属性2}}$）】= 俄

该字甲骨文作。董莲池（2005：319）解释为：字由缺足的正面人形“大”（粥）和斧钺“我”（掎）构成，意为砍足而斜；“行顷也”为引申义。综合起来看，许说更符合《说文》以具体表抽象概念的基本原则（对比“鱻”及其构成成分“魚”与特征“鲜”，以及“吅”及其构成“口”与特征“驚呼”之间的关系）。

（56）肁 zhào 始開也。从戶从聿。治矯切

【（X$_{\text{动作者1}}$）·开$_{\text{过程1}}$·户$_{\text{目标1}}$】×【（X$_{\text{动作者1}}$·持$_{\text{过程2}}$）·聿$_{\text{目标2}}$】=

【（[X]$_{\text{动作者1+2}}$）·开$_{\text{过程1}}$/（持$_{\text{过程2}}$）·户$_{\text{目标1}}$/聿$_{\text{目标2}}$】= 肁（同“肇”）

段玉裁（2006：587）解为“凡始之称”，其引申义内涵变窄而外延拓宽。

（57）啟 qí/qǐ 教也。从攴启聲。康礼切

“啟”甲骨文为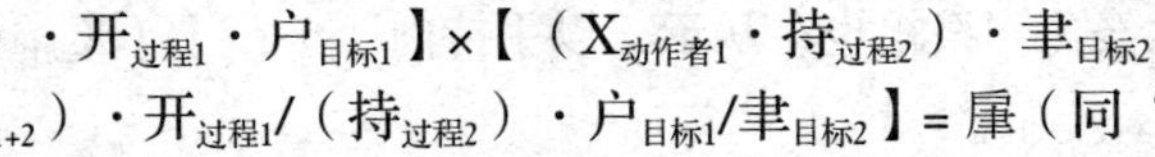，从户从口，或从又。据此，有三种描述方法。第一，没有“口”的情况：【（X$_{\text{动作者}}$·开$_{\text{过程}}$）·户$_{\text{目标}}$·又$_{\text{手段方式环境}}$】；第二，有“口”的情况，有人解释为“打开门以口说话”，据此：【（X$_{\text{动作者}}$·开$_{\text{过程}}$）·户$_{\text{目标}}$·〖又$_{\text{手段方式环境}}$ +（说$_{\text{目的原因环境}}$）+ 口$_{\text{手段方式环境}}$〗】，这应该包括“啟”的另一种写法“啓”；第三，还可以就有“口”的写法做出一种解释。根据《说文》中出现的大量隐喻构字情况，我们有理由把带“口”的“啟”解释为：开门如同开口：【（[X]$_{\text{动作者1/行为者2}}$·开$_{\text{过程1/2}}$）·户$_{\text{目标1}}$/口$_{\text{目标2}}$·又$_{\text{方式环境1}}$】= 啟。而有“口”无“攴”者可以描述为：【（X$_{\text{行为者}}$·说话$_{\text{过程}}$）·口$_{\text{手段方式环境}}$】，不再是物质过程，而是行为过程。

（58）皮 pí 剥取獸革者謂之皮。从又，爲省聲。符羈切

【（$X_{\text{动作者}}$·剥$_{\text{过程}}$）·獸革$_{\text{目标}}$·又$_{\text{手段方式环境}}$】×【獸革$_{\text{载体}}$·$Y_{\text{属性}}$】=

【（$X_{\text{动作者}}$·剥$_{\text{过程}}$）·獸革$_{\text{目标}}$·〖又$_{\text{手段方式环境}}$ + $Y_{\text{成品角色环境}}$〗】= 皮

上述解释从金文或（董莲池, 2005：122）；“属性”是由“獸革”变来的成品。

最后看动作者、过程和目标三者同时缺失、只有环境成分显现的范畴，不少是复合框架。

（59）罰 fá 辠之小者。从刀从詈。未以刀有所賊，但持刀罵詈，則應罰。房越切

徐灏的解释是：“罰，从网从言从刀。网者罪之省也；言者爰书定罪之意；刀者自大辟以至剕刵髡黥之属，皆刑其肢体也。析言之，则重者为刑，轻者为罰。”（转引自徐中舒, 1996：1219）。据此，“罰”的及物性过程为：【（$X_{\text{动作者}}$·刑$_{\text{过程}}$·$Y_{\text{目标}}$）·〖网$_{\text{原因环境}}$ + 言$_{\text{角度环境}}$ + 刀$_{\text{手段环境}}$〗】。

（60）辱 rǔ 耻也。从寸在辰下。失耕時，於封畺上戮之也。辰者，農之時也。故房星爲辰，田候也。而蜀切

董莲池（2005：586-587）认为：“辱”的意思应该是“手持辰以行农事”，即甲骨文“農”（）所从，“甲骨文从又之字至篆文常变作从寸”，可能是“耨”字初文。“辱”的及物性模式可以写作：【（$X_{\text{动作者}}$·行$_{\text{过程}}$·农事$_{\text{目标}}$）·〖辰$_{\text{手段方式环境}}$+ 又$_{\text{手段方式环境}}$〗】。

（61）買 mǎi 市也。从网、貝。莫蟹切

【（$X_{\text{动作者1}}$·获得$_{\text{过程1}}$·货物$_{\text{目标1}}$）·貝$_{\text{手段方式环境1}}$】×

【（$X_{\text{动作者2}}$·扑捉$_{\text{过程2}}$·鳥獸$_{\text{目标2}}$）·网$_{\text{手段方式环境2}}$】=

【（[X]$_{\text{动作者1/2}}$·获得$_{\text{过程1}}$/扑捉$_{\text{过程2}}$·货物$_{\text{目标1}}$/鳥獸$_{\text{目标2}}$）·貝$_{\text{环境1}}$·网$_{\text{环境2}}$】= 買

跟“買”语义相对、图示相当的是“賣”（mài，“出物貨也；从出从買”）。不同点在于过程的“获得”与“给出”关涉的方向性，即矢量特征有别。

（62）等 děng 齊簡也。从竹从寺。寺，官曹之等平也。多肯切

王钧在《句读》中解释为“整齊其簡牘也”（见徐中舒, 1996：212, 1235），可见“竹”在这个范畴的形成中所发挥的是转喻作用：用材料表征成品“簡牘”：

【（$X_{\text{动作者1}}$·加工$_{\text{过程1}}$）·竹$_{\text{目标1}}$·（簡$_{\text{结果属性1}}$）】+

【（$Y_{\text{动作者2}}$·整理$_{\text{过程2}}$·簡$_{\text{目标2}}$）·〖寺：：齊〗$_{\text{结果属性2}}$】=

【（$X_{\text{动作者1}}$·加工$_{\text{过程1}}$）·竹$_{\text{目标1}}$·（簡$_{\text{结果属性1/目标2}}$

·（被）整理$_{\text{过程2}}$）·〖寺：：齊〗$_{\text{结果属性2}}$】= 等。

该类存在形声字的实例。

（63）剪 jiǎn 齊斷也。从刀歬聲。子善切

【（$X_{\text{动作者}}$·斷$_{\text{过程}}$·$Y_{\text{目标}}$）·〖刀$_{\text{手段方式环境}}$ + 齊$_{\text{比较方式环境}}$〗·|歬s】= 剪

（64）攘 ràng 推也。从手襄聲。汝羊切

【（$X_{\text{动作者}}$·推$_{\text{过程}}$·$Y_{\text{目标}}$）·手$_{\text{手段方式环境}}$·|襄s】= 攘

5. 结语

分析表明，通过系统功能语法的及物性模式恢复的隐没成分，能充分体现系统功能语言学以句为出发点的理论优势，否则补足相关成分的做法以及成分之间的关系就会失去支撑平台；但如果没有及物过程，我们有很难找到合适的框架来解释词义化涉及的“填充”机制。此前的研究发现，及物性过程在现代汉语的小句分布中占有绝对优势（彭宣维，2000），它在词义化过程中仍然是主要的。

此外，及物性涉及的词汇语法关系所起的作用也是明显的。比如，（1）人、身体器官和日用工具：“人”“大”“又”“手”“口”“足”“目”“心”“止”“頁”“肉”“女”“貝”“刀”“火”“糸”“車”；（2）处所：“宀”“穴”“尸”“邑”“囗”；（3）常见动植物以及非生物：“犬”“魚”“馬”“豕”“鳥”“牛”“羊”“艸”“木”“禾”“竹”“水”“日”“金”；它们是在及物性框架的导入下形成词义概念的。

鸣谢：本文系教育部人文社科重点研究基地民俗典籍文字研究中心2013年度重大项目（项目批准号：13JJD740004）阶段性成果。蒙北京师范大学文学院王宁教授和卜师霞博士审阅，谨此致谢。

参考文献

Halliday, M. A. K. 1994. *An Introduction to Functional Grammar* (2nd edition). London: Arnold.

董莲池，2005，《说文解字考正》。北京：作家出版社。

董莲池，2007，《说文部首形义新证》。北京：作家出版社。

胡壮麟、朱永生、张德禄、李战子，2005，《系统功能语言学概论》。北京：北京大学出版社。

龙日金、彭宣维，2012，《现代汉语及物性研究》。北京：北京大学出版社。

马如森，2008，《殷墟甲骨文实用字典》。上海：上海大学出版社。

孟世凯，2009，《甲骨学辞典》。上海：上海人民出版社。

彭宣维，2000，《英汉语篇综合对比》。上海：上海外语教育出版社。

容庚，1985，《金文编》。北京：中华书局。

许慎（汉）著、段玉裁（清）注，2006，《说文解字注》。上海：上海古籍出版社。

徐中舒主编，1996，《汉语大字典》（缩印本）。成都：四川辞书出版社；武汉：湖北辞书出版社。

曾宪通，1992，《长沙楚帛书文字编》。北京：中华书局。

标示–价值结构的功能句法分析

——以“谁是NP？”和“NP是谁？”为例[1]

王　遥

山东理工大学/上海外国语大学

1.引言

根据Halliday为代表的系统功能语法，及物性系统能够将现实模型化为不同的经验过程，如物质过程是事物动作和事件发生的过程（a process of doing and happening），而心理过程构建的则是与感觉认知等相关的意识经验（a process of sensing）。不同的过程在语言的语法体系中反映出不同的特点。其中，关系过程小句（以下简称关系小句）表现的是一个对象与其自身或是与其他对象在特征属性以及情境等方面的关系（a process of being）。传统语法对关系小句的描述往往过于简单，甚至在很大程度上忽视了对其内在结构和语义关系的解释（Bloor & Bloor, 1995; Thompson, 1996）。作为关系小句的描述方式之一，标示–价值结构（Token-Value structure）[2]反映了关系双方在表达和内容层面的逻辑语义关系，这一结构与同为关系小句描述方式的被认同者–认同者结构以及语篇功能的主位及信息结构等既有联系又有区别。标示–价值结构在整个及物性系统中是“最费解然而却同时又是最重要的一部分”，通过对这一结构的分析往往能有助于对价值倾向性语域（如科技性、商务性、政治性以及官方性语篇）的理解和评价（Halliday, 1994: 126; Halliday & Matthiessen, 2004: 234）。正是由于这一结构的复杂性和争议性，国内外学界对关系小句标示-价值结构有限的研究多以引述观点为主，其关注点在于对结构本身的划分理据进行功能句法分析（Matthiessen, 1991; Davidse, 1992, 1996; 何伟, 2002; 袁鑫, 2004; 何恒幸, 2007），而对该结构的实践应用分析则相对较为鲜见，文献检索发现仅有张和友（2003）利用标示–价值结构对两种汉语语法结构的阐释及王遥和李景娜（2007）尝试将标示–价值结构应用于语篇分析两项研究。鉴于此，本文拟对这一结构展开功能语义的阐释，正确把握其含义以进一步理解关系小句的本质所在。

1 本文曾在“第40届国际系统功能语言学大会”（中国广州，2013年7月）上宣读，主要内容发表在《当代外语研究》，2014年第3期，15-19。

2 国内文献对关系小句种种概念的译法较为混乱，如“标示–价值”也译作“标记–价值”等等（何伟，2002; 张璘，2007等），本文术语统一参照黄国文(2000)与胡壮麟(2008)的译法。

2. 关系小句的分类

关系小句主要用来将对象做特征化和认同化处理。Halliday & Matthiessen（2004: 211）从两个角度对关系小句进行了考察：从小句以上层面来看，关系小句的作用在于把人们对于客观世界和主观世界的经验模型化为一种关系（而不是动作或是感觉），而在小句以下层面，典型的关系小句由体现过程的不同时态的系动词和两个参与者构成。关系小句的作用在于把经验识解为一种没有能量介入因而不产生相的变化的均衡状态，这样识解的关键就落在了两个参与者上，而过程只不过是参与者之间的一种高度概括化的联系，因而体现过程的动词是非突显的，在语音上往往表现为非重读特征（如*Tom's a student*中的/z/，或者“小明是个学生”中的“是”）[3]。

在Halliday & Matthiessen（2004）看来，关系小句的两个参与对象x与a之间的语义关系可以是归属的、环境的或者是属有的，对应地就有了三种类型的关系小句，即集约型（x is a）、环境型（x is at a）和属有型（x has a）；这三种类型又可以进一步分为两种模式，即修饰式（a is an attribute of x）和认同式（a is the identity of x）。Halliday同时指出两个参与者在修饰式小句中的位置不可互换，而在认同式中则可以，两个系统互相交叉，构成了关系小句的六种范畴，如表1所示：

表1 关系小句范畴体系（Halliday & Matthiessen, 2004: 216）

	修饰式	认同式
集约型	Sarah is wise	Sarah is the leader The leader is Sarah
环境型	The fair is on a Tuesday	Tomorrow is the 10th The 10th is tomorrow
属有型	Peter has a piano	The Piano is Peter's Peter's is the piano

3. 标示–价值结构

3.1 标示–价值结构的界定

在传统的系统功能语法框架下，标示–价值结构是认同式关系小句的描述方式之一。就其本质而言，认同关系就是把一个具体的概念形式与一个概括的功能范畴联系起来，而标示–价值结构的配置便是依据这种经验体现功能，二者的确定正是以人们对经验世界的认识为前提，表示概括的或更为抽象的一般性内容是价值，而特指

3 动词弱化的极端形式就是缺省，在英语中表现为非限定小句（如 *Tom came in, with a book in hand* 中 *with* 引导的小句），而汉语中则往往是以无标记的形式体现为动词的直接缺省（如“小娜人很好”）。

的或者说具体化的成分则是标示，试看下例分析：

(1) Tom is the treasurer.
[Tk ^ Vl][4]
(2) Tom is the tall one.
[Vl ^ Tk]

在例（1）中，*Tom*被认同为一个更抽象的范畴*the treasurer*的具体体现形式，之所以说*the treasurer*这一范畴是更抽象和更概括的，是因为这一范畴从理论上来说可以有其他具体的体现形式，即从理论上来说可以指称其他除*Tom*以外的人。例（1）相当于对提问“*What is Tom?*”的应答，即已经知道有一个具体的*Tom*，下面要对*Tom*的抽象身份做一定的了解。与之相反，在例（2）中，*Tom*作为相对抽象的范畴被认同为具体的体现形式*the tall one*，这里相当于有人提问“*Which is Tom?*”，即已经知道了有具体的一些人，接下来要做的则是把其中一个具体的人找出来认同为其抽象的身份*Tom*。

根据Halliday & Matthiessen（2004）的观点，认同式关系小句存在着方向性，标示和价值的不同配置方式决定了小句能够以编码或解码的方式展现关系双方的认同关系：

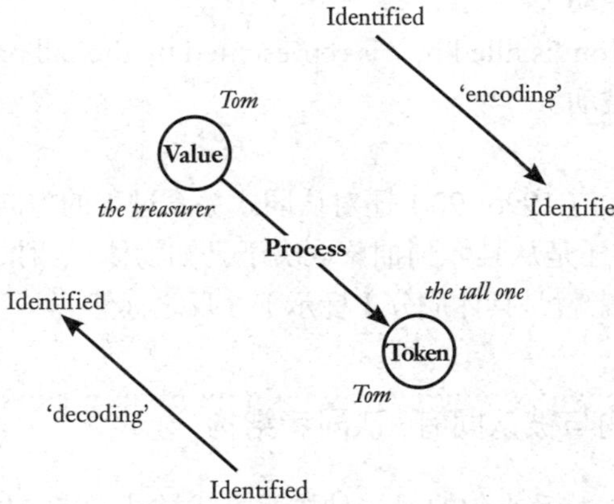

图1 关系小句的编码与解码认同方式（Halliday & Matthiessen, 2004: 230）

如图1所示，标示被认同为价值，关系小句体现为解码形式（*Tom is the treasure*）；价值被认同为标示，关系小句则体现为编码形式（*Tom is the tall one*）。由此可见，认同关系或者通过参照价值来解码标示，或者通过参照标示来编码价值。这也同时解释了以下（3）和（4）二例不合格的原因所在，因为*the tall one*一般被识解为标示，而*the treasurer*则为价值，二者不可以并列出现：

4 文中缩略语的全称为：Tk=Token, Vl=Value, Id=Identified, Ir=Identifier, G=Given, N=New。

(3)* Tom is the tall one and the treasurer.
(4)* The tall one and the treasurer is Tom.

此外，Halliday & Matthiessen（2004: 231）还认为，标示–价值结构决定了小句语态的选择，主语是标示则小句为主动语态，而主语是价值则小句为被动语态，以（1）和（2）两句为例：

(1) Tom is the treasurer.
[Tk ^ Vl]（主动）
(2) Tom is the tall one.
[Vl ^ Tk]（被动）

按照Thompson（1996: 90）的建议，可以用*represent*，*play*及*fill the role of*等实义动词或词组把原有的系词进行替换，因此（1）和（2）两个小句可以分别转写为（5）和（6），这样小句的语态就变得直观和清晰：

(5) Tom fills the role of / represents the treasurer.
[Tk ^ Vl]（主动）
(6) The role of Tom is filled by / is represented by the tall one.
[Vl ^ Tk]（被动）

另外，Thompson（1996: 90）还对认同式关系过程的方向性做出了进一步的解释，是从抽象到具体还是从具体到抽象取决于已知物体：如果已知物体是抽象概念（价值），则其认同者就是具体成分（标示），反之亦然。

3.2 标示–价值结构与被认同者–认同者结构

标示–价值结构与关系小句的另一种描述方式被认同者–认同者结构的配置依据都是经验体现功能，但二者之间有着本质上的区别。

被认同者和认同者的区分取决于语言事件的进展，其中，已经出现过的成分指称方式，即需要确定或辩明身份的对象是被认同者，而新的成分指称方式，或者说起确定或辩明身份的对象则是认同者，因此被认同者–认同者的配置分析能够有助于对特定语篇展开方式的了解和把握。相比之下，标示与价值的区分则取决于两种指称成分的原本已经存在的语义特征，二者中更概括化的方式是价值，而更具体化的方式则是标示，因此标示–价值结构分析体现的往往是作者乃至整个文化用来衡量和评价其所处理的标示的价值取向，正如Halliday（1994: 126）所说，“科技、商务、政治及官方话语等领域中，对认同式关系小句的概念性价值的分析对意识形态价值观的研究是非常有帮助的”。

标示–价值结构与被认同者–认同者结构在认同式关系小句中是结合在一起的，同一个小句由于这两种结构的不同配置组合可以产生四种不同的解释，试比较：

(7) Halliday is the systemic functional linguist.
[Id/Tk ^ Ir/Vl]
(8) Halliday is the systemic functional linguist.
[Ir/Tk ^ Id/Vl]
(9) Halliday is the systemic functional linguist.
[Id/Vl ^ Ir/Tk]
(10) Halliday is the systemic functional linguist.
[Ir/Vl ^ Id/Tk]

3.3 标示–价值结构与信息结构

信息结构体现着人们在交际中所传递内容的组织方式，结构由已知信息和新信息组成。信息结构由声调突出得以体现，而不是通过语言单位的排列来表示。在一个信息单位中，声调重音所在的成分便是信息中心。信息结构是从人们使用语言时对信息的组织角度出发，体现的是语言的语篇功能，这显然与体现语言概念功能的标示–价值结构不同（标示与价值的确定是从关系双方的语义基础出发的）。在把信息结构纳入考虑范围后，关系小句的分析在原有的标示–价值结构以及被认同者–认同者结构组配的基础上就又多出了一个维度，然而尽管如此，在实际的句法操作中，小句的解释方式并没有实质性的增加，因为在具体的语境中被认同者往往总是与已知信息重合，而认同者则总是与新信息相吻合。试比较：

(11) Halliday is the greatest systemic functional linguist.
[Id/Tk/G ^ Ir/Vl/N]
(12) Halliday is the greatest systemic functional linguist.
[Id/Vl/G ^ Ir/Tk/N]
(13) Halliday is the greatest systemic functional linguist.
[Ir/Tk/N ^ Id/Vl/G]
(14) Halliday is the greatest systemic functional linguist.
[Ir/Vl/N ^ Id/Tk/G]

4. 标示–价值结构的功能句法分析

“张老三是谁？”是否等于“谁是张老三？”？从表面来看，的确很难说清两句话的区别，毕竟二者有着相同的概念意义。然而，小句最终以这样而并非那样的方式出现，在很大程度上取决于具体的情景语境中预设所表达的内容以及焦点的选取；小句的表述方式之所以出现种种差异和不同，必定是在某种功能动因的作用和影响下产生的结果。正如杉村博文（2002: 14）所说，作为一种重要的句法手段，语序“无疑占着一个至高无上的地位，词序（语序）的变化总是伴随着语法意义的变化发生”。

最早对“谁是NP？”和“NP是谁？”的对应关系这一语言现象进行说明的是吕叔湘（1984）。吕先生受方言的启发，以“谁”可以分为“哪个”和“啥人”为例指出了“张老三是谁？”不一定等于“谁是张老三？”。杉村博文（2002）和张和友（2003）随后分别从语篇和功能的角度对这一现象进行了一定的阐释。通过对这一语言现象的进一步观察，可以发现，标示–价值这一组概念与认同式关系小句的被认同者–认同者配置以及信息结构的结合分析能够对这一问题进行更为明确和合理的解读。

先看“谁是张老三？”。在这个句子中，“张老三”作为待定成分，是被认同者，我们需要把“张老三”认同为一个特定对象，因为这时候我们已经知道有这样一个“张老三”，但并不知道哪一个人是“张老三”，因此“张老三”与其识别成分相比处于一个更加抽象的地位，因此，“谁”充当了小句的标示，而“张老三”则充当了价值：

(15) 谁是张老三？
[Ir/Tk ^ Id/Vl]

在具体的语境中，由于小句的形式受到情景预设表达内容的影响，我们可以通过对小句进行扩展分布的方法（如增补答句的方式）对其做出进一步的观察。扩展后的小句如例（16）和例（17）所示：

(16) 张老三是那个戴帽子的。
[Id/Vl/G ^ Ir/Tk/N]
(17) 那个戴帽子的是张老三。
[Id/Vl/N ^ Ir/Tk/G]

可以看出，例（16）和例（17）两个小句都是合格的。根据之前的分析，关系小句同样具有语态，而语态的选择取决于小句的标示–价值结构的不同配置，主语是标示则小句为主动，而主语是价值小句则为被动，因此例（16）表达被动意义，而例（17）则表达主动意义。从语态的标记性上讲，被动表达的例（16）明显具有更高的标记性。另一方面，从小句的信息结构来看，情况却恰恰相反，相对于例（17）信息组织结构的显著标记性特征（新信息在已知信息之前），例（16）却又体现为未标记形式（已知信息在新信息之前）。可见，正是由于两个小句或者在语态上（如例17）或者在信息结构上（如例16）的未标记特征决定了两个小句的语法合格性。

再来看“张老三是谁？”。在这个句子中，“张老三”仍然是待定成分，同样是作为被认同者，被认同为另一个特定的对象，虽然此时我们已经知道有一个“张老三”，但却不知道“张老三”是何许人也，因此对“张老三”的识别成分处在了一个更为抽象的层次，因此，“张老三”充当了小句的标示，而“谁”则充当价值：

(18) 张老三是谁？
[Id/Tk ^ Ir/Vl]

同样可以通过扩展分布的方法，以补充答句的方式来对小句进行观察，如例（19）和例（20）所示：

(19) 张老三是那个戴帽子的。
[Id/Tk/G ^ Ir/Vl/N]
(20) *那个戴帽子的是张老三。
[Ir/Vl/N ^ Id/Tk/G]

进一步的观察可以看出，例（20）明显是不合格的，其原因同样可以通过对小句的标示–价值结构进行分析，并通过对其语态和信息结构的标记性特征进行观察而得以阐释。例（20）的主语是价值，小句由于表达被动意义，因而带有语态的标记性特征；然而与此同时，其信息编码采用的是新信息在已知信息之前的组织方式，因而就信息结构来看也带有显著的标记性。我们知道，语言的标记性在实际运用中往往要受到各种条件的制约，正是这种在语态和信息结构上的双重标记性让（20）小句会在受话者看来有种非常别扭的感觉。与之相对，例（19）则无论是在语态上（主语是标示）还是在信息结构上（已知信息在前）都具有未标记性特征，因而更有可能作为“张老三是谁？”的正常应答方式。

5. 标示–价值结构的语义功能

标示–价值结构与被认同者–认同者结构及信息结构的结合可以实现关系小句的复杂语义功能，如预设或含意等。

预设是言语交际中发话者在发话前对话语的假设，可以是双方都已知道的常识或是发话者认为自身与受话者共享的信息，而这种常识或信息往往包含在语句的意思之中，无须表现在字面上。标示–价值结构可以体现关系小句的不同预设功能，例如，小句“谁是张老三？”的预设可以是：我们已经知道某一个人唤作“张老三”，但是却不知道哪一个人是“张老三”，“张老三”比其识别成分处在更抽象的位置，这时候的问句实际上要求对“张老三”进行指别和识认；而小句“张老三是谁？”的预设则有所不同：我们虽然同样已经听说过某人名为“张老三”，但却并不熟知“张老三”是何等人物，因此对“张老三”的识别成分要具有一种更为抽象的含义，这里问句的应答相当于对“张老三”进行一定程度的描述和说明。

此外，标示–价值结构的不同配置也可以实现小句的不同含意。含意或者说会话含意指的是发话者的话语或话语中词语的暗含或提示与字面意义有所差别的意义，往往生成于受话者对话语的理解过程中，具有主观性、动态性和可延伸性等特征。标示–价值结构同样可以表达这种语义功能，如下例所示：

(21) The best students are the greatest worriers.

例（21）因为标示与价值的不同配置可以出现以下两种含意：

(22) The best students are the greatest worriers.
（学习最好的学生往往忧虑最多。）
[Tk ^ Vl]

(23) The best students are the greatest worriers.
（忧虑最多的学生往往学习最好。）
[Vl ^ Tk]

6. 关系小句的本质

Halliday对于关系小句的分类研究始源于对英语动词be[5]的分析（何中清，2009）。Halliday（1967）早期对关系小句双方的划分没有以小句的表面形式作为出发点，而是从参与对象的语义关系角度出发，这符合功能语法的理念和原则，而后来Halliday（1994）对修饰式和认同式关系小句的区分却是以形式作为依据（参与者的位置是否可以互换）。我们认为，关系小句修饰式和认同式的确立并没有构成显著区别，尤其是考虑到环境型和属有型关系小句在这两种范式上的差别微乎其微，在这两种类型的关系小句中修饰式和认同式的区分更显得意义不大。以属有型关系小句为例：

(24) Peter has a piano.

(25) a. Peter's is the piano.
b. The piano is Peter's.

5 不包括在动词词组中的语法操作词 *be*，这时的 *be* 仅仅起到实现时态或语态特征，与及物性无关。

根据Halliday的观点，例（24）是修饰式关系小句，表达*Peter*对*a piano*的领属关系，而例（25）则是关系小句的认同式，体现着*Peter's*与*the piano*的等同关系；例（24）中两个参与者的位置不可互换，这很容易理解，然而例（25）中参与者的位置可以互换的论述却值得进一步推敲和商榷。从小句的表面形式来看，*Peter's is the piano*等于说*The piano is Peter's*，然而实际上两个参与者的语义关系发生了很大的变化，整个小句的含义也发生了相应的改变。比如，例（25）a预设的是*Peter*拥有的是*the piano*，而不是*guitar*或*drum*等其他的乐器，而例（25）b突显的则是*the piano*的拥有者是*Peter*，而不是*Tom*或*Mary*等其他人。

从语义关系变化的角度来看，在集约型关系小句方面，修饰式和认同式的区别意义也不显著，Thompson（1996: 93）举过这样一个例子来说明修饰式与认同式区分的不明确性：

(26) This little pattern is a common building block of spoken interaction.

就上例来看，很难说清小句到底是修饰式关系小句还是认同式关系小句。此外，类似“张三就是张三”“冰是冰”“火是火”等的同语反复，也很难讲清它们是属于修饰式还是认同式。基于以上考虑，可以把关系小句简单看作表明两个成分x与a之间的属性、环境或者属有关系的小句，具体把a当作x的属性还是把a看成x的认同的区分意义不大，毕竟，认同本身就可以看作一种属性，只不过是一种唯一的属性而已。Fawcett（1987）以及程晓堂（2002）的研究也部分地证明了这一观点。

在Halliday（1994: 124）看来，标示–价值结构体现的是一种“形式与功能”的区分，任何一方都可以用来去认同另一方。然而，这种形式与功能的双重标准大大降低了标示和价值这一对概念的研究价值。事实上，形式的划分并没有必要，而且也违背了功能主义的基本理念。Halliday对于修饰式和认同式关系小句的区分标准之一就在于修饰式关系的双方位置不可互换，认同式关系双方的位置则可以互换，而在实际分析中可以发现情况往往并非如此。认同式关系双方的位置在形式上的确可以互换，但是就事实来看互换后的意义已经发生了实质上的改变（程晓堂, 2002）。也许是意识到了这个问题，Halliday & Matthiessen（2004: 230）后来修改了表述，标示和价值不再体现“形式与功能”的区分，而是一种“表达和内容”的区分。

此外，从标示–价值结构的方向性方面来看，传统意义上的认同式自然可以实现标示和价值位置的互换，而实际上，修饰式关系双方的位置也并不是完全不可以互换，Wise is Linda在古英语中是未标记语序之一，而且在现代英语也并非完全不可以出现，尤其是当形容词前面出现程度副词的时候更是如此，如So wise is Linda；而在汉语中，类似的例子也举不胜举，如“很聪明啊小明”“不错啊你”等等。因此，有理由认为，标示–价值结构所反映的就是意义问题，而不应该过多地考虑形式问题，价值指的就是实质、意义、职能和身份，而标示指的则是外表、符号、形式和名称。从这个意义上讲，*Tom is the tallest*固然有标示–价值结构（相当于*Tom is the* *monitor*），*Tom is the taller one*似乎也有着标示–价值结构，那么同样地，*Tom is tall*应该也有标示–价值结构。

7. 结语

作为认同式关系小句的描述方式之一，标示–价值结构体现着客观世界的具体与抽象、殊相与共相之分，二者的确定以语义为基础，以人们对世界经验的认识为前提，表现特指的或者具体的成分是标示，而表示概括抽象的一般性内容则为价值。换言之，价值指的是抽象的实质和意义，而标示指的则是具体的形式和名称。此外，从语用角度来看，作为语义表达的句法表现形式，标示–价值结构可以实现预设以及含意等语义关系。

参考文献

Bloor, T. & M. Bloor. 1995. *The Functional Analysis of English: A Hallidayan Approach*. London: Arnold.

Davidse, K. 1992. A Semiotic Approach to Relational Clauses. *Occasional Papers in Systemic Linguistics*, 6: 99-131.

Davidse, K. 1996. Turning Grammar on Itself: Identifying Clauses in Linguistic Discourse. In M. Berry, C. Butler, R. Fawcett & G. W. Huang (eds.) *Meaning and Form: Systemic Functional Interpretations*. Norwood, NJ: Ablex, 367-393.

Fawcett, R. 1987. The Semantics of Clause and Verb for Relational Processes in English. In M. A. K. Halliday & R. Fawcett (eds.) *New Developments in Systemic Linguistics, Volume 1: Theory and Description*. London: Frances Pinter Publishers, 130-183.

Halliday, M. A. K. 1967. Notes on Transitivity and Theme in English: Part 1. *Journal of Linguistics*, 3: 37-81.

Halliday, M. A. K. 1994. *An Introduction to Functional Grammar* (2nd edition). London: Arnold.

Halliday, M. A. K & C. M. I.M. Matthiessen. 2004. *An Introduction to Functional Grammar* (3rd edition). London: Arnold.

Matthiessen, C. M. I. M. 1991. Language on Language: The Grammar of Semiosis. *Social Semiotics*, 12: 69-111.

Thompson, G. 1996. *Introducing Functional Grammar*. London: Arnold.

程晓堂，2002，关于及物性系统中关系过程的两点存疑，《现代外语》（3）：311-17。

何恒幸，2007，系统功能语法中英语认同型小句的构建理据，《外语学刊》（3）：60-64。

何伟，2002，英语识别小句中的“标记 – 价值”配置结构之研究，《解放军外国语学院学报》（1）：5-9。

何中清，2009，英语关系过程分类中的两个存疑，《北京科技大学学报（社会科学版）》（4）：117-24。

胡壮麟，2008，《功能语法导论》导读. In M. A. K. Halliday & C. M. I. M. Matthiessen. *An Introduction to Functional Grammar*（3rd edition）. 北京：外语教学与研究出版社，vi-xxv.

黄国文，2000，《功能语法入门》导读. In G. Thompson. *Introducing Functional Grammar*. 北京：外语教学与研究出版社，F13-48.

杉村博文，2002，论现代汉语特指疑问判断句，《中国语文》（1）：14-21。

吕叔湘，1984，“谁是张老三？”=“张老三是谁？”，《中国语文》（4）：305。

袁鑫，2004，论英语识别小句中的标记 – 价值关系的双向性，《天津外国语学院学报》（6）：56-59。

王遥、李景娜，2007，英语认同型关系小句中价值 / 标示结构分析，《忻州师范学院学报》（2）：69-72。

张和友，2003，“标示 – 价值”和“被认同者 – 认同者”及汉语语法研究二三例，《外语与外语教学》（2）：40-43, 53。

张璘，2007，英语识别型小句中标记和价值划分的理据及其他，《江苏大学学报（社会科学版）》（6）：73-76。

汉语「的」字结构的三种类型及其互补性

徐富美

台湾元智大学

1. 本文的互补理论基础

汉语「的」是出现频率最多的虚词，其用法也最复杂多样。历来处理「的」字的各种用法多半分开处理，彼此之间没有关系。本文讨论汉语三种「的」字结构，并认为这三种类型构成互补性，可以统整为一个更高的统一体。本文理论基础来自Halliday（2008），下面先说明这个互补理论。

1.1 互补的概念

我们先从Halliday（2008）书中所举例说明互补概念。Halliday（2008：34）分别用颜色、补角，以及量子力学的波、粒二象性三种例子说明互补概念。在互补色方面，若两种颜色结合在一起时能产生白色，则该两种颜色互为补色。例如红色与绿色为互补色，外科医生穿绿衣进行手术见血也是这个道理。在补角方面，两个角的度数之和等于90度，即为一个补角。在光的波、粒二象性方面，光有时显示出波动性，有时又显示出粒子性，在不同条件下分别表现为波动和粒子的性质。

互补概念具有普遍性，我们举中国传统典籍的互补例子。《易经 · 系辞传》有所谓「一阴一阳之谓道」。我们且不论「阴」「阳」和「道」是怎样的内涵，至少「道」的运作要由互补的一阴一阳构成。佛经《金刚经》所说的「是名」状态「庄严即非庄严，是名庄严」，「庄严」与「非庄严」也产生互补。互补不只由两个成分形成，也可以由多个成分组成。佛经上所说的「瞎子摸象」故事，几个瞎子所摸到的大象都只是一部分，拼凑起来才成为整个大象的形象。

回到语言现象。互补概念在语言学上其来有自，很为大家所熟悉的是音韵学（phonology）上的互补关系。英语塞音的送气与不送气构成互补，送气与不送气是同位音（allophones），构成一个音位（phoneme）。例如英语的「p」有两个同位音，在「s-」后面发成不送气的〔p〕，如speak、spy；其他则发成送气的〔p'〕，如people、pay。〔p〕和〔p'〕二者构成同一个音位 / p' /。在句法方面，汉语「的」

「地」「得」也构成互补。「的」连接定语和中心语，「地」连接状语和谓语动词，「得」连接谓语动词和补语。

Halliday（2008：33）说具有互补性的两个方面是互不兼容甚至是互相矛盾，但两者都涉入语言的每一个表现，它们同时分享更为普遍、更为本质的某种东西，是语言根本属性的某种东西。他（Halliday, 2008：36）又说互补性是把「析取」转为「合取」，选择一种看待事物的方式，也可以选择另一种看待事物的方式。Halliday从更高的语言角度看三种关系的互补，即语法和词汇（grammar and lexis）的互补、系统和语篇（system and text）的互补，以及口语和书面语（speaking and writing）的互补。在词汇和语法的互补方面，词汇和语法分别是整个语义资源的不同方面，语法与语义自然糅合在一起。它们之间的互补性主要体现在对现实世界和经验进行解释的概念功能，也就是说，既可以采取词汇的手段，也可以采取语法的手段。在系统和语篇的互补方面，语篇是系统的例示化（instantiation），系统是语篇的意义潜势（potential）。无论如何关注系统，都要以具体的语篇作为实例来说明问题。在书面语和口语的互补方面，主要体现在组织意义上的不同手段以及复杂现象的不同策略。Halliday（2008：184）分别从所形成的互补性及其相反性质上说明这三者的不同：

表1 三种互补关系

	形成互补	相反性质
语法和词汇	焦点（focus）上的互补	精密度的相反
系统和语篇	角度（angle）上的互补	例示化的相反
口语和书面语	状态（state）上的互补	体现方式的相反

1.2 提出互补概念的意义

Halliday（2008：3）说只有同时用多种方式进行识解，我们才得以见到令人满意的全景图。就语法而言（Halliday, 2008：35），每个语言的语法都是人类经验的一种识解，语法把我们的经验转换为意义，借以建构我们的实相（reality）。他（Halliday, 2008：169）又说语言不是以部分来运作，它是作为整体才具有功能的。这也就是为什么Halliday的Complementarities是复数形式。本书的汉语书名由Halliday本人翻译，提出「互补」也强调「并协」，是因为所涉及的选择都以对方的存在为前提。简单说，互补的核心就是系统化，几个不同部分可以构成一个系统。

Halliday讨论三种互补，有两个面向，一个是彼此不同的选择，一个是更为系统本质的东西。这些互补都有一个前提，即是在更高的层次上统合这两种（或更多）的迥然不同。作为识解语言系统，互补概念不只是为了经济性，更有其心理真实性。讨论词汇和语法现象的互补，其更本质的是语义资源系统；讨论系统和语篇的互补，其更本质的是对语言系统的关注；讨论口语和书面的互补，其更本质的是表达模式。

2. 汉语「的」字结构的三种类型

本文讨论汉语「的」字结构三种类型。第一种「的」字结构是「的」的一般用法，「的」主要联系定语和中心语，「的」帮助前面的成分作定语用，修饰或限定后面的中心语。中心语一般是名词组，而充任定语的成分则能表达各种语义。例子如下：

（1）〔你〕的工作怎么样？（表所属）
（2）后边传来了〔姊姊〕的喊声。（表来源）
（3）中国人民要加强〔同世界各国人民〕的友谊。（表对象）
（4）孙先生是一个〔谦虚〕的人。（表个性描写）
（5）他买了一条〔三斤〕的鲤鱼。（表性质）
（6）靠墙摆着〔装满书籍〕的柜子。（表状态）

例子（1–3）以人为对象，表示其所属、来源或对象；例子（4–6 ）则不限定人，基本上语义表示性质或限定。这些都是我们一般常用「的」字结构用法，简单来说，「的」有两个基本用法，即表「所属」和「限定」。

本文讨论「的」后面跟有名词成分，不讨论「的」后面省略中心语的情形，如（7–8）；也不讨论「的」放在句末、作为语气用法的情形，如（9–10）。

（7）吃的、穿的，样样都有。
（8）我看过那个穿红衣服的。
（9）这种东西我是见过的。
（10）这水果很好吃的。

第二种类型的「的」字结构是一个动词后面跟着一个宾语（我们把处所也当宾语），动词和宾语之间有个「的」的情形。例子如下：

（11）是你引诱的我！
（12）姊姊让我进的屋。
（13）你什么时候结的婚？
（14）昨天初五，我去女婿家吃的饺子。
（15）我在外语学院学的英语。
（16）他昨天到的北京。

上面这些例子的「的」前面都有一个动词，后面有一个名词成分。例如例子（11）「的」插在「引诱」和「我」之间。这些句子都有具体的时间、空间或对象，表示动作已经实现或完成，预设已知。

第三种类型主要连接指人的名词和代词，其后面表示职务、身份等，表示某人承担某职务或具有某种身份等。例子如下：

（17）这次开会，你的主席，我的纪录。（你当主席，我当记录）
（18）今天晚上的京剧，马连良的诸葛亮，裘盛戎的……（马连良演诸葛亮，裘盛戎演……）
（19）他的老师当的好。（他当老师当的好）

例子（17-19）不是表示限定，也不是表示所属，是一种特殊的「的」。像例子（19）有歧义，可以是「他的老师」，也可以是「他当老师」。这里指的是他这个人本身，「他的老师」是「他当老师」，而不是「他的老师」。例子（17）「你的主席」和例子（18）「马连良的诸葛亮」也分别是「你当主席」以及「马连良演诸葛亮」。

3. 三种类型的功能互补性

下面我们讨论这三种「的」字结构。第一种类型的「的」是作定语，这一类用法是「的」的典型用法，是「真定语」，我们称为「标准型」定语。第二种类型标志某一些成分的信息焦点，我们称之为「凸显型」。第三种类型动词隐蔽了，我们称之为「隐蔽型」。我们把这三种类型简列如下：

表2 三种「的」字结构

类型		例子
1	标准型	（1）
2	凸显型	（11）
3	隐蔽型	（17）

处理这三种「的」字结构可以有两种方式。第一种方式是这三种用法彼此之间没有关系，需一一个别处理，这也是传统的处理方式。第二种方式则是把这三种用法统一起来，看作彼此之间具有互补关系。本文实行第二种办法；也就是说，这三种「的」字结构形成互补关系，三种「的」字功能可以统一起来，共构一个整体。

那么，这三种类型的统一特征是什么？其更为本质的整体是什么？我们认为，这三种「的」字结构的功能是定语化及名物化（nominalization），也就是说，「的」把整个小句变成名词组（nominal group）。

第一种类型固然不论，本来就是名词组。第二种类型则是把小句降阶（rankshift）为名词组。试看下面对比例子：

（20a）昨天初五，我去女婿家吃饺子。

（20b）昨天初五，我去女婿家吃的饺子。

例子（20a）的「我去女婿家吃饺子」是个小句形式；而（20b）「我去女婿家吃的饺子」则变成了名词性成分。就语言形式上，「的」字把（20a）的小句降阶为（20b）的名词性成分。就功能上，我们认为这种类型的「的」是「弱化」标记，「的」把前面动词的语义「弱化」了，表示已知信息，并凸显动词前面的成分成为信息焦点，例如例子（11）凸显「你」，（15）凸显「在外语学院」，（16）凸显「昨天」。所凸显的成分前面还可以用焦点标记「是」标示出来。如：

（21）昨天初五，我是去女婿家吃的饺子。

上面例子的信息焦点是「去女婿家」。如果动词前面没有其他成分，那么所凸显的焦点往往在「的」后面的对比成分。如：

（22）老大是学的历史，老二是学的水利。

（23）今天中午我们是吃的饺子。

例子（22）的「学」弱化了，其所凸显的焦点在对比的「历史」和「水利」。例子（23）虽然没有出现两个对比成分，其焦点也是在「的」后面的「饺子」。

这种类型和所谓的「离合词」不同。「离合词」是动宾关系中间可以再插进若干动貌（aspect）成分，例如「结婚」是合词，「结过两次婚」是离词。「离合词」当中的动词并没有弱化，其动词语义反而因动貌而得到强化效果。相对而言，本文所说第二种类型的动词则是弱化了。另外，这种类型的「的」字结构与放在句末、表语气的「的」用法也不同。我们看下面例子：

（24a）是你引诱的我！

（24b）是你引诱我的！

（24a）的「的」来自上面例子（11）。（24a）和（24b）这两句话的意思差不多，但所强调的信息焦点有些不同。（24a）的「的」有弱化功能，焦点只强调「你」，而（24b）的「的」没有弱化作用，「是」和「的」中间的「你引诱我」整个句子都是信息焦点。（24b）的「的」是语气助词，而（24a）的「的」则是一种结构助词。「你引诱的我」，用「的」把结构「定语化」，这是「的」字的非典用法。

上面（24a）和（24b）这两句话的意思虽然差不多，也可以互相替换，但第二类型并不都能与句末语气词的「的」字结构互相替换。如下面例子：

（25a）今天晚饭我是吃的馒头，不是吃的米饭。
（25b）*今天晚饭我是吃馒头的，不是吃米饭的。
（26a）他们害怕主公，他们先见的我。
（26b）*他们害怕主公，他们先见我的。
（27a）我昨天刚下的飞机。
（27b）?我昨天刚下飞机的。

上面例子（25—27）当中的（a）句似乎很难换成（b）句。这是第二种类型不同于句末「的」字结构的主要原因。即使（27b）勉强可以说，也总不如（27a）自然顺当。

下面看第三种类型。我们认为第三种类型也是从小句降阶成名词组，是从第二种类型隐省动词而来。看下面例子：

（28a）这次开会，你当主席，我当纪录。
（28b）这次开会，你当的主席，我当的纪录。（第二种类型）
（28c）这次开会，你的主席，我的纪录。（第三种类型）

我们认为「的」把（28a）降阶成（28b），也就是第二种类型，而（28c）则直接隐省了动词「当」。第三种类型的动词隐蔽了，把「的」前面和后面的成分都变成了对比。例子（28c）「你的主席，我的纪录」当中的「你」和「我」对比，「主席」和「记录」对比，都成了信息焦点。

第三种类型所隐省的动词及物性多半是关系（relational）过程；其他动词隐省的情形比较少。我们看下面例子：

（29a）完后我们去吃晚餐，主任开车。
（29b）完后我们去吃晚餐，主任开的车。
（29c）完后我们去吃晚餐，主任的车。
（30a）晚上我们还小聚了一下，林老师泡茶。
（30b）晚上我们还小聚了一下，林老师泡的茶。
（30c）晚上我们还小聚了一下，林老师的茶。

上面例子的（29b）和（30b）如果说成（29c）和（30c），意义已经有所改变。（29c）「主任的车」未必是主任开，（30c）「林老师的茶」未必是林老师泡。

第三种类型隐省动词的情形也常常出现在包孕句（embedded clauses）中，但往往为我们所忽略。如下面例子：

（31a）谢谢你提供意见！
（31b）谢谢你的意见！
（32a）我很欣赏你有幽默感。
（32b）我很欣赏你的幽默感。

我们认为（31b）和（32b）分别是从（31a）和（32a）而来；（31b）和（32b）甚至更为常见。如果把（31b）和（32b）中的定语「你的」拿掉，定语是修饰语，可有可无，那么例子（31b）要谢谢的不是「人」，变成了「意见」，（32b）所欣赏的就变成了「幽默感」。其实这样的句子也是因为隐省动词而使用「的」字而来。

回到（28）的例子。（28a—c）分别表达了从「动词组」到「名词组」，以及从「名词组」到「名词」的阶段。如下简表：

表3 从「动词组」到「名词组」，从「名词组」到「名词」各阶段

阶段	1	2	3
语言形式	VO	V的O	O
举例	（28a）	（28b）	（28c）
变化	动词性强	动词弱化	动词消失

一路过来，动词语义逐渐弱化，甚至消失。也就是说，它们形成中间过渡形式，分别表达语法和词汇之间词汇化（lexicalization）的不同阶段。这种词汇化过渡阶段，也与互补性有关。

汉语的名词组可以作为小句，是小句的非典型形式；换句话说，以名词组作为小句是汉语的特色。这些定语化及名物化的「的」字结构可以独立存在，单独作为一个小句。Hsu（forthcoming）认为，像上面例子（29b）「主任开的车」以及（30b）「林老师泡的茶」都是小句。这些小句降级为名词组成分的效果是可以造成复句（clause complex）逻辑语义关系（logico-semantic relation）有所不同。例如（29a）和（30a）是增强（enhancement）关系，而（29b）和（30b）则是详述（elaboration）关系。

总结来说，第一种类型是「的」的典型用法，第二和第三种类型则都是「的」的非典型用法。之所以称为非典型用法，乃因为「的」并非直接连接定语和中心语，其功能是要凸显小句中某些成分作为信息焦点。这三种「的」字类型的语言形式虽然不同，但同样表达定语化和名物化功能。也就是说，这三种类型形成互补，属于词汇和语法上的互补。第二种和第三种类型的非典型「的」字结构在口语中更为常见，有语境可以提供说话者和受话者的理解，也可以是口语和书面语的互补。

4. 结语

本文讨论汉语三种「的」字结构及其互补性，第一种类型是定语的典型用法，第二种和第三种是非典型用法。第一种类型的典型用法和第二、第三种类型的非典型用法构成互补，而第二种类型动词的「现」与第三种类型动词的「隐」又构成互补，三者彼此之间构成两个层次的互补。我们简列成下表：

表4 三种「的」字结构

语法功能	定语化、名物化		
信息焦点	自然焦点	凸显焦点、对比焦点	
「的」字类型	第一种类型	第二种类型（现）	第三种类型（隐）

这三种不同「的」字结构其更具普遍性的语法功能是定语化及名物化，在语义上减低了动词语义。第一种类型的信息焦点一般落在「的」后面的成分，属于自然焦点；第二种和第三种类型则要凸显某些成分，可能在「的」前面或是后面，属于对比焦点。

王品（2010：25）在述介Halliday（2008）这本书文末提出自己的看法，认为可以考虑汉语当中的互补性是怎样体现的，可以应用它来做什么等。本文即是以汉语为尝试，以互补观点的联系，把这三种看似很不一样的「的」字用法整合起来，得到统一的解释。

参考文献

Halliday, M. A. K. 1994. *An Introduction to Functional Grammar* (2nd edition). London: Arnold.

Halliday, M. A. K. 2008. *Complementarities in Language*. Beijing: The Commercial Press.

Halliday, M. A. K. & C. M. I. M. Matthiessen. 2004. *An Introduction to Functional Grammar* (3rd edition). London: Hodder Arnold.

Hsu, Fu-mei. (forthcoming) *Chinese Characteristics of Clause Complex: A SF Perspective of Achievements from Former Accounts*.

王品，2010，系统功能语言学的互补思想——M. A. K. Halliday 新著 *Complementarities in Language* 述介，《外国语》33.2: 20-26。

李力，2010，语言阐释上何以殊途同归——《语言系统的并协与互补》介绍，《外语教学与研究》（3）：232-235。

黄正德，2008，从「他的老师当得好」谈起，《语言科学》（3）：225-241。

刘月华、潘文娱、故韡，2001/2007，《实用现代汉语语法》。北京：商务印书馆。

汉语存在句句首成分的功能语法研究

邓仁华 梁素莲

华南理工大学

1. 引言

汉语的存在小句（以下简称为“存在句”）是一种很有特色的句式，自《马氏文通》问世以来，汉语存在句一直是语言学界研究的热点。近年来，随着国外语言学理论的引入，存在句研究的深度和广度都有明显的进展。然而，由于学者们的理论背景不同，对存在句的界定和分类至今仍众说纷纭，莫衷一是；对句首成分的语法地位和语义角色（semantic role）也没有达成一致的看法。另外，从系统功能语法的角度对汉语存在句进行的研究不多。迄今为止，国内外大多数学者都是把系统功能语法应用于英语的研究，如邓仁华（2012）在系统功能语言学的理论框架下对英语存在句进行了系统的研究。参加2013年在中山大学召开的第40届国际系统功能大会的国内学者普遍认为系统功能语法的“本土化”研究方面还非常欠缺。因此，本文从系统功能语法的角度对汉语存在句句首成分的句法地位和语义角色进行探讨，试图在系统功能语法的“本土化”研究方面做出尝试。

2. 汉语存在句的研究回顾

存在句的主要功能是呈现存在的人或物（Fawcett, 2003：54; Forthcoming：75）。“存在”本身应该是一个过程，包括“存在的开始”（出现）、“存在状态的持续”以及“存在的终结”（消失）。本文研究的是广义上的存在句，相当于传统语法中所说的“存现句”。

吕叔湘（1943/1982）在《中国文法要略》中第一次提出“有无句”，并通过有无起词来对有无句进行分类，从而提出了“存在句”这个概念。陈庭（1957）提出事物的存在还应包括“出现”和“消失”，“存现句”这个概念随着得以确立。随后，不少学者对存在句的分类进行探讨。张学成（1982）指出存在句有四种类型，包括“有”字句、“是”字句、静态动词句和动态动词句。宋玉柱（1991, 2007）则对存在句进行系统分类总结，提出存在句可分为静态存在句（“有”字句、“是”字句、“着”字句、经历体存在句、定心谓语句、名词谓语句）和动态存在句（进行体动态存在句、完成体动态存在句）。雷涛（1993）对存在句的A（处所词语）、B（动词或动词性词语）、C（名词或名词性词组）段进行分析，并根据三段间的关系对存在句进行分类，他认为除了C段是必不可少以外，其他部分则可有可无。

对于汉语存在句主语的认定，在传统语法中主要可分为两大派别，一个是根据语义以及施受事关系来判定主语，称之为意义派（如吕叔湘、王力、允川、岑麒麟）；另一个是根据词序或者形式，把句首成分看作主语，叫做词序（如张志公、邢公畹、陈庭珍、唐启运、宋玉柱）。

对于存在句句首处所词，有的学者认为它是“状语”（或“附加语”），有的学者认为它是“主语”，还有的学者认为它是“话题”。吕叔湘（1953）根据意义或者施受关系把句首处所词看成“状语”，把动词后的名词（词组）当作“主语”。持有这种观点的学者还包括允川（1955）、黎锦熙（1955）、岑麒（1955）。但陈庭珍（1955）和唐启运（1955）提出“语法结构决定主语和宾语”的看法，认为存在句句首处所词才是“主语”。持同样观点的学者还有黄伯荣、廖序（2002）、吕冀平（1955：9）、周祖谟（1955）、朱德熙（1999）。甚至连丁声树、吕叔湘等（1961/1979：34）也把存在句的动词前的处所词当作主语。王力（1956）和张先亮、范晓等（2010）则认为，当存在句句首的处所词是名词时，它就作“主语”；如果是介词短语，则作“状语”。[但王力认为此类存在句是无主句，吕叔湘（1999：31-42）和杨国文（2013）也持相同的观点]。

此外，赵元任（1979：5）认为汉语里的主语、谓语宜分别当作“话题”（Topic）和“说明”（Comment）来看待，持类似观点的学者还包括邢公畹（1995）、沈家煊（1999）、石毓智（2001），他们倾向把存在句句首的成分当作“话题”或者“主题”。

虽然汉语存在句的研究取得丰富的成果，但是关于存在句本身的定义和分类等问题仍然没有得到妥善解决；存在句句首成分的句法地位和语义角色仍有待探讨。因此，本文从系统功能语法的视角重新审视汉语存在句句首成分的句法作用（功能）及其不同的语义角色。

3. 系统功能语法中的三种“主语”及其认定

3.1 句首处所词作主语存在的问题

把句首处所词当作“主语”至少存在三个问题：（1）汉语存在句中的动词通常是非宾格（unaccusative）动词和非作格（unergative）动词，这样的动词后面无法接“宾语”，因此不宜把句首的成分当作“主语”。（2）汉语存在句中的动词即便是及物动词（如“放、挂、摆、贴、写、唱、煮”等），它后面也总是跟着“着”，因此使动词体现的动作“状态化”（彭宣维, 2011：312），它并不表示具体的动作。如“土豆”在“锅里煮着土豆”和“他正在煮土豆呢”这两个小句中的作用是不同的，前者交代“土豆”所在的位置是在锅里，而且正处在（被）煮着的状态；而后者描述“他”正在进行煮土豆这一动作，后者中的“土豆”可以作传统语法的“宾语”，但前者中的“土豆”是存在的主体，应作“主语”。（3）句首的成分不论是名词还是介词短语，都起到交代存在的人或物的地点（或移动的人或物的移动方向）的作用，因此它们的语义角色和句法地位应该是相同的（曹逢甫, 1995：5-6）。系统功能语法认为，同一个句法成分可以由不同的语言单位体现，而同一语言单位也可能体现不同的句法成分或语义角色（参见例14）。

另外，一些带有显性格标记的语言（如芬兰语和日语）的存在句也可以佐证汉语“地点型”存在句中的名词（词组）是“主语”（这表明首的处所词不是“主语”）：

芬兰语存在句：

（9）Piha- llä on poika.

院子–近处格 系词 现在时 单数第三人称 男孩 **主格**

“院子里有个男孩。”

日语存在句：

（10）Tsukue-no-ue-ni （wa） hon-ga anu.

桌子–的–上面–方位格（**话题标记**）书–**主语标记** 存在

“桌子上有一本书。”

（周迎芳、王勇 2012, 黑体为本文作者所加）

从上两例可知，与汉语的存在句一样，芬兰语和日语中的存在句的处所词语占据句首的位置，芬兰语存在句动词后的名词词组带主格，因此是“主语”，因此也就排除了句首的处所词语作“主语”的可能。日语存在句句首的处所词语后接方位格助词“ni”和话题格助词“wa”（即两个助词叠加在一起）表明它既是“地点”又是小句的“话题”[系统功能语法因此把它称为“主题主位”[1]（Topical Theme）]，而动词前的名词接的是“主语”格助词“ga”，表明它是小句的“主语”。

3.2 “逻辑主语”“语法主语”和“心理主语”及其认定

Halliday（1978）认为语言是多功能（意义）的社会符号，每一个小句都同时表达概念意义、人际意义以及语篇意义这三种意义。语言的多功能（multifunctionality）在小句中的体现是小句中的每一个句法成分可能具有上述一种或一种以上的意义，小句的句首成分也不例外。如表1所示，小句的句首成分可能

1 主位通常分为“简单主位”和“复项（multiple）主位”，它们都必须包含一个具有经验意义的成分，这样的主位通常是语篇中的主题，因此被称为“主题主位”。“复项主位”还有人际意义和语篇意义的成分，因此是“人际主位”和“语篇主位”。

同时是“语法主语”（Grammatical Subject）、“逻辑主语”（Logical Subject）和“心理主语”（Psychological Subject）：

表1 小句中的“语法主语”“逻辑主语”和“心理主语”

（1）	The lion	chased	the tourists
句法分析	主语（语法主语）	限定词 / 谓体	补语
及物性 / 作格分析	动作者 / 施事（逻辑主语）	过程：物质过程	目标 / 中介
主位分析	主位（心理主语）	述位	

系统功能语法中的“语法主语”是小句“断言的对象”，是“说话者用来对其所说内容的有效性负责的成分”（Halliday & Matthiessen 2014：83）；“逻辑主语”是指小句经验（experiential）意义中的“动作的发出者”，即小句的及物性（transitivity）分析中的“动作者”（Actor）或者作格（ergativity）分析中的“施事”（Agent）；“心理主语”是“小句涉及的对象”，是“说话人心里所想的出发点”（Halliday & Matthiessen, 2014：79），即“主位”（Theme）。（语法）“主语”是指它的句法作用，后两者分别属于概念意义和语篇意义。汉语中的“主语”不参与表达人际意义，因此没有人际意义（Halliday & McDonald, 2004）。

“主位”（“心理主语”）和“动作者”或“施事”（“逻辑主语”）的认定较容易：在没有明显的格标记的语言中，“主位”通常是小句句首的成分；而“动作者”或“施事”通过施受事关系就可以确定。汉语（语法）“主语”的确定则较复杂，但彭宣维（2011）提出的“将小句及物性分析中的主导（leading）参与者当作主语”的方法较好地解决了这一问题。彭宣维（2011：308）认为“主语在小句范围内既是一个形式范畴，又是一个功能概念”。他指出，小句相关过程的“主导参与者是过程得以展开的基础和立足点”（彭宣维, 2011：305），因此是小句的“主语”。此外，系统功能语法还把在小句中对“主语”或过程（“谓体”）进行补充说明的句法成分叫做“补语”（包括传统语法中的“宾语”和“补语”）。而且，要充分说明汉语存在句句首成分的功能，还必须探讨动词后的名词词组的功能，因为确定它的功能都有助于说明句首成分的功能。

4. 汉语存在句的分类

在Fawcett（1987, 2003, Forthcoming; 黄国文等, 2008）的“加的夫（模式的系统功能）语法”（the Cardiff Grammar, CG）中，常见的英语（“地点型”）存在句是“地点型”关系过程小句（Fawcett, 1987, 2003），其中的两个参与者是“载体”和“地点”（Location），但加夫语法中的“地点”是“参与者角色”[2]（Participant Role），而不是“环境角色”（Circumstantial Role）。加的夫语法对

2 文中具有参与者角色地位的“地点”用斜黑体表示，以区别于悉尼语法中充当环境成分的“地点”。

“地点型”存在句的及物性分析如下：

表2 加的夫语法的“地点型”存在句及物性分析

（2）	There	was	a sheep	in the garden.
CG		地点型关系过程	载体	地点

根据Neale（2002：164），加的夫语法的关系过程分为五个子过程——地点型（locational）、属性型（attributive）、方向型（directional）、属有型（possessive）和匹配（matching）型关系过程。这五个子过程共有的参与者为“载体”，另一参与者角色分别为“地点”“属性”（Attribute）、“方向”（Direction）、“被属有者”（Possessed）和“受匹配者”（Matchee）。五个子过程又根据“载体”的不同形式分为四类：“（简单）载体”（simple Carrier）、“施事–载体”（Agent-Carrier）、“受事–载体”（Affected-Carrier）、“第三者（充当）施事”（third party Agent）。根据Neale对关系过程的分类，邓仁华（2012：162-174）曾提出：英语中至少有“地点型”“属性型”“方向型”和“属有型”四种存在句，加上（3）e这样的“动作型”存在句，英语中就有五种存在句：

（3）a. There's [地点型关系过程] a man [载体] at the door [地点].

b. ... there were [属性型关系过程] one or two of them [载体] really interesting [属性].

c. There swam [方向型关系过程] towards me [方向] someone carrying a harpoon [施事–载体].

d. There was presented [属有型关系过程]（to the winner）[受事–载体] by the mayor [施事] a gold medal [被属有者].

e. At this point, there hit [动作过程] the embankment [受事] a shell from our lines [施事].

根据我们对存在句的及物性分析方面的观察，汉语中有“存在型”“方向型”和“属有型”三种存在句：

（4）a. 北京城里有 [地点型关系过程] 一座故宫。（地点型）

b. 东边来了 [方向型关系过程] 一个人。（方向型）

c. 北京有 [属有型关系过程]（一）个天安门。（属有型）

下面我们将从加的夫语法的视角探讨这三种存在句句首成分的句法地位和语义角色。

5. 汉语存在句句首成分的功能语法研究

5.1 “地点型”存在句的功能语法研究

汉语“地点型”存在句表达的基本语义是“某处有（存在）某人/物”。如例

（5）所示，在一定的语境中，不论英语还是汉语的“地点型”存在句，“人”或“物”存在的处所可以不用交代，因此存在的“人”或“物”才是整个小句要表达的语义重心，因此也是存在句的“信息焦点”（Halliday & McDonald, 2004），是“地点型”关系过程的主导参与者，应为“地点型”存在句的“主语”。句首的处所词对存在的“人”或“物”的位置进行必要的说明，因此它在存在句起着“补语”的作用。因此，（5）b中的“一个人”是（语法）“主语”，“门口”是“补语”。

（5）a. There is a man (at the door).

b. （门口）有一个人。

“门口”位于句首，是小句的信息的出发点，因此是小句主位分析中的“心理主语”——主位 [大量的语料证明了存在句的信息起点（即“主位”）基本上都是由句首处所词来体现，处所词作主位的概率最高，因此它在存在句中实际上是一个无标记的主位]；它同时又是小句及物性分析中的“地点”；而句中的名词词组“一个人”是“简单载体”，因此可把该类小句称为“简单载体”类“地点型”存在句。

“是”字存在句也是“地点型”存在句。“是”字表示“存在”，“是”字句有“穷尽”（exhaustiveness）之意——表示除了存在的东西之外别无他物，而“有”字句表示还有其他东西（Tsao, 1990：77），这在宋玉柱（2007：41）所说的“名词谓语”（存在）句（例6和7）体现得尤为明显：

表3 “是”字存在句的及物性分析

（6）	满脸	（都）（是）	青春美丽痘儿
（7）	满地	（都）（是）	垃圾
（8）	山下	（是）	一片肥沃的良田
CG	地点	地点型关系过程	简单载体

例（6）、（7）尽管没有出现谓语动词，但完全可以加入“是”或“都是”，因此我们把它们归入“地点型”存在句。此类存在句中表示处所的名词词组带有“周遍性”（宋玉柱, 2007：45），表明存在的事物之多。宋玉柱（2007：36）所说的“定心谓语”（存在）句则需根据具体的语境来判定：有的也可以加入“是”字（见例8），因此也可以归为“地点型”存在句；有的则只能加入“传来”或“传出”，如“屋外（传来）阵阵松涛”和“人群里（传出）一片嬉笑声”，因此是“方向型”存在句（参见4.2）。

根据加的夫语法，“地点型”存在句“台上坐着主席团”和“方位句”“主席团坐在台上”具有相同的经验意义，都是关系过程小句，都有“施事–载体”和“地点”这两个参与者角色，但两者的主位组织和信息组织方式不同：“地点型”存在句基本的语义是“某地有某人/物”，句首的“地点”是小句表达的信息的出发点，因此是“主位”，也是“已知（Given）信息”，而“存在的人/物”是新信息，也是小句的“信息焦点”；“方位句”基本的语义是“某人/物在某地”，句首的“存在的人/物”是小句表达的信息的出发点，因此是“主位”，也是“已知信息”，而存在的“地点”是新信息，也是小句的“信息焦点”。但是，“台上”在这两个小句中都是“地点”，而“主席团”在两个小句中都是“施事–载体”（因为他们是“坐”这一动作的发出者, 因此可称此类小句为“施事–载体”类“地点型”存在句）。因在一定的语境下“地点”可不用交代，因此“主席团”是主导的参与者，在两个小句中都是“主语”，“台上”则是“补语”。也就是说，语序的变化没有改变它们的句法地位和参与者角色（participant role）。试比较：

（9）a. 台上[地点/主位/补语]坐着[地点型关系过程]**主席团**[施事－载体/信息焦点/主语]。

b. 主席团[施事－载体/主位/主语]坐[地点型关系过程]**在台上**[地点/信息焦点/补语]。

像“墙上挂着一幅画”这样的小句也是“地点型”存在句，它与（9）a这样的存在句区别在于：前者中的“载体”是“受事–载体”（因为“一幅画”是被人挂上去的, 此类小句因此是“受事–载体”类“地点型”存在句），而后者的“载体”是“施事–载体”：

（10）墙上[地点/主位/补语]挂着[地点型关系过程]**一幅画**[受事－载体/信息焦点/主语]。

宋玉柱（2007：30）所说的经历体存在句也是“地点型”存在句，只不过它表示的是过去的“存在”，存在的人或物往往已不复存在：

（11）窗子上[地点]曾经贴过[地点型关系过程]两张贴纸[受事–载体]。

综上所述，“简单载体”类（12a、12b、12c）、“施事–载体”类（12d和12e）和“受事–载体”类（12f和12g）“地点型”存在句句首的成分的功能是“补语”“地点”“主位”和“已知信息”的重合（conflation），即它同时具有这四种功能。这三类“地点型”存在句的句法–语义分析可用表4表示：

图4“地点型”存在句的句法–语义分析

例（12）／句法－语义分析		a. 桌子上面	有	一个古瓷花瓶
		b. 山下	（是）	一片肥沃的良田
		c. 满地	（都）（是）	垃圾
		d. 台上	坐着	主席团［施事］
		e. 天上	飞着	一只鸟［施事］
		f. 墙上	挂着	一幅画［受事］
		g. 窗子上	（曾经）贴过	两张贴纸［受事］
句法分析		补语	主要动词	主语
语义分析	及物性分析	地点	地点型关系过程	载体
	主位分析	主位	述位	
	信息结构分析	已知信息	新信息	

5.2 “方向型”存在句的功能语法研究

根据加的夫语法对关系过程的分类，“方向型”存在句属于“方向型”关系过程。在这类过程中有两个基本的参与者：“方向”和“载体”（邓仁华, 2012：172）。“方向型”存在句基本的经验意义是“某人/物在某个方向出现或者消失”，也就是涉及“存在”系统里面的“存在的开始”以及“存在的终结”。根据Neale（2002：164），“方向”主要包括“来源（Source）”“路径（Path）”或“目的地（Destination）”。例如：

（13）a. 东边[方向：来源]来了[方向型关系过程]一个人[施动者–载体]。

b. 学校里[方向：来源]走了[方向型关系过程]一批毕业生[施动者–载体]。

c. 公路上[方向：路径]驶来[方向型关系过程]一辆胶轮拖拉机[施动者–载体]。

d. 屋子里[方向：目的地]飞进[方向型关系过程]一只蜜蜂[施动者–载体]。

e. 打葡萄架上[来源]掉[方向型关系过程]他脖子里头[目的地]一个蝎子[施动者–载体]。

值得注意的是，在例（13）e中“来源”和“目的地”一起出现在“方向型”关系过程里。

“方向型”存在句的动词通常是“飞”“跑”“滚”这样的表示移动意义的动词和/或“来”“去”“进”等趋向动词。另外，存在句同一句首成分会因动词的不同而充当不同的参与者角色。例如：

（14）a. 屋子里[方向：目的地]飞进一只蜜蜂[施动者–载体]。（出现）（“方向型”存在句）

b. 屋子里[地点]飞着一只蜜蜂[施动者–载体]。（存在）（“地点型”存在句）

c. 屋子里[方向：来源]飞出一只蜜蜂[施动者–载体]。（消失）（“方向型”存在句）

“方向型”存在句的及物性（经验意义）分析表明，此类存在句的句首处所词或方向意义的词语充当“方向型”关系过程的参与者“方向”（可能是“路径”“来源”或“目的地”），而句末的名词词组充当“施事–载体”。“方向型”存在句可以不说明人或物移动的“方向”，如我们也可以说“来了一个人”或“走了一批毕业生”。因此，此类存在句的“施动者–载体”是这一过程的主导参与者，因此是句中的“主语”（和“信息焦点”），而充当“来源”“路径”或“目的地”的句首成分则是“补语”，也是此类小句的信息的出发点，因此是“方向型”存在句的“主位”，同时也是句中的“已知信息”。因此，“方向型”存在句的句首成分同时是“补语”“方向”“主位”和“已知信息”：

表5 “方向型”存在句的句法–语义分析

例（15） 句法－语义分析		a. 东边［来源］	来了	一个人
		b. 屋子里［目的地］	飞进	一只蜜蜂
		c. 学校里［来源］	走了	一批毕业生
		d. 公路上［路径］	驶来	一辆胶轮拖拉机
句法分析		补语	主要动词	主语
语义分析	及物性分析	方向	方向型关系过程	施事－载体
	主位分析	主位	述位	
	信息结构分析	已知信息	新信息	

5.3 “属有型”存在句的功能语法研究

我们认为像“三亚有天涯海角风景区”和“广州有上下九步行街”这样的存在句可作两种解读：一是可理解为“地点型”存在句，因此“三亚”和“广州”是“地点”，“天涯海角”和“上下九步行街”是“简单载体”；一是可理解为“属有型”存在句，是“属有型”关系过程小句，“三亚”和“广州”是“施事–载体”，“天涯海角”和“上下九步行街”则是“被属有者”。在“属有型”存在句中，“施事–载体”和“被属有者”都是这一过程的基本参与者，因“施事–载体”是“被属有者”的“属有者”（Possessor），因此是主导参与者和“主语”。

动词“有”在“地点型”存在句和“属有型”存在句的属性是大不相同的：“地点型”存在句中的“有”意为“存在”，是不及物动词（如“地球上有/存在多少秘密?”），存在的人或物是存在的主体，它只能作“有”的“主语”；而“属有型”存在句中的“有”作“拥有”解，是及物动词，“被属有者”是“（拥）有”的对象，因此是“有”的“补语”（传统语法中的“宾语”）。试比较这两种解读在语义和句法上的差异：

（16）a. 三亚[地点/补语]有[**地点型**关系过程]天涯海角风景区[简单载体/主语]。

b. 三亚[施动者–载体/主语]有[**属有型**关系过程]天涯海角风景区[被属有者/补语]。

（17）a. 广州[地点/补语]有[**地点型**关系过程]上下九步行街[简单载体/主语]。

b. 广州[受事–载体/主语]有[**属有型**关系过程]上下九步行街[被属有者/补语]。

或许是因为没有注意到上述“有”的两种不同属性的区别，汉语界的学者可能误把“地点型”存在句中的动词“有”当作及物动词，因此通常把“有”之后的名词（词组）当作“宾语”，把句首的处所词语当作“主语”：

（18）*北京城里[主语]有[谓语]一座故宫[宾语]。

实际上，“某人或地拥有某物”意味着“某物在某人/地那”，也是“存在”意义的表现形式之一。根据加的夫语法，本文认为“属有型”存在句是属有型关系过程小句，主要表达“某地拥有某物”的经验意义，它与典型的“属有型”关系过程的差异在于：后者中的“施动者–载体”（即悉尼语法中“属有者”）通常是有生命的人或物；而前者中的“施动者–载体”却是一个无生命的（如“这张桌子有四条腿”）地点名词。尽管如此，语义上“三亚”和“广州”分别是“天涯海角风景区”和“上下九步行街”的“属有者”，因此是此类小句中的主导参与者，也因此是“主语”，“被属有者”“天涯海角”和“上下九步行街”则是“补语”。而且“施事–载体”处于句首的位置，是小句信息的出发点，因此是“主位”，同时也是“已知信息”；而“被属有者”则是小句的“信息焦点”。“属有型”存在句句首成分同时是“主语”“施事–载体”“主位”和“已知信息”：

表6 “属有型”存在句的句法–语义分析

<table>
<tr><td colspan="2" rowspan="2">例子
句法－语义分析</td><td>（16）b. 三亚</td><td>有</td><td>天涯海角风景区</td></tr>
<tr><td>（17）b. 广州</td><td>有</td><td>上下九步行街</td></tr>
<tr><td colspan="2">句法分析</td><td>主语</td><td>主要动词</td><td>补语</td></tr>
<tr><td rowspan="3">语义分析</td><td>及物性分析</td><td>施事－载体</td><td>属有型关系过程</td><td>被属有者</td></tr>
<tr><td>主位分析</td><td>主位</td><td colspan="2">述位</td></tr>
<tr><td>信息结构分析</td><td>已知信息</td><td colspan="2">新信息</td></tr>
</table>

“属有型”存在句尽管与前两种存在句在句法结构上不同，但它们在语义上有相同之处：（1）句首都有表示处所意义的词语；（2）句中有表示“存在”意义的动词；（3）句末有表示“存在的事物”的词语。因此，它们都可以当作汉语存在句。

6. 结语

本文从系统功能语法的角度探讨了汉语存在句句首成分的句法地位和语义角色，并对存在句句进行了及物性、主位组织和信息组织分析。本文认为汉语中主要有“地点型”“方向型”和“属有型”三种存在句，它们分别属于“地点型”“方向型”和“属有型”关系过程小句；前两种存在句的句首成分分别是及物性分析中的“地点”或“方向”，为非主导参与者是“补语”，因此是“补语”（它们的动词后的名词词组体现的是主导参与“载体”——“简单载体”“施事–载体”或“受事–载体”，是“主语”），因此驳斥了传统语法把存在句句首成分当作“主语”的观点；句首成分同时充当小句的无标记主位和“已知信息”；“属有型”存在句在动词的属性和句法结构上都与“地点型”和“方向型”存在不同，句首的地点名词体现的是“施事–载体”（即“属有者”）的语义角色，同时是已知信息，是这一过程的主导参与者，因此是“主语”，动词后的名词词组充当“被属有者”和信息焦点，为非主导参与者，因此是“补语”。但这三种存在句在语义上都有相同之处，因此都是汉语中的存在句。通过对存在句句首成分的句法地位和语义角色进行分析，本研究或许能一定程度上解决了关于汉语存在句的部分分歧。

参考文献

Fawcett, R.P. 1987. The Semantics of Clause and Verb for Relational Processes in English. In M. A. K. Halliday & R. P. Fawcett (eds.) *New Developments in Systemic Linguistics*. London: Pinter, 130-183.

Fawcett, R. P. 2003. The Many Types of 'Theme' in English: Their Semantic Systems and Functional Syntax. http: //www.wagsoft.com/ Systemics/ Archive/Fawcett-ThemePaper.rtf.

Fawcett, R. P. Forthcoming. *The Many Types of 'Theme' in English: Their Syntax, Semantics and Discourse Functions*. London: Equinox.

Halliday, M. A. K. & C. M. I. M. Matthiessen. 2004. *An Introduction to Functional Grammar*（3rd edition）. London: Arnold.

Halliday, M.A.K. & C. M. I. M. Matthiessen. 2014. *An Introduction to Functional Grammar*（4th edition）. London & New York: Routledge.

Halliday, M. A. K. & E. McDonald. 2004. Metafunctional Profile of the Grammar of Chinese. In A. Caffarel, J. R. Martin & C. M. I. M. Matthiessen. *Language Typology: A Functional Perspective*. Amsterdam: John Benjamins, 305-396.

Neale, A. C. 2002. More Delicate Transitivity: Extending the PROCESS TYPES System Networks for English to Include Full Semantic Classifications. Unpublished PhD Thesis, Cardiff University.

Tsao, F. F. 1990. *Sentence and Clause Structure in Chinese: A Functional Perspective*. Taipei: Student Book Co., Ltd.

曹逢甫，1995，《主题在汉语中的功能研究》。北京：语文出版社。

岑麟祥，1955，讨论主语宾语问题的几个原则，《语文学习》（10）：19-20。

陈庭珍，1957，汉语中处所词作主语的存在句，《中国语文》（8）：15-19。

邓仁华，2012，《系统功能语法的存在句研究》。广州：中山大学出版社。

丁声树、吕叔湘等，1961/1979，《现代汉语语法讲话》（中国语文杂志社编）。北京：商务印书馆。

黄伯荣、廖序东，2002，《现代汉语（下册）》。北京：高等教育出版社。

黄国文、何伟、廖楚燕，2008，《系统功能语法入门：加的夫语法》. 北京：北京大学出版社。

雷涛，1993，存在句的范围、构成和分类.《中国语文》（4）：244-251。

黎锦熙，1955，主宾小集（下），《语文学习》（12）：36-40。

吕冀平，1955，主语和宾语的问题，《语文学习》（7）：8-12。

吕叔湘，1943/1982，《中国文法要略》。北京：商务印书馆。

吕叔湘，1953，《语法学习》。北京：中国青年出版社。

吕叔湘主编，1999，《现代汉语八百词》（增订版）。北京：商务印书馆。

彭宣维，2011，《语言与语言学概论》。北京：北京大学出版社。

沈家煊，1999,《不对称和标记论》。南昌：江西教育出版社。
石毓智，2001, 汉语的主语和话题之辨,《语言研究》（2）: 82-91。
宋玉柱，1991,《现代汉语特殊句式》。太原：山西教育出版社。
宋玉柱，2007,《现代汉语存在句》。北京：语文出版社。
唐启运，1955, 语法结构决定主语宾语,《语文学习》（9）: 35-36。
王力，1956, 主语的定义及其在汉语中的运用,《语文学习》（1）: 21-25。
邢公畹，1955, 论汉语造句法上的主语和宾语,《语文学习》（9）: 25-27。
杨国文，2013, 主谓语段的主语界定,《世界汉语教学》（4）: 435-453。
允川，1955, 主语宾语的位置问题,《语文学习》（8）: 33。
张学成，1982, 存在句,《语言学年刊》（5）: 48-55。
赵元任，1979,《汉语口语语法》, 吕叔湘译。北京：商务印书馆。
周迎芳、王勇，2012, 存在小句的几种类型,《外国语》（3）: 59-67。
张先亮、范晓，2010,《现代汉语存在句研究》。北京：中国社会科学出版社。
周祖谟，1955, 关于主语和宾语的问题,《语文学习》（12）: 29-31。
朱德熙，1999,《语法答问》。北京：商务印书馆。

识读资源再分配的动因及其效率分析

汤　斌

东南大学

1. 引言

悉尼学派20世纪80、90年代所完成的科研项目旨在通过识读资源再分配（redistribution of literacy resources），使处于社会弱势的学习者掌握识读资源、提高识读能力，从而能够在社会中为自身重新定位（Martin, 2011：38）。识读资源指能够提高识读能力的语言学资源。个体之间对识读资源的掌握有所不同，因而个体识读能力之间也存在着差别。识读资源的不平衡分配强化了权力在个体之间的不平衡分布，而识读资源再分配的目的在于：通过拉近个体识读能力之间的差距，促进权力在社会中的平衡分布。识读资源之所以需要再分配是因为识读资源分配的不平衡。虽然Martin等一批学者在20世纪80年代就认清这一事实，但他们还无法从SFL理论上对识读资源的不平衡分配做出解释。自2008年以来，Martin（2008, 2009, 2010）提出了SFL中又一重要概念——“个体化”（individuation）。个体化为研究识读资源的不平衡分配提供了全新的视角。个体化理论探讨的是语义资源在社会组群或个体之间的分布特点（Martin & 王振华, 2008）。厘清社会符号资源如何分配至个体是探讨识读资源再分配的前提。鉴于此，本文试图回答以下三个问题：（1）社会符号资源在个体化过程中以何种模式分配至个体？（2）识读资源再分配的动因是什么？（3）如何提高识读资源再分配的效率？

2. 个体化过程中的社会符号资源分配模式

Martin（2009：564）分别从“符号资源的分配”（allocation of semiotic resources）与“亲和关系的建立”（affiliation）角度分析了语义资源在个体之间的分布。前者为个体化过程，探讨社会符号资源如何分配给个体，从而使其身份得以建构；后者为社会化过程，探讨个体如何使用社会符号资源与其他成员建立亲和关系（朱永生, 2012）。个体所掌握的社会符号资源是建构其社会文化身份的前提，并为其亲和关系的建立提供了保证。如图1所示，社会符号资源是按照等级关系，从宏观到具体逐渐分配至个体，从而使其身份得以建构。资源分配的等级关系对应社会文化身份的等级关系。个体的社会文化身份从属于特定的亚文化，特定的亚文化又从属于主流身份，而主流身份又构成了整个文化体系中的一部分。

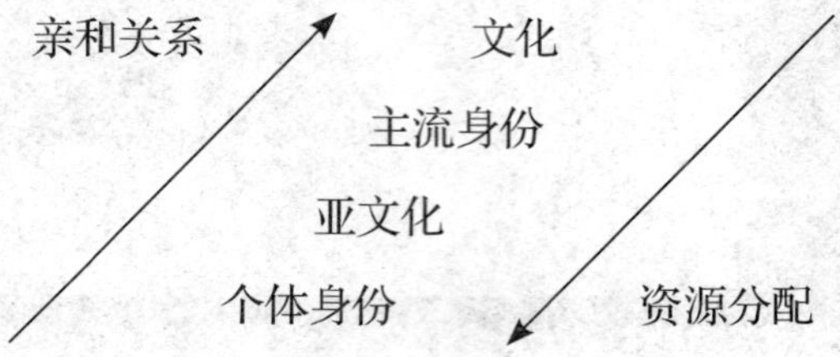

图1 个体化是亲和关系与资源分配的等级体现（朱永生, 2012）

Martin（2009）主要从社会文化身份角度探讨了符号资源的分配过程。我们将从社会符号资源特点、资源分配方式两个角度对个体化理论进行拓展，揭示社会符号资源在个体化过程中以何种模式分配至个体。社会符号资源的分配是个体从“集体意库”（reservoir）获取语义资源形成“个体意库”（repertoire）的过程；集体意库是社会团体中所有成员的语义资源总和，而个体意库指个人的语义资源总和；社会团体中各成员的个体意库均共享一些核心特征，但也存在着差异（Bernstein, 1999：159-160）。非共享的社会符号资源形成了个体意库之间的差异，体现了社会文化身份的差别。资源分配方式可分为“习得”（acquisition）与“传授”（transmission）。习得强调个人对知识的学习与掌握，习得者在此过程中对隐秘而有利于学习的活动发挥积极的调控作用；传授强调传授者为学习者制订出明确而有效的知识学习顺序（Bernstein, 1990：214）。习得注重学习者在知识学习中的主观能动作用，而传授强调教师在知识学习中的主观能动作用。

社会符号资源特点与资源分配方式相互组合，构成了不同的符号资源分配模式。如图2所示，垂直区域表示分配至个体的是共享资源，还是非共享资源；水平区域表示资源分配的方式是习得，还是传授。两者交差后形成四类符号资源分配模式：共享资源的习得与非共享资源的习得；共享资源的传授与非共享资源的传授。

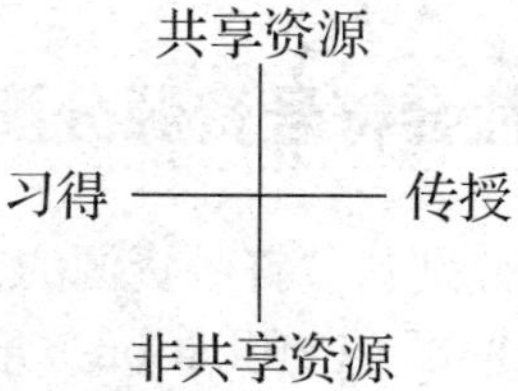

图2 社会符号资源的分配模式

根据Hasan（1996：384）的观点，个体的识读能力通常在普通生活语境（context of mundane activities）与正式教育语境（official pedagogic context）中得到发展。这一点与我们提出的社会符号资源分配模式形成对应。在普通生活语境与正式教育语境中，个体分别通过习得与传授方式获取社会符号资源，促成其识读能力的发展。一般而言，正常的儿童在普通生活语境中均能习得自己的母语。这一过程体现为共享资源的习得。个体对表义方式的学习是终身学习的过程（Hasan, 1996：384）。作为共享资源，母语的习得是表义方式学习中的一部分。习得母语后，个体继续在普通生活语境中学习表义方式。普通生活语境中的识读能力发展很大程度上取决于个体的社会取位（social positioning）（Hasan, 1996：385）。不同的社会取位决定了个体会参与不同的社会化过程，不同的社会化过程会影响个体的表义方式，使其习得不同的社会符号资源。个体编码取向的形成是典型的非共享资源习得过程。拥有不同社会取位的个体在家庭生活中习得不同的语义资源，形成不同的编码取向。编码取向可分为："限制型语码"（Restricted Code）与"精致型语码"（Elaborated Code）。限制型语码依赖于具体的语境，句法简单，词语范围狭小，不适合表达抽象的概念；精致型语码不囿于具体的语境，句法结构复杂，措辞严谨，适用于分析、推理与表达抽象的概念（朱永生, 2011）。编码取向既能促进也能阻碍个体识读能力的发展。这也解释了为什么对母语的习得并不代表每个人都掌握了相同的、以母语为载体的识读能力。

从时间角度看，正式教育语境中的识读能力发展要滞后于普通生活语境中的识读能力发展；从逻辑关系看，正式教育语境中的识读能力发展又以普通生活语境中的识读能力发展为基础（Hasan, 1996：385）。也就是说，个体在进入学校教育前已经掌握了特定的表义方式。当个体的表义方式顺应教学话语时，学校教育会促进个体识读能力的发展；反之，则会阻碍其发展。促进与阻碍均体现为非共享资源的传授过程。显然，非共享资源的传授强化了个体社会取位之间的差异。与普通生活语境相比，正式的学校教育同样会受到个体社会取位的影响。不考虑个体的社会取位，采用相同的教学目标与方式，只会强化个体之间识读能力的差异。与之相反，如果学校教育能够考虑社会取位对个体表义方式的影响，并在教学中通过识读资源再分配拉近不同表义方式之间的差距，个体之间识读能力的发展将会更为均衡。这一过程体现为共享资源的传授。

3. 识读资源再分配的动因

个体在普通生活语境与正式教育语境中的识读能力发展均会受到其社会取位的影响。换言之，不同的社会文化身份使个体在其表义方式的形成过程中获取不同的识读资源。如图2所示，个体在普通生活语境中既能够习得共享资源，也能够习得非共享资源。非共享资源的习得造成了识读资源在个体之间的不平衡分配。社会文化身份的差别是导致识读资源不平衡分配的根本原因。这一点已由Hasan（2005,

2009）的研究得到证实。Hasan通过分析不同社会阶层的母亲与子女的对话，发现社会文化身份与个体语义表达方式之间存在密切的关联。从亲和关系角度看，由于个体掌握的是对应自己身份的识读资源，所以当个体使用这些资源建立亲和关系时也巩固了社会对不同身份的划分。身份的差别使识读资源无法在个体之间得到平衡分配；识读资源的不平衡分配又通过个体对亲和关系的建立，强化了身份之间的差别。

在社会符号资源的传授过程中，社会文化身份同样会影响到识读资源的分配，从而形成非共享资源的传授。如上文所述，个体在步入学校教育前就已掌握了特定的表义方式。不同的社会文化身份使个体在普通生活语境中获取不同的识读资源，形成不同的表义方式。如果课堂语文教学不考虑个体之间文化身份、表义方式的差别，顺应教学语言的表义方式会促进个体识读能力的发展，反之则会阻碍其发展。此时的课堂语文教学便形成了非共享资源的传授，强化了个体之间社会文化身份的差别。

社会团体成员之间的隔阂或排斥越深，个体意库与集体意库发展所需的社会基础越薄弱（Bernstein, 1999：160）。社会文化身份的差别越大，识读资源的分配越不平衡，识读资源再分配的必要性也就越明显。Martin的个体化理论揭示了个体身份差别与识读资源不平衡分配之间的相互强化关系，为识读资源再分配提供了动因。识读资源再分配的目的是实现权力在社会中的平衡分布（Martin, 2011），因为权力的差别分配是个体社会文化身份差异形成的根本原因。

4. 如何提高识读资源再分配的效率

识读资源的分配对应个体的社会文化身份。在普通生活语境中，身份的差别使个体无法回避非共享资源的习得；在正式教育语境中，身份的差别亦会造成非共享资源的传授，二者均强化了个体之间社会取位的差别。由于非共享资源的传授以非共享资源的习得为基础，因此非共享资源的习得是识读资源再分配亟待解决的核心问题。非共享资源被个体内化后形成编码取向，不同的编码取向会潜移默化地影响个体识读能力的发展，阻碍识读资源的再次分配。共享资源的传授为识读资源再分配提供了有效的模式，因为它充分考虑到个体的社会文化身份对其表义方式的影响，通过显性的教学方法将识读资源重新分配给个体，弥补个体之间表义方式的差别，从而使拥有不同社会文化身份的个体掌握顺应教学话语的表义方式。

4.1 在识读资源再分配中抑制编码取向的影响

非共享资源的习得使个体形成不同的编码取向。儿童时期是编码取向形成的关键阶段。编码取向不同并不表明来自不同社会阶层的儿童在智商上有所差（Bernstein, 1958, 1960; Halliday, 1988）。由于编码取向已经被个体内化，如果不实施干预与抑制，编码取向便会阻碍识读资源的再次分配。教学语言属于精致型语码，因此学校教育对于持精致型语码的个体来说是符号性与社会性的发展（symbolic and social development），而对于持限制型语码的个体来说则是符号性与社会性的改变（symbolic and social change）（Bernstein, 1971：143-144）。因编码取向的差异所导致的文化断层（cultural discontinuity）使得持限制型语码的个体在学校教育中处于劣势，无法享受到平等的教育机会。

个体的学习可以理解为表义资源的建构过程，个体通过语言学习知识，并同时在此过程中学习语言（Halliday, 1993）。个体掌握的识读资源越多，知识学习的效果越好。同时，个体的识读资源也会不断地巩固与丰富，从而形成识读能力与知识学习之间的良性循环。与之相反，识读资源的缺失会使个体无法有效地掌握知识，知识学习的失败又限制了个体识读能力的发展。编码取向的差异使个体无法获得成功的教育，其真正原因是个体识读资源的匮乏。与限制型语码相比，精致型语码赋予了个体更为丰富的识读资源。我们认为，抑制编码取向的影响就是通过识读资源再分配拉近编码取向之间的差距，从而有效抑制限制型语码对个体知识学习造成的阻碍作用，促进识读资源在个体之间的平衡分配。抑制编码取向的影响构成了识读资源再分配的核心环节。

4.2 把共享资源的传授作为抑制编码取向影响的有效途径

如图2所示，共享资源的传授是社会符号资源分配至个体的模式之一。共享资源的传授旨在将社会符号资源公平地分配给拥有不同社会文化身份的个体。编码取向是社会符号资源按照不同的社会文化身份分配至个体的结果。在此过程中，个体习得与其身份相对应的社会符号资源。通过共享资源的传授抑制编码取向的影响就是在课堂语文教学中将精致型语码作为共享资源传授给持限制型语码的个体。但是这一过程并非轻而易举，因为个体在学习精致型语码的过程中仍然会受到自身限制型语码的影响。选择适当的语言教学方法与正确的语言教学目标直接关系到共享资源的传授效果，并最终影响到识读资源再分配的效率。我们认为，提高教学法的可见度与语义资源的共享程度能够有效地缩小编码取向之间的差距。

4.2.1 提高教学法的可见度

Bernstein（1975：116-117）区分了不可见的教学法（invisible pedagogy）与可见的教学法（visible pedagogy）：知识传授方式越隐秘、教学评价标准越宽泛，教学法的可见度越低；知识传授方式越明显、教学评价标准越具体，教学法的可见度越高。不可见的教学法以拥有长期的教育生涯与对精致型语码的掌握为前提，认为对学生具体能力的培养可以延迟或是学生在精致型语码的帮助下已经掌握了这些技能（Bernstein, 1975：124）。不可见的教学法降低了对具体文化技能、识读能力传授与习得的关注，是对编码取向的默认与强化。它将“社会符号资源按照社会文化身份分配的特性”延续到课堂语文教学之中，极大地降低了识读资源再分配的效率。

建构主义教学法（constructivism）是典型的不可见教学法。该教学法否定了教师在教学中的权威地位，强调由学生自主决定学习的内容、方法与目标。Rose & Martin（2012：3）发现，建构主义教学法在澳大利亚仅为职业化、中产阶层家庭的利益诉求服务，却无法为被边缘化的社会群体提供良好的教育。来自中产阶层家庭的学生由于已经掌握了与教学语言相近的精致型语码，所以能够很容易地适应从家庭到学校语境的转换并在知识学习中取得成功；来自被边缘化家庭的学生通常掌握限制型语码，家庭与学校之间的语码差异使他们无法较快地适应学校教育，并在知识学习中取得成功。就后者而言，如果教学的内容、方法、目标与评价标准无法向这些学生明示，他们将只能停留于家庭语境之中，从而巩固了他们在家庭生活中形成的限制型语码。其结果是他们无法在知识学习中获得成功（Rothery, 1996; Martin, 1999）。不可见的教学法实质是非共享资源的传授过程、是对原有权力结构的再造与强化，有悖于识读资源再分配的初衷，因此识读资源再分配应该采用可见的教学法。

在个体获取社会符号资源的过程中，可见的教学法是一种外界干预。虽然它无法改变社会符号资源按照社会文化身份分配的特性，但可以明示限制型语码与精致型语码的差别，使个体意识到新的社会符号资源的存在。提高教学法的可见度实际就是提高识读资源再分配的可见度。

4.2.2 提高语义资源的共享程度

除提高教学法的可见度外，我们还应该关注社会取位的差别对于个体表义方式的影响，即不同编码取向之间的差别。仅仅提高教学法的可见度，不考虑编码取向之间的差异，同样会形成非共享资源的传授，从而阻碍识读资源的再次分配。与建构主义教学法相比，传统的语言教学法注重语言形式与语法的精确性，因而具有较强的可见度。然而，该类教学法忽略了语言作为社会符号行为这一现实，并最终发展成为由教师给学生反复灌输语言标准的过程（Hasan, 1996：388-389）。语法是表义资源，语言的学习是表义资源的建构过程（Halliday, 1975, 1993, 1994）。否定语言是表义资源，我们将失去解释个体之间表义方式差别的重要视角。将语言学习等同于语言标准的灌输又会强化个体之间表义方式的差别，因为有些人在普通生活语境中已经习得了与语言标准相吻合的表义方式，而有些则没有。为了提高识读资源再分配的效率，语言的使用应该被视为个体使用语义资源表达意义的社会行为。只有这样，我们才能解释个体之间表义方式的差别、不同编码取向的形成原因。

提高语义资源的共享程度旨在通过缩小精致型语码与限制型语码之间的差距，提高识读资源再分配的效率。因此，在语言教学目标的选择上，我们需关注哪些语义资源能够有效地拉近精致型语码与限制型语码之间的距离。根据Bernstein（1971）对这两类语码的定义，精致型语码区别于限制型语码较为明显的特征是语境独立性。精致型语码能够较早地引导儿童意识到独立于语境的意义的重要性（Bernstein, 1975：124），而且与限制型语码相比，精致型语码的句法特征很难从语境角度加以预测（Bernstein, 1990：96）。我们认为，在识读资源再分配中，传授独立于语境的语义资源应成为课堂语文教学的目标，如语法隐喻的教学。试比较下面两例：

Wealthy families manufactured garum in Pompei.
Wealthy families controlled the manufacture of garum in Pompei.
(Martin & Matruglio, 2013: 85)

在前句中，话语对经验的建构与现实完全一致；在后句中，现实中的动作过程（manufactured）被话语识解为抽象的个体（the manufacture）。虽然名词化短语建构了相同的经验，但与现实中的经验模式完全不同。作为精致型语码的典型体现，概念语法隐喻建构的经验模式已经摆脱了现实语境的束缚，从而能够帮助学生建立概念之间的逻辑关系，为知识结构的形成奠定基础。如果学生在中学阶段没能掌握独立于语境的语义资源，他们将无法获取相关的专业知识，因为在教科书、讲义、网络中，这些知识的建构均依赖独立于语境的语义资源；不但如此，他们也将无法在考核中展示自己对专业知识的掌握（Martin, 2013; Martin & Matruglio, 2013）。与持限制型语码的个体相比，已掌握精致型语码的个体在专业知识学习与考核中都会更胜一筹。缩小两种语码之间的差别也就是将独立于语境的语义资源重新分配给持限制型语码的个体。

5. 结论

识读资源再分配是社会符号资源重新分配至个体的过程。个体化与识读资源再分配的区别在于：前者强调了社会文化身份的差别在社会符号资源分配中的影响；后者的目的恰恰是在社会符号资源分配中削弱社会文化身份差别带来的影响。在个体化中，社会符号资源的差别分配强化了权力在社会阶层中的不平衡分布，而识读资源再分配的作用恰恰在于改变这种状况，促进权力在社会中的平衡分布。个体化理论揭示了社会符号资源按照社会文化身份分配的特性，为识读资源再分配提供了动因。在个体化过程中，不同的社会符号资源分配模式为识读资源再分配提供了指导。在识读资源再分配的过程中，应有效地抑制编码取向的影响。在课堂语文教学中，提高教学法的可见度、拉近不同编码之间的差距，能够减少编码取向在语言教学中的负面影响，提高识读资源再分配的效率。

参考文献

Bernstein, B. 1958. Some Sociological Determinants of Perception: An Enquiry into Sub-Cultural Differences. *The British Journal of Sociology*, 9(2): 159-174.

Bernstein, B. 1960. Language and Social Class. *The British Journal of Sociology*, 11(3): 271-276.

Bernstein, B. 1971. *Class, Codes and Control: Theoretical Studies Towards a Sociology of Language, Volume 1*. London: Routledge and Kegan Paul.

Bernstein, B. 1975. *Class, Codes and Control: Towards a Theory of Educational Transmission, Volume 3*. London: Routledge and Kegan Paul.

Bernstein, B. 1990. *The Structuring of Pedagogic Discourse: Class, Codes and Control, Volume 4*. London and New York: Routledge.

Bernstein, B. 1999. Vertical and Horizontal Discourse: An Essay. *British Journal of Sociology of Education*, 20(2): 266-279.

Halliday, M.A.K. 1975. *Learning How to Mean: Explorations in the Development of Language*. London: Arnold.

Halliday, M.A.K. 1988. Language and Socialization: Home and School. In L. Gerot, J. Oldenburg& T. van Leeuwen (eds.) *Language and Socialisation, Home and School: Proceedings from the Working Conference on Language in Education*. North Ryde, N.S.W: Macquarie University.

Halliday, M.A.K. 1993. Towards a Language-based Theory of Learning. *Linguistics and Education*, 5: 93-116.

Halliday, M.A.K. 1994. *Introduction to Functional Grammar* (2nd edition). London: Arnold.

Hasan, R. 1996. Literacy, Everyday Talk and Society. In R. Hasan&G. Williams (eds.) *Literacy in Society*. London: Longman.

Hasan, R. 2005. *Language, Society and Consciousness*. London: Equinox (*The Collected Works of Ruqaiya Hasan* edited by J. Webster, Volume 1).

Hasan, R. 2009. *Semantic Variation: Meaning in Society and Sociolinguistics*. London: Equinox (*The Collected Works of Ruqaiya Hasan* edited by J. Webster, Volume 2).

Martin, J.R. 1999. Mentoring Semogenesis: "Genre-based" Literacy Pedagogy. In F. Christie (ed.) *Pedagogy and the Shaping of Consciousness: Linguistic and Social Processes*. London: Cassel.

Martin, J.R. 2008. Innocence: Realisation, Instantiation and Individuation in a Botswanan Town. In N. Knight, &A. Mahboob (eds.) *Questioning Linguistics*. Cambridge: Cambridge Scholars Publishing.

Martin, J.R. 2009. Realisation, Instantiation and Individuation: Some Thoughts on Identity in Youth Justice Conferencing. *DELTA-Documentação de EstudosemLinguisticaTeorica e Aplicada* 25: 549-583.

Martin, J.R. 2010. Semantic Variation: Modelling Realisation,Instantiation and Individuation in Social Semiosis. In M. Bednarek&J.R. Martin (eds.) *New Discourse on Language: Functional Perspectives on Multimodality, Identity and Affiliation*. London:

Continuum.

Martin, J.R. 2011. Bridging Troubled Waters: Interdisciplinarity and What Makes it Stick. In F. Christie & K. Maton (eds.) *Disciplinarity: Functional Linguistic and Sociological Perspectives*. London: Continuum.

Martin, J.R. 2013. Embedded Literacy: Knowledge as Meaning. *Linguistics and Education*, 24(1): 23-37.

Martin, J.R. & E. Matruglio. 2013. Revisiting Mode: Context In/dependency in Ancient History Classroom Discourse. In Z. Li& D. Lu (eds.). *Studies in Functional Linguistics and Discourse Analysis, Volume 5*. Beijing: Higher Education Press.

Rose, D. & J. R. Martin. 2012. *Learning to Write, Reading to Learn: Genre, Knowledge and Pedagogy in the Sydney School*. Sheffield: Equinox.

Rothery, J. 1996. Making Changes: Developing an Educational Linguistics. In R. Hasan & G. Williams (eds.) *Literacy in Society*. London: Longman.

Martin、王振华，2008, 实现化、实例化和个性化——系统功能语言学的三种层次关系，《上海交通大学学报（哲学社会科学版）》（5）: 73-81。

朱永生，2011, Bernstein 的教育社会学理论对系统功能语言学的影响，《外语教学》（4）: 6-12。

朱永生，2012, 系统功能语言学个体化研究的动因及哲学指导思想，《现代外语》（4）: 331-337。

古典藏语语气系统的系统功能分析

王　品

上海交通大学

1. 古典藏语概述

藏语属于汉藏语系藏缅语族藏语支，主要分布于中国的青藏高原地区和印度次大陆北部，包括尼泊尔、不丹、巴基斯坦、印度等国家。现代藏语分为三大方言：卫藏方言、安多方言、康方言。

本文的研究对象——古典藏语——指的是藏语发展演化过程中三个主要阶段（上古期、古典期和现代期）中的中间阶段。有的学者认为上古藏语之前还有一个远古（archaic）藏语期，古典期和现代期之间还有一个中古（medieval）藏语期（Hodge, 1993：vii）。具体地说，古典藏语是指公元九世纪左右主要为翻译来自印度的梵语佛经而标准化的藏语。古典藏语用以记录大量的宗教、文学以及医学文献，为现代藏语奠定了词汇与语法基础。因此，古典藏语在藏语历史上占有极其重要的地位。

古典藏语的词汇可大致分为实义词和助词。实义词包括名词、动词、形容词等；而助词则附加在实义词之后，体现实义词之间的概念、人际与语篇关系，如名助词、格助词、独立助词等。

古典藏语采用SOV语序[1]，是一种作格（ergative）语言，并且没有主动语态和被动语态的区分。小句根据动原（agency）的存在与否分为使役态（effective）和中间态（middle）。关于古典藏语作格与语态的系统功能语言学分析可参见Wang（2012）。

下面是古典藏语的一个例句：

（1）	*da ltar*	*Ni*	*Dag*	*gis*	*khyim*	*la*	*dur*	*tsam*	*du*	*'dzin*	*no*[2]
	现在	主题助词	我	作格助词	家	向格助词	坟墓	仅	终格助词	看作	终助词

1 古典藏语作为一种作通格语言（ergative-absolutive language），而非主宾格语言（nominative-accusative language），是否适用印欧语传统下的“主语”（Subject）和“宾语”（Object）这样的术语尚还有待商榷。这里只是权且采用 SOV 这种通行的说法。

2 本文古典藏语采用威利（Wylie）式转写方案。

"现在家对我来说只是一座坟墓。"

从例（1）可以明显看出古典藏语小句中实义词与助词的交互作用，除了dur一词后为零助词标记外[3]，其余实义词成分后均带有助词。因此，助词可以看作是实义词之间的黏合剂，对小句的意义构建起到至关重要的作用。下节将从三大纯理功能的角度简要探讨古典藏语助词的功能。

2. 古典藏语助词的纯理功能

在例（1）中，助词ni起到提示主题的作用，表示其前的成分为话语的出发点，即主位系统中的主位（Theme）。因此它所起到的功能是语篇的，我们可以将它称作语篇助词。

助词gis的作用发生在及物性系统层面，表示其前的成分为小句的施事（Agent）。除了表示施事外，它还可以体现手段（Means）、质量（Quality）、原因（Cause），或者体现两个小句之间的因果逻辑关系。助词la表示过程的方向、对象，使其前的成分行使小句的地点（Location）、受益者（Beneficiary）等功能。助词du在这里使其前的成分起到方式（Manner）的功能，在其他情况下还可能表示地点（Location）或范围（Range）。它们所起到的功能是经验或逻辑的，我们可以将它们称作概念助词。

小句末尾的助词（n）o表示小句为陈述语气，在语气系统中发挥作用。它起到的功能是人际的，我们可以将它称为人际助词。

综上所述，古典藏语的助词虽然可以出现于同一个横组合结构中，但它们所起到的纯理功能却不尽相同。古典藏语的助词自然不限于例（1）中出现的五个，但任何一个助词都可以归入上述按照纯理功能划分的三大类别之一。本文探讨的主题是古典藏语的语气系统，所以我们要重点探究人际助词，更确切地说，我们要关注的是那些在语气系统中起作用的助词。这些助词实际上是协商小句语气的最关键部分，小句的语气主要靠它们来体现。我们可以按照系统功能语言学的惯例将这些语气助词赋予功能名称——协商语（Negotiator）。

3. 协商语的类别

协商语是古典藏语语气的主要体现手段，共分为三类：陈述协商语（Declarative Negotiator）用以体现叙述；疑问协商语（Interrogative Negotiator）用以体现提问；祈使协商语（Imperative Negotiator）用以体现命令。下面对它们逐一进行介绍。

3 概念功能的作格分析法中的媒介（Medium）不带有任何助词，详见Wang（2012）。

3.1 陈述协商语

陈述协商语的基本形态是'o，但在位于其前的音素或形态的影响下，存在不同的形态变体。

a. 如果前面的词以元音结尾，*'o*直接附于其后。例如：
'dre（混合）→*'dre'o*

b. 如果前面的词以字母'a结尾，将*'a*去掉，后接*'o*。例如：
bda'[4]（赶出）→*bda'o*

c. 如果前面的词以辅音结尾，需要将该辅音重复一次，后拼*o*。例如：
'tshong（卖）→*'tshongngo*
Smras（说）→*smras so*

d. c的例外：有些以辅音n，r，l结尾的动词最初还有一个d作为其祈使词干[5]的落尾，但到古典藏语阶段d发生脱落。这样的词后接陈述协商语*to*。例如：
stor（丢失）→*stor to*

3.2 疑问协商语

疑问协商语的基本形态是*'am*。与陈述协商语类似，疑问协商语在位于其前的音素或形态的影响下，也存在不同的形态变体。

a. 如果前面的词以元音结尾，*'am*直接附于其后。例如：
'dre→*'dre'am*

b. 如果前面的词以字母*'a*结尾，将*'a*去掉，后接*'am*。例如：
bda'→*bda'am*

c. 如果前面的词以辅音结尾，需要将该辅音重复一次，后拼*am*。例如：
'tshong→*'tshongngam*
smras→*smrassam*

d. c的例外：古典藏语阶段词尾d发生脱落的词后接疑问协商语*tam*。例如：
stor→*stor tam*

3.3 祈使协商语

祈使协商语的基本形态是*cig*。根据其前具体音素或形态的不同，同样有不同的形态变体，但变体出现的环境以及变化的方式与陈述协商语和疑问协商语并不一致。

---

4 *'a* 为藏语字母འ（字母名称为 *a-chung*）独立形式的转写方案，当该字母位于一个完整的音节形式但不做该音节的主要元音时，转写为 '。

5 关于祈使词干见第 4 节。

a. *cig*用于词尾g、d或b后。例如：

sod（杀）→*sod cig*

b. zhig用于词尾ng、n、m、'、r或l后。例如：

nyon（听）→*nyonzhig*

c. *shig*用于词尾s后。例如：

byos（做）→*byosshig*

需要强调的是，尽管古典藏语的语气主要靠协商语来体现，但并非完全依赖协商语，协商语并非决定小句语气的唯一要素。三种语气的具体体现方式见下文第5节。

4. 祈使词干

在绘制古典藏语语气系统网络前，还有一项与古典藏语语气有关的背景知识需要先行交代。尽管古典藏语的三种语气主要由协商语决定，但其中的祈使语气除了要求使用祈使协商语之外，动词本身也要使用专门的祈使词干。

古典藏语的词干包含四个类别，分别是：现在词干（present stem）、完成词干（perfective stem）、将来词干（future stem）、祈使词干（imperative stem）。对于有些动词来说，这四个词干在形式上可能有部分或完全重叠的情况。表1提供了一些具体的例子（引自Hahn, 2005：53）。

表1 古典藏语动词的词干

	词义	现在词干	完成词干	将来词干	祈使词干	
四个词干形式	做	*byed*	*byas*	*bya*	*Byos*	词干形式各不相同
三个词干形式	获得	*rnyed*	*brnyes*	*brnyed*	*Rnyed*	现在词干与祈使词干形式相同
	拉长	*snar*	*bsnar*	*bsnar*	*Snor*	完成词干与将来词干形式相同
	役使	*'khol*	*bkol*	*'khol*	*khol*	现在词干与将来词干形式相同
两个词干形式	给	*sbyin*	*byin*	*sbyin*	*byin*	现在词干与将来词干形式相同；完成词干与祈使词干形式相同
	会面	*'phrad*	*phrad*	*phrad*	*phrad*	完成词干、将来词干与祈使词干形式相同
一个词干形式	看见	*mthong*	*mthong*	*mthong*	*mthong*	所有词干形式相同

各种词干的功能分述如下。现在词干可以看作动词的词根形式，也就是词典或词汇表的词条形式，它用于没有任何时态、体、语气或情态限制的环境。完成词干体现完成体，表示某个动作业已结束。古典藏语语法上所谓的将来词干实际上并不体现时态，而是体现一种必要或意愿的情态（Modality），表示某个尚未开始的动作需要被执行或有被执行的愿望。祈使词干，顾名思义，是用于体现命令的词干，是祈使语气必要的体现形式。

5. 古典藏语的语气系统网络

本节将对古典藏语的语气系统进行尝试性的形式化描述，即利用系统网络来表现系统与结构的关系，并制定相应的体现规则。

5.1 祈使语气

首先，古典藏语的小句需要在[直陈]和[祈使]之间做出选择，[直陈]体现的是命题（proposition），而[祈使]体现的是提议（proposal）。古典藏语的动词并不按照人称和数进行屈折变化，没有限定性这一语法系统，因此也没有限定成分这一功能。但如上节所述，祈使语气要求动词使用祈使词干；祈使词干后面再加上祈使协商语来构成祈使语气的完整体现形式。于是我们可以首先得到具有两个选项的系统网络，并为[祈使]添加体现规则[6]，如图1所示。例句（2）是一个祈使小句。

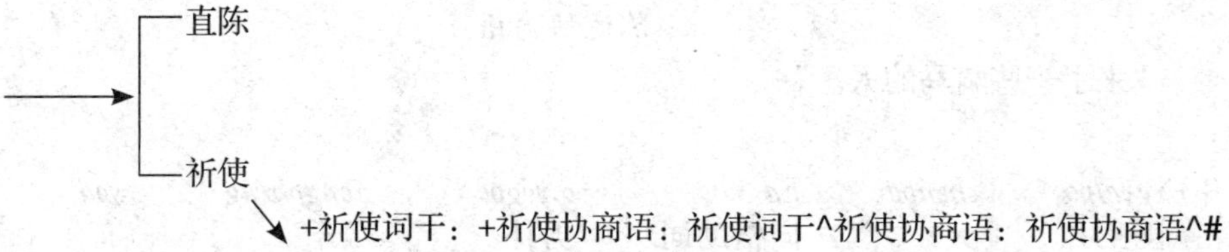

图1 古典藏语的祈使语气

（2）*chubo*	*gting*	*zabpo*	*'di*	*ltos*	*Shig*
河	底	深	这	看	
				祈使词干	祈使协商语

"看这深河！"

6 体现规则中的符号的意义见 Martin（2013：163）。

5.2 陈述语气

接下来，[直陈]分为体现叙述的[陈述]和体现提问的[疑问]两个子系统。在这个精密阶上，古典藏语的语气系统网络看起来和英语的语气系统网络十分相像，都有相同的系统选项（Martin, 2013：43）。但它们在结构上的体现方式却有很大不同。英语的语气主要通过主语和限定成分的加入和排序来体现，但古典藏语并没有限定成分，同时主语[7]也不一定出现，这一点和汉语的情况类似。

古典藏语的陈述语气在大多数情况下依赖于陈述协商语；但在关系过程小句中，陈述协商语省略，这种情况下动词通常为*yin*（在）或*yod*（有）。我们把这两种情况分别称为[终结式]和[非终结式]。于是我们得到如图2所示的系统网络及体现规则。例句（3）和（4）分别是终结式和非终结式陈述小句。

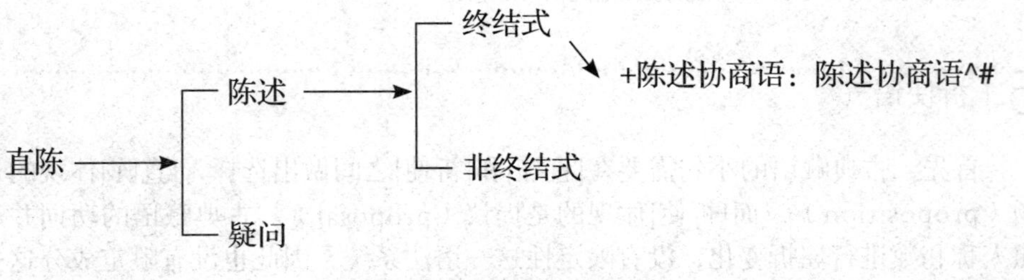

图2 古典藏语的陈述语气

（3）	*rta pa*	*kha cig*	*'ong*	*ngo*
	骑马的人	一些	来	
				陈述协商语

“来了一些骑马的人。”

（4）	*rgyalpo*	*chenpo*	*La*	*g.yogpo*	*stongphrag*	*yod*
	国王	大	向格助词	男仆	数千	有

“大国王有数千男仆。”

5.3 疑问语气

古典藏语中有三种疑问小句，分别是是非疑问、选择疑问和特指疑问。例如：

（5）	*mi*	*de*	*dgra*	*yin*	*nam*
	人	那	敌人	是	
					疑问协商语

“那个人是敌人吗？”

7 同注1。

(6) *mi de dgra 'am gnyen*

人 那 敌人 朋友

疑问协商语

“那个人是敌人还是朋友？”

(7) *mi de su yin*

人 那 谁 是

特指疑问语

“那个人是谁？”

我们发现，三种疑问小句的共同特点是：它们在结构上都具有一个表示疑问的语言形式。据此我们可以在[疑问]这一较低精密阶的选项上先插入疑问语作为体现规则，以区别于同一精密阶的[陈述]。疑问语包括疑问协商语和特指疑问语两个类别。

例（5）的是非疑问小句和例（6）的选择疑问小句都出现了3.2节介绍的疑问协商语。换句话说，疑问协商语这一功能既要出现在[是非]这一选项的体现规则中，又要出现在[选择]这一选项的体现规则中。因此，如果疑问语气的系统网络直接分为[是非][选择]和[特指]三个选项的话，[是非]和[选择]体现规则的重复说明系统网络缺乏概括。这两个选项应该在精密阶上逆推一步，用[非特指]这一选项先行概括，然后再行细分。是非疑问将疑问协商语置于小句最末；选择疑问将疑问协商语置于两个选项之间。

特指疑问小句方面，古典藏语与汉语类似，寻求未知信息的特指疑问语保留在由该疑问语提问的未知信息在陈述句的原有位置，无需语序的调整。所以只需要在体现规则中加入特指疑问语，并将其与某项未知信息所体现的功能合并即可。

根据以上讨论，我们可以绘制出如图3所示的古典藏语的疑问语气系统网络，并制定相应的体现规则。

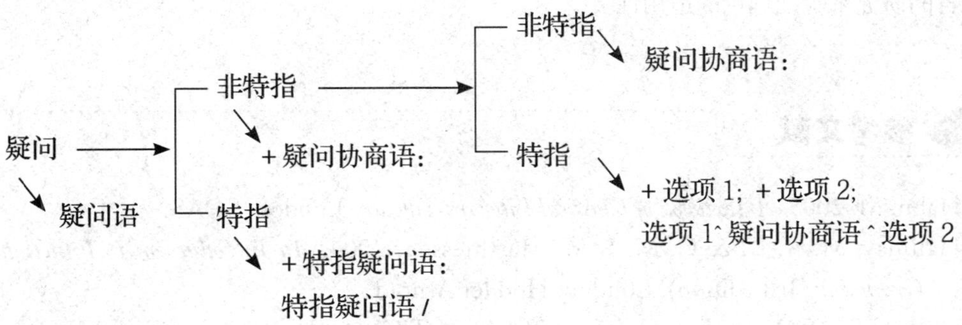

图3 古典藏语的疑问语气

在本节的最后，综合以上对祈使语气、陈述语气和疑问语气的讨论，我们可以尝试绘制一幅综合反映古典藏语语气系统运作及选择的系统网络。

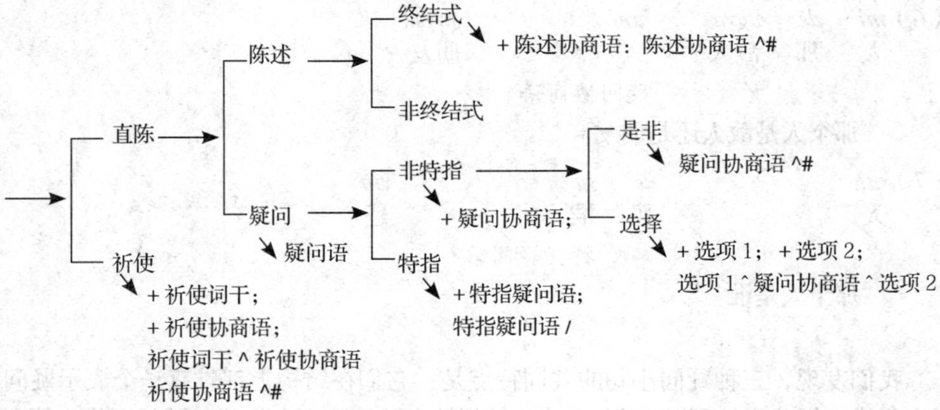

图4 古典藏语的语气系统

6. 结语

本文尝试分析了古典藏语的语气系统，探讨了不同的言语功能（命令、叙述和提问）是如何由古典藏语的词汇语法资源来协商和体现的。古典藏语主要通过语气协商语和动词词干的变化来体现语气，这一点与我们熟悉的英语或汉语都不尽相同。本研究的初衷也正是利用系统功能语言学这一适用性的理论工具来描述和解释英语或汉语这样的大语种之外的语言现象，而这也是许多系统功能类型学家面临的挑战和致力从事的工作。这种工作的至关重要的一点是将系统功能语言学的理论原则和描写范式本地化。概括性的理论框架与具体的语言在逻辑上自然形成互补：系统功能类型学家一方面用理论解释具体语言表达意义的方式，另一方面用对具体语言的研究来验证理论的适用性。

参考文献

Hahn, M. 2005. *A Textbook of Classical Literary Tibetan*. London: SOAS.

Halliday, M. A. K. & C. M. I. M. Matthiessen. 2004. *An Introduction to Functional Grammar* (3rd edition). London: Hodder Arnold.

Hodge, S. 1993. *An Introduction to Classical Tibetan*. Warminster, England: Aris& Phillips.

Jäschke, H. A. 1883. *Tibetan Grammar* (2nd edition). London: Trübner& Co.

Martin, J. R. 2013. *Systemic Functional Grammar: A Next Step into the Theory — Axial Relations* (Translated and expanded by Wang Pin and Zhu Yongsheng). Beijing: Higher Education Press.

Matthiessen, C. M. I. M. 2004. Descriptive Motifs and Generalizations. In A. Caffarel, J. R. Martin & C. M. I. M. Matthiessen (eds.) *Language Typology: A Functional Perspective*. Amsterdam/Philadelphia: John Benjamins, 537-673.

Wang, P. 2012. A Systemic Functional Interpretation of Ergativity in Classical Tibetan. In Knox, J. (ed.) *To Boldly Proceed: Papers from the 39th International Systemic Functional Congress*. Sydney: UTS, 105-110.

以《石青嫂子》为例探究汉语中及物性过程的评价价值

刘玉洁

北京师范大学

1. 引言

在功能语法中，小句通过及物性表达语言的概念功能。及物性分析涉及三个成分——参与者、过程和环境，其中过程是核心。及物系统包括六个过程类型：物质过程、心理过程、行为过程、言语过程、关系过程和存在过程（Halliday, 1994：106-108）。评价系统与人际意义有关，涉及语篇中作者或说话者的主观立场。这一立场可以针对他们所呈现的材料，也可以针对他们所交流的对象（Martin & White, 2005：1）。本文结合及物性过程和评价系统的观点，从评价语料库中选取小说《石青嫂子》，研究其中及物性过程的评价价值。

2. 评价意义的体现方式

系统功能语言学认为，语言是一个多层次的复杂符号系统，包括音系层、词汇语法层和语义层，它们之间是体现关系（Halliday, 1994：F46）。系统功能语言学语法研究的基本单位是小句，而Martin（1992：16-21）强调要研究超越小句（即语篇）的意义，从而指出语篇的重要性，并将语义层改为语篇语义层。评价系统是语篇语义层面表达人际意义的三个系统之一，与作者或说话者在语篇中的主观态度有关，可用来协商社会关系（Martin & White, 2005：9）。Martin将评价意义范畴化，分为态度、介入和级差三个子系统。态度是评价系统的核心，即使是客观的态度也含有某种情感意义（刘世铸, 2009：22），级差是对态度的调节，介入则指明态度的来源（Martin & White, 2005：35）。

态度意义有显性和隐性两种，相应的评价方式也有两种：一种是直接而明确地表达，称为铭刻性评价方式；另一种则是由表示概念意义的词汇激发某种态度，称为引发性评价方式。前者通过明显的评价词汇或句式表达态度，如态度修饰词（a beautiful girl）、关系过程中的属性（his smile seemed fake）或评论附加语（Sadly, she walked back upstairs）等。而引发性评价方式又包括激发性和邀约性两种：前者主要通过词汇隐喻激发读者的态度反应，如we fenced them in like sheep；后者则通过融有方式的非核心词汇旗示隐含的态度意义，如we smashed their way of life，或通过上下文或阅读定位来致使某种态度，如we brought the diseases（Martin & White, 2005：61-67）。

Halliday的系统功能语言学专注于语法研究，而Martin把人际意义的研究从语法层面扩展到词汇层面，克服了纯语法研究的局限性，从而丰富了系统功能语言学理论（Martin, 2000; 朱永生、严世清, 2011）。词汇和语法属于同一现象，是两个互补的研究视角（Halliday, 2008：48-49）。尽管评价意义主要是词汇体现的，但其表达方式并不局限于词汇层面，语法层、音系层等也可以表达评价意义。

朱永生和严世清指出评价研究对概念功能中的评价意义不够关注，也忽视了隐性评价、讲话者的交际目的及句式的评价意义等（朱永生、严世清, 2011：94-100）。很多学者也注意到这些问题，并展开讨论研究。Hunston & Sinclair（2000）提出评价的局部语法，认为评价意义的基本语义范畴包括评价者、评价对象和评价范畴，它们之间通过连接（hinge）相互联系。他们共识别6种语法模式，对识别形容词的评价意义及语篇的自动分析有重要意义。刘世铸（2007）关注表达评价意义的句式，发现英语中有10个句式可以表达情感意义，有12个句式可以表达判断意义。Bednarek（2008）采用局部语法研究情感，并总结出不同语域中最重要的情感表达模式及其功能。这些研究把词汇和句式联系在一起考察评价意义的表达，说明词汇和语法可以相互配合来表达评价意义。

王振华（2004）将物质过程和评价系统结合，认为物质过程小句可以体现评价意义，且它们的评价价值有三个维度：积极的、消极的和中立的。他还指出，只通过物质过程小句的评价价值分析是单一的，要全面考察人物形象，必须要考虑整个及物系统中小句的评价价值。朱永生（2009）则从概念意义的角度出发，探讨描写性词汇和语义结构如何表达隐性的评价意义。这两项研究都关注隐性态度意义的表达，将及物过程、语境等因素纳入评价研究，提供了新的视角。但都只涉及部分过程，没有全面分析。

本文从具体语篇出发，探究词汇语法层的及物过程与语篇语义层的评价系统之间的关系，从而探讨及物过程的评价价值。

3.《石青嫂子》态度资源的统计：基于评价语料库

本文从评价语料库中选取小说《石青嫂子》进行个案研究。该语篇长度适中，含有大量的评价成分，包括不少的隐性评价。

评价语料库（汉英对应评价语料库的简称）是运用评价理论研制的一个双语对应语料库，是北京师范大学彭宣维教授主持的国家社科基金项目“评价理论在文体学中的应用及评价语料库的研制”的成果之一。评价语料库容量为100多万词次，包括11种不同体裁的118个文本，有近50%的语料是文学作品。所有文本中表达评价意义（包括显性和隐性评价意义）的资源都已通过UAM CorpusTool软件标注好，包括词、词组、小句、复合句等，并开发研制了一个相应的语料库检索统计软件（AMParaConc）。评价语料库的标注结果是经过研究人员分组反复讨论确定的，准确率较高。它一方面可以为明确某一语言资源的具体评价范畴提供标准，另一方面可以在标注好的语料基础上进行词典编纂、语篇分析和教学等研究，实用性很强。

研究过程包括四个方面：首先，通过检索软件找出语篇中所有表达态度意义的资源，包括词、词组、小句等；其次，剔除表达显性态度意义的资源，主要是明显的态度词汇和词组；再次，去除表达隐性态度意义的特殊句式，如祈使句、反问句等；最后，把表达隐性态度意义的及物过程罗列出来并详细阐释。

《石青嫂子》中表达态度意义的资源丰富，共598例。其中，情感和判断分别占39%，鉴赏占22%。经过甄别筛选，表达隐性态度意义的及物过程共有85例。因为篇幅问题，这里不一一列举，在第三部分会举例说明。语篇中表达隐性态度意义的及物过程在三个态度范畴的分布如表1所示：

表1 体现隐性态度意义的过程类型分布

态度范畴 / 及物过程	情感	判断	鉴赏
物质过程	8	26	7
心理过程	0	3	0
行为过程	10	4	0
关系过程	4	2	3
言语过程	2	0	0
存在过程	1	1	4

由此可见，这一语篇中表达隐性情感意义和隐性判断意义的过程类型主要是物质过程和行为过程，体现隐性鉴赏意义的过程数量较少，包括物质过程、关系过程、存在过程。态度系统中的判断主要是对人的行为的评估，而物质过程和行为过程的参与者都可以是人，都可以表达人的作为；情感涉及人的感情、情绪等，这可通过人的行为动作间接表现出来，因此也可以通过物质和行为过程体现；鉴赏则是对事物美学价值的评价，可以通过表达事物状态的物质、关系和存在过程实现。

4. 及物过程评价价值的具体分析

系统功能语言学把语言系统和语言实例的关系看作是一个渐进体，由系统、语域、语篇类型和实例组成。Martin & Rose（2003/2007：312）则把阅读作为这一渐进体的末端，阅读指根据读者的主观性从语篇中确定的意义。Martin & White（2005：164）认为，就评价资源而言，实例渐进体则由评价、基调、站位、具体评估和反应组成。其中，反应是读者对语篇中评价意义的阅读。他们区分不同的阅读策略，包括顺从式阅读、抵制性阅读和策略阅读（同上：206）。一般情况下，为了与作者所在的社团达成一致性，研究者采取顺从式阅读策略，即接纳语篇中自然形成的阅读定位。

本文对《石青嫂子》采取顺从式阅读定位，与作者保持一致。文学作品中一般有三类参与者：隐含作者、叙述者和叙述对象。在评价分析时，他们都可能以评价者身份出现。他们之间的评价立场可能一致，也可能对立。对立的情况下，作者的评价意图是隐含的，需要深度挖掘。在《石青嫂子》这一语篇中，隐含作者与叙述者的评价立场是一致的，他们与石青嫂子一致，但站在了吴大老爷的对立面。通过评价语料库检索统计软件，可发现在所有的态度意义资源中，情感和判断所占比例较大，前者主要是石青嫂子的伤心、不安与愿望等，后者主要聚焦于石青嫂子一家的遭遇和对吴大老爷行为的批判。从整个语篇来看，作者的评价意图是对石青嫂子为代表的农民阶级深表同情，对吴大老爷为代表的封建势力强烈谴责。

评价分析时，要考虑四个参数：（1）评价来源；（2）评价对象；（3）评价范畴；（4）评价价值（积极/消极）。对及物过程进行分析时，则要考虑：（1）过程类型；（2）主要参与者。对及物过程体现的隐性态度意义分析时，要将这几个参数结合起来。下面看具体实例的分析。

（1）日子就放在勤劳和希望里，一天天过了下去，只是她那张太阳晒黑的胖脸，慢慢地瘦了。

例（1）是一个关系过程小句，载体是“她那张太阳晒黑的胖脸”，属性是“瘦了”。这一过程的评价价值是消极愉悦性。石青嫂子在丈夫被拉走之后，强忍痛苦，辛勤劳作，努力养活自己的孩子们，但是她的痛苦依然还在，因此才会逐渐消瘦下来。这一情感意义在前文语境中通过“伤心”“痛哭”等明显词汇表达过，由于评价意义是韵律性分布的，因此关系过程也带有了这样的情感意义。同时，通过关系过程表达的情感意义更为客观，可以使读者感受她的痛苦，激发读者对她的同情。

（2）说得伤心的时候，泪珠便成串地滚在黄瘦的脸上。

例（2）是一个物质过程小句。“泪珠”可以是因为伤心，也可以是由于喜悦。在这一语境中，“伤心”表达的是消极愉悦性，这使得物质过程也带上了这一情感色彩，体现了石青嫂子的伤心和痛苦。因此这一物质过程的评价价值是消极愉悦性。其中，物质过程的动作者是“泪珠”，与“石青嫂子”这一情感者是所属关系。通过这一物质过程，石青嫂子的情感更为生动地表现在读者面前，比“伤心”“痛苦”等词汇表达的意义更为深刻。

（3）她终天头上包着一张蓝布帕子，不是拿锄头挖地、镰刀割草，就是手腕上挂个篮子，采摘什么东西。

例（3）中有两个物质过程小句，动作者是“石青嫂子”。作者没有使用“勤劳”“辛勤”等词汇表达对石青嫂子的赞赏，而是通过两个物质过程说明石青嫂子十分勤劳，整天不辞辛苦劳作。这是作者或叙述者对石青嫂子的积极评价，属于判断范畴中的积极可靠性。与单纯的态度词汇相比，通过物质过程表达的隐性判断意义较为客观，犹如事实一样，读者更容易接受。

（4）石青嫂子见这三个人莫名其妙地跑来践踏菜地，又大模大样地气势凌人。

例（4）中有一个物质过程小句“这三个人莫名其妙跑来践踏菜地”、一个关系过程小句“大模大样地气势凌人”。这是从石青嫂子的视角看“这三个人”，把他们无理取闹、恃强凌弱的样子生动表达出来，评价价值为判断范畴的消极恰当性。作者或叙述者借用石青嫂子的视角对他们的行为进行谴责，通过对他们行为、样貌的描写来突出这一意图，使得读者更容易接纳作者的评价意图。

（5）“我们那个地方，实在生得好，泥土肥不消说了，河水挑起来又很方便！”

上例中的“泥土肥”“河水跳起来又很方便”是两个关系过程。“好”是石青嫂子对小河边土地价值的赞赏，在她的眼里这个地方简直是个宝，属于鉴赏范畴的积极价值性。这一评价意义的韵律性分布也影响了后面的两个关系过程，它们表达的也是这个地方的优势，评价价值为积极价值性。

从以上五个例句可以看出，及物过程体现的评价价值要受语境和评价的韵律性分布影响。语境包括情景语境、文化语境和语篇语境（即上下文语境）（彭宣维，2011：29），可以激发潜在的评价意义；评价意义呈韵律性分布，可以使得某些语言成分带有某种评价意义，是确定隐性评价的重要因素。再看下面几个例句：

（6）现在当家人没有了，恐怕永远不回来了，她夜来大声嚎过，捶过她的胸口，扯过她的头发，白天则痴痴地在河边站过，伸手摸过可以挂索子的树枝，都因了五个孩子的影子，掩映在眼前，各样娇小幼稚声音，萦绕在耳边，使她一时忍不下心的。

从上文语境中可以知道，石青被拉走，石青嫂子几乎绝望，因此例（6）表现的是她的伤心欲绝，且这一情感呈韵律性分布在语篇中。但这里，作者并没有采用明确的态度词汇（如伤心、难过、悲痛等）表达这一情感，而是通过对石青嫂子行为动作的描写来表现。“她夜来大声嚎过”“痴痴地在河边站过”是两个行为过程，行为者是石青嫂子，这两个行为可以表现她的无助与悲痛；“捶过她的胸口”“扯过她的头发”“伸手摸过可以挂索子的树枝”是三个物质过程，动作者是石青嫂子，她通过虐待自己来发泄心中的痛苦，甚至不想活下去。因此，这几个过程的评价价值是消极愉悦性，情感发出者是过程的主要参与者，即石青嫂子。

通过对石青嫂子行为动作的描写来体现她的伤心，这样使得这一情感的表达较为客观、生动，作为读者也更容易体会她的情感，对她产生同情，这样就与作者的评价立场一致。

（7）看见斜坡的泥土肥得发黑，便不禁眼睛红了挑。

在例（7）中，看到肥沃的土地，石青嫂子特别想要，属于积极的意愿性。但作者并没有使用明显的态度词汇，如想、想要、渴望等，而是通过关系过程“眼睛红了挑”来体现，“眼红”指见别人有好条件或好东西非常羡慕和忌妒。这一关系过程属于归属性的，载体是眼睛。关系过程所表达的情感是石青嫂子的情感，眼睛与石青嫂子是整体和部分的关系。这样表达的情感比直接的态度词汇要客观，使得石青嫂子的形象更为生动。

（8）他做的好事，扯我的菜，烧我的房子。

例（8）是石青嫂子话语中的一部分，“他”指代吴大老爷。从上文语境中可以看出，吴大老爷派人糟蹋石青嫂子的菜地，烧毁了她的茅屋，千方百计要逼迫她离开这个地方，使她几乎无法生存。作者没有使用“坏”“狠毒”“残酷”等词汇表达她对吴大老爷的谴责，而是从石青嫂子的视角通过两个物质过程“扯我的菜”“烧我的房子”来体现，评价价值属于判断范畴的消极恰当性。“好事”本来是对人的赞扬，应属于积极恰当性范畴，但在这里评价者使用了反讽修辞，“好事”与后面的两个物质过程相对应，评价价值是相同的，因此也属于消极恰当性。

通过石青嫂子的视角，对吴大老爷行为的描写，使他的形象更加鲜明。行为往往是人的品德的外在表现，通过行为表达对这个人的谴责，比通过直接的态度词汇表达更为客观，读者也更容易接纳这样客观的评判。

（9）她觉得就是拼命也得把这片斜坡、这个峡谷好好守住。

例（9）是一个心理过程小句，“她”指石青嫂子。这个小句表达了石青嫂子的决心，为了孩子们无论怎样也要坚守这个家，体现了石青嫂子的坚韧。作者或叙述者与石青嫂子的立场是一致的，因此这个心理过程小句的评价价值为判断范畴的积极可靠性。

（10）再没有歌声缭绕在树间了，黄昏的河边上，也再没有散步的人影子。

例（10）有两个存在过程小句，说明学校搬走以后，石青嫂子一家所在的峡谷不再热闹，而是显得凄凉、寂寞，体现的评价价值是鉴赏范畴的消极反应性。这与上文语境中峡谷的热闹形成对比：有学校的时候，峡谷里有快活的学生散步、唱歌，使得峡谷充满生机，有积极的反应性价值；但学校搬走之后，峡谷变得凄凉，属于消极反应性范畴。评价价值的对比通过两个存在过程小句表达。

Thompson & Hunston（2000：9）认为，评价意义越不明显，就越可能成功地控制读者，因为隐性评价更为客观，更容易为读者接纳。因此，语篇中的隐性评价也很重要，与显性评价一起构建人物关系，使人物形象更加生动丰满。及物过程是体现隐性评价的重要资源，在语篇分析时不容忽视。从上面的例句可知，分析及物过程小句的评价价值，需要从及物过程和评价两个视角同时分析，把不同的参数结合在一起，同时要重视语境的作用。

5. 结语

本文通过对《石青嫂子》这一语篇中体现隐性评价的及物过程小句的分析，可以明确及物过程的评价价值对于小说中人物形象的塑造和人物关系的建构是很重要的。分析及物过程小句的评价价值需要考虑以下几个因素：

第一，小说中的评价者可以是作者、叙述者或人物角色，要清楚三者之间的评价立场是否一致，在《石青嫂子》中作者、叙述者的评价立场一致：同情石青嫂子为代表的农民阶级，谴责吴大老爷为代表的地主阶级。

第二，及物过程表达的是隐性评价，评价价值有积极和消极之分。分析及物过程的评价价值时，及物过程的主要参与者与评价分析的参数都要考虑在内。

第三，过程的参与者与评价对象之间会有一定关系，要么是同指关系，要么是整体–部分关系等。

第四，隐性评价意义要结合语境和评价的韵律分布才能确定，但首先要确定好分析者的阅读定位，对《石青嫂子》采取的是顺从式阅读定位，接纳作者在语篇中自然形成的评价意图。

总之，及物过程体现的隐性评价，更为客观地表现人物情感或对人物的评判，可以使人物的性格更为丰满，更好地体现作者意图，同时也能更好地为读者接纳。

参考文献

Bednarek, M. 2008. *Emotion Talk across Corpora*. New York: Macmillan.

Halliday, M. A. K. 1994. *An Introduction to Functional Grammar* (2nd edition). London: Arnold.

Halliday, M. A. K. 2008. *Complementarities in Language*. Beijing: The Commercial Press.

Hunston, S. & J. Sinclair. 2000. A Local Grammar of Evaluation. In S. Hunston & G. Thompson (eds.) *Evaluation in Text: Authorial Stance and the Construction of Discourse*. Oxford: Oxford University Press, 74-101.

Martin, J. R. 1992. *English Text: System and Structure*. Amsterdam: Benjamins.

Martin, J. R. 2000. Beyond Exchange: Appraisal Systems in English. In S. Hunston & G. Thompson (eds.) *Evaluation in Text: Authorial Stance and the Construction of Discourse*. Oxford: Oxford University Press, 142-175.

Martin, J. R. & D. Rose. 2003/2007. *Working with Discourse: Meaning beyond the Clause*. London: Continuum.

Martin, J. R. & P. R. R. White. 2005. *The Language of Evaluation: Appraisal in English*. London: Macmillan.

Thompson, G. & S. Hunston. 2000. Evaluation: An Introduction. In S. Hunston & G. Thompson (eds.) *Evaluation in Text: Authorial Stance and the Construction of Discourse*. Oxford: Oxford University Press, 1-27.

刘世铸 , 2007,《态度的结构潜势 —— 话语评价的语法视角》。北京 : 中国社会科学出版社。

刘世铸 , 2009, 基于语料库的情感评价意义构型研究 ,《外语教学》(2) : 22-25。

彭宣维 , 2011,《语言与语言学概论 —— 汉语系统功能语法》。北京 : 北京大学出版社。

王振华 , 2004, "物质过程" 的评价价值 —— 以分析小说人物形象为例 ,《外国语》(5): 41-47。

朱永生 , 2009, 概念意义中的隐性评价 ,《外语教学》(4) : 1-5。

朱永生、严世清 , 2011,《系统功能语言学再思考》。上海 : 复旦大学出版社。

投射语言翻译的“级阶”对等评估初探

曾　蕾　杨慕文

中山大学

王梦婉

香港中文大学

1. 引言

“对等”是翻译理论与研究中的一个核心概念，也是翻译研究领域中引起不断争论的一个问题。纵观历史，各种研究学派给翻译对等下了不同的定义，因而就有了诸如“功能对等”“文体对等”“形式对等”“语用对等”等等相对应的术语。翻译研究领域中的对等，不同于数学术语中的绝对对等，一般都指的是相对对等，只是相对对等概念都比较模糊化，并经历了从全面接受、到质疑、到不断补充的过程，也就是由认同性接受到批判性接受的过程，至今对这概念的争论与探讨并未停止，可谓是“路漫漫其修远兮，吾将上下而求索”。“相对对等”的不同观点，缘于不同的理论背景（杨柳, 2006）。目前国内外已有不少学者运用系统功能语言学理论探讨翻译的相对对等，但仍然需要进一步验证其适用性。为此，本文试图从系统功能语言学的“级阶”视角，以《论语》原文与辜鸿铭（1989）的译文为分析对象，阐述汉英投射语言翻译的“对等”。

2. 理论依据

基于系统功能语言学的翻译对等探讨始于20世纪60年代，最早的主要代表人物是Halliday（1962）和Catford（1965）。之后Baker（1992）和House（1977）等学者都开始运用系统功能语言学的一些理论框架探讨翻译问题；在国内，黄国文（2002a; 2002b）也在十多年前就开始倡导系统功能语言学理论的翻译研究途径。Halliday（2001; 2009）强调翻译的意义对等是相对的，对等评估需要依据于语境。功能语境指导下的翻译系统选择，旨在根据不同的体裁在目的语系统中进行选择，而这种选择，因为文化语境、情景语境、语言等因素，不一定与原语系统的选择完全对等。基于此，Halliday（2001）提出了翻译对等评估的基本模式与参数，包括级阶、层次、元功能：

To summarize the discussion of "equivalence value": in any particular instance of translation, value may be attached to equivalence at different ranks, different strata, different metafunctions.（Halliday 2001: 17）

级阶、层次、元功能都是系统功能语言学的重要思想，它们之间并不是彼此孤立，而是一个系统下的不同层面，是互为涵盖、互为交错、互为实现的。级阶与元功能分别是层次中的词汇语法和语义层面。Halliday（2001）界定了这三个概念及其内在联系：

Stratification is the organization of language in ordered strata：phonetic, phonological, lexicogrammatical and semantic — and one or more contextual strata outside of language proper. Metafunction is the organization of the content strata（lexicogrammar and semantics）in functional components：ideational, interpersonal and textual — roughly, the parts of the system that have to do with construing human experience, enacting social relationships, and creating discourse. Rank is the organization of the formal strata（phonology and lexicogrammar）in a compositional hierarchy: for example, in the grammar of English, clause complexes, clauses, phrases, groups, words and morphemes.（Halliday, 2001: 15）

由以上可以看出这三个参数之间的关系，其中，层次指的是语言为多层次的系统，有语义、词汇语法、音系等各语言层次，各层次之间是一种有序和体现关系。元功能为内容层面，包括语义层和词汇语法层，而语义层由词汇语法层体现。级阶为形式层面，包括词汇语法层和音系层，而词汇语法层又体现于音系层。这种互相接应的语言各上下层次的清晰划分及其体现关系有助于对语言与语篇进行系统的研究，使得整个复杂语言分析理论框架脉络清晰，方便于对语篇各个层面的功能分析能面面俱到，更能彰显出其语篇分析研究的系统性、多层性、精细性。由于篇幅有限，本文只从词汇–语法层次的级阶层面探讨投射语言的对等问题。根据Halliday（2001）的观点，一般情况下，原文与译文的相对对等值的高低与语境层次及语言级阶高低成正比。也就是说层次方面，文化语境高于情景语境，语义对等值高于词汇语法。在级阶层面上，Halliday通过分析相关俄语的例子后，指出：

Here again we can observe that equivalence at different ranks carries differential values; and that, again, the value tends to go up the higher the rank — clause complex（sentence）equivalence is valued more highly than clausal, clausal than phrasal and so on; ....（Halliday, 2001: 16）

在提出小句复合体对等值高于小句、小句对等值高于短语的一般评估模式时，Halliday（2001）进一步补充说明了这种对等观并不一定适用于所有语篇翻译的评估，很可能为了特殊的交际目的，语境因素的变量会影响这个评估模式，某种语篇的低级阶的相对对等值有可能高于其他高级阶。

3. 汉英投射语言翻译的“级阶”对等分析

在分析汉英投射语言翻译的级阶对等时，本文所选取的分析对象是《论语》及辜鸿铭的《论语》译本（下面简称译文）。首先我们简单介绍投射语言级阶结构在《论语》原文与译文的主要体现类型，然后根据我们所考察的主要《论语》投射级阶结构类型，分析出相关对等值，最后从功能语境翻译的角度，探讨各级阶对等值的功能结构与语义的相对对等评估的有效性与可行性。

3.1 《论语》原文和译文投射语言级阶结构类型及体现形式

投射语言指的是一种逻辑语义关系，存在于小句复合体、嵌入、动词短语等结构中（Halliday, 1994）。“投射”小句复合体的功能与语义分析方法对汉语相似结构的分析是可行而有效的（曾蕾, 2000）。本文主要分析投射语言的相关级阶层面，包括英汉投射小句复合体、英汉投射小句及英汉投射动词的对等。这几种级阶的投射结构都频繁出现在《论语》原文与译文中（见表1）。

表1 《论语》中投射语言现象的级阶结构

小句复合体	简单小句	动词
并列述说 主从述说	投射小句 言语过程小句	投射动词

由表1可以看出投射语言现象在各种级阶的基本结构。投射小句复合体级阶主要体现了小句与小句之间呈现出的两种功能关系：投射关系与相互依存关系。相互依存关系包括并列（paratactic）关系和主从（hypotactic）关系。在《论语》原文和译文中的投射小句复合体主要是并列述说和主从述说。小句级阶的结构主要包括投射小句复合体中的投射小句和言语过程小句，统称为投射简单小句。投射类短语主要是投射动词。表2展示了原文与译文中各投射级阶结构类型的基本实现方式与例句。

表2 原文和译文的投射级阶实现方式与例句

级阶（Ranks）	原文与译文例句
投射小句复合体	（1a）子曰：孝哉闵子骞，人不间于其父母昆弟之言。（并列述说） （1b）Confucius remarked of another disciple, saying: “He was indeed a good son. People found nothing in him different from what his parents said of him.”（并列述说） （2a）子张问十世可知也。（主从述说） （2b）A disciple asked Confucius whether ten generations after their time the state of the civilization of the world could be known.（主从述说） （3a）冉子为其母请粟。（主从述说） （3b）Another disciple then asked Confucius to provide her with grain.（主从述说）

（续表）

级阶（Ranks）	原文与译文例句
投射简单小句	（4a）季康子问：……（投射小句） （4b）A minister who was in power in Confucius's native State asked him ...（投射小句） （5a）或问褅之说。（言语过程小句） （5b）Somebody asked Confucius for the meaning of the great Ti sacrifice mentioned above.（言语过程小句）
投射动词	（6a）子张问崇德辨惑。（粗体部分：投射动词） （6b）A disciple of Confucius **enquired** how to raise the moral sentiment and to dispel delusions in life.（粗体部分：投射动词）

3.2《论语》原文和译文中投射级阶的对等分析结果

在分析中，我们根据表1所列出的各种投射语言级阶结构类型对比了《论语》原文与译文在各级阶层面的异同。表3展示出《论语》原文和译文中投射级阶的对等分析结果：

表3 投射语言的级阶结构对等

级阶对比	总数	对等	不对等	对等值
投射小句复合体	805	733	72	91%
投射简单小句	823	739	84	90%
投射动词	815	235	580	30%

从表3可以看出，《论语》原文和译文中投射级阶的对等结果显示投射小句复合体级阶上的对等是比较高的（91%）；投射简单小句的对等值稍低（90%），投射动词短语对等值最低（30%）。少部分相关英汉投射小句复合体不对等现象的产生主要有两个原因：第一，虽然原文中的绝大多数并列投射小句复合体被译成了同一级阶，但是在"投射小句的取舍"上仍有所不同：原文投射小句省略，而译文中添加了这些投射小句，相反，原文的投射小句在译文中被省略；这就造成了部分汉英投射小句复合体不对等现象的存在。第二，原文的投射小句复合体被译成了英语投射简单小句，而原文中的投射简单小句被译成了投射小句复合体，后者比例较大。试看以下四个例子[1]：

（7a）子曰：管仲之器小哉。或曰：管仲俭乎。曰：管式有三归，官事不摄，焉得俭。<u>然则管仲知礼乎（a）</u>。曰：邦君树塞门，管氏亦树塞门，邦君为两君之好，有反坫，管氏亦有反坫。管氏而知礼，孰不知礼。

（7b）Confucius, speaking of a famous statesman (the Bismarck of the time),

1 例句中的斜体、下画线、粗体及括号内的其他字母数字符号均为本文所添加，以方便于下文的解释。

remarked, “Kuan Chung was by no means a great-minded man!”

“But,” (d^1) said somebody, “Kuan Chung was simple in his life: was he not?” (a’)

“Why,” (d^2) replied Confucius, “Kuan Chung had that magnificent Sansouci Pleasaunce of his. Besides, he had a special officer appointed to every function in his household. How can one say that he was simple in his life?” *“Well,” (d^3)* rejoined the enquirer, “but still, Kuan Chung was a man of taste who observed the correct forms; was he not?”

“No,” (d^4) answered Confucius, “The reigning princes have walls built before their palace gates. Kuan Chung also had a wall built before his door. When two reigning princes meet, each has a special buffet. Kuan Chung also had his special buffet. If you say Kuan Chung was a man of taste, who is not a man of taste?”

（8a）樊迟请学稼。子曰：吾不如老农。请学为圃。曰：吾不如老圃。樊迟出。子曰（c）：小人哉。樊须也。上好礼，则民莫敢不敬。……

（8b）*A disciple of Confucius* requested to be taught farming. Confucius answered, “For that I am not as good as an old farmer.”

The disciple then asked to be taught gardening. *“For that,” (d^5)* replied Confucius, “I’m not as good as an old gardening.”

After the disciple had left, *Confucius remarked (c^1)*, “What a petty-minded man he is!”

“When the rulers of a country,” (d^6) he then *went on to say (c^2)*, “encourage education and good manners the people will never fail in respect! ....”

（9a）子贡问曰：赐也何如。子曰：女器也。曰（f）：何器也。曰：（e）瑚琏也。

（9b）*Another disciple* who heard the above remarks said then to Confucius, “And I, what do you say of me?” *“You are,” (d^7)* answered Confucius, “a work of art.” “What work of art?” asked the other. (f’) “A rich jewelled work of art,” *was the reply. (e’)*

（10a）冉子退朝。子曰：何晏也。对曰：有政。子曰：其事也。如有政，虽不吾以，吾其与闻之。（b）

（10b）On one occasion when a *disciple* who was in official employment returned from the palace, Confucius said to him, “Why are you so late?” *“Oh!” (d^8)* answered the disciple, “We have just had State affairs.” *“You mean ‘business’! For if there had been State affairs, although I am not now in office, I should still have been consulted.” (b’)*

从以上的例句中，不难发现，投射小句复合体在级阶层面的少部分不对等现象主要是该结构中投射小句的不够对等造成的。在对原文投射小句的处理上，译文有以下几个主要特点：一是原文无投射小句，但译文中有，如（a）—（a’）。二是原文有投射小句，但译文中无，如（b）—（b’）。三是原文中，数个并列或递进关系的句子共用一个投射小句，但译文中一个投射小句衍生成多个，此时原文中单个的投射复合体分裂成了多个投射复合体，如（c）—（c^1）（c^2）。四是原文由投射动词和被投射小句实现的投射结构被译成了由嵌入述说或嵌入观点或嵌入事实名词实现的投射结构如（e）—（e'）。上面的例句还展示了译文中投射小句位置的灵活处理，如（d^1），（d^2），（d^3），（d^4），（d^5），（d^6），（d^7），（d^8），（f）—（f'）。

以上的分析也同样说明了少部分相关投射简单小句中的不对等的主要因素。原文与译文的投射简单小句对比包括无依存关系的言语过程小句和投射小句复合体中的投射小句，后者为投射简单小句级阶的主要实现方式，前者所占比例较少，但是，这两种实现方式几乎全部由言语过程体现，极少数情况下译者采用了关系过程小句，如在例（9a）和（9b）对话中，在话轮的最后一个小句复合体中，原文的言语过程小句被翻译成了关系过程小句。又如：

（11a）厩毁。子退朝，曰：伤人乎。不问马。

（11b）On one occasion when, as he was returning from an audience at the palace, he heard that the State stable was on fire, *his first question was*, *"Has any men been injured?"* He did not ask about the horses.

另外，原文的言语过程小句被译成了投射小句复合体，下面例（12a）到例（14a）原文为言语过程的小句，而与之对应的译文（12b）到例（14b）均是小句复合体。

（12a）樊迟问知。

（12b）A disciple enquired what constituted understanding.

（13a）樊迟问仁。

（13b）The same disciple mentioned above asked, "What does a moral life consist in?"

（14a）南容三复白圭。

（14b）A disciple of Confucius was fond of repeating the *verse*: "A flock on the stone may be ground away; A word misspoken will remain alway."

投射动词对等值较低的部分原因也是受投射小句变化的影响，如原文或译文投射小句省略，投射小句中"言语过程"转换成了译文中的"关系过程"，投射动词被"be"所取代。但最为主要的原因是由于投射动词的语义及使用常规性的问题（见表4），其中也包括投射动词被译为"乏词义动词"的现象，也就是原文中投射动词的意义由乏词义动词后的名词成分来体现。

表4 原文与译文投射动词的对比

原文		译文		常规性：±	
投射动词	数量	投射动词（短语）	数量	常规：+	非常规：-
辞	2	say	1		-
		decline	1	+	
诵	1	repeat	1	+	
复	1	repeat	1	+	
告	1	report	1		-

（续表）

原文		译文		常规性：±	
投射动词	数量	投射动词（短语）	数量	常规：+	非常规：-
欲	5	wish	1	+	
		propose	1		-
		express（a wish to）	1		-
		was inclined to	1		-
		wish to	1		-
命	1	give（him charge）	1		-
请	6	ask	4	+	
		beg	1		-
		request	1		-
对曰	28	reply	12		-
		answer	15	+	
		say	1		-
问于……曰	3	say	1		-
		ask	1	+	
		enquire	1		-
问曰	10	ask	2	+	
		say	8		-
谓	5	say	5	+	
问	68	ask	35	+	
		enquire	29		-
		say	3		-
		remark	1		-
曰	676	say	154	+	
		remark	297		-
		其他	233		-

3.3 从功能语境观看《论语》原文和译文中投射级阶的对等分析

功能语境是系统功能语言学的重要观点。语言在一定的语境中发生，语言和语境之间的关系是体现的关系，即上面一个层次由下面一个层次来体现：文化语境由情景语境体现，情景语境由词汇–语法体现，词汇–语法最后由音系系统（口语）或拼写系统（书面语言）体现（Martin, 1992; Eggins, 1994）。

在《论语》原文和译文中，作为上一级阶的投射小句复合体基本达到了对等，这与Halliday（2001）的评估模式一致。小句复合体上的对等是受文化语境的影响。《论语》的语篇体裁为典型的语录体，总体话语方式为"师–生""生–生""孔子–

时人”之间口头问答式的对话体。据此，《论语》的情景语境的三要素为：语场是孔子向其弟子、孔子弟子之间、孔子或其弟子对其余人讲述、辩论自己在政治、教育、文学、哲学以及立身处世等方面的见解。语旨是话语授受双方，主要为“师–生”，即孔子向其弟子“传道、授业、解惑”；少数情况下为“生–生”和“孔子–时人”。语式是口头对话为主的方式。可以看出《论语》中对话的模式为“教–学”的情景语境。辜鸿铭作为儒家经典思想的捍卫者，在学习和翻译《论语》的过程中，视自己为孔子嫡传弟子，同“相与辑而论纂”的孔子弟子或门人的师弟一起亲临对话现场聆听孔子授业；辜鸿铭作为华人独自全译《论语》的第一人，其享誉国内外的“标准译本”无异于两千年前孔子弟子对孔子授业解惑现场的记录——经典古籍《论语》。只是两者在语码上有所不同，前者为现代英语，而后者为古汉语；另外，他翻译儒家经典，是要在“西学东渐、东学西渐、中西文明冲撞交汇”的时代把中国传统思想文化的真谛传播到西方。他同孔子门人、弟子记述的目的（即将孔子及其弟子具有深刻思想内涵的儒家思想传承下去）基本一致。在一定的语言运用中，某些语言特征会从具有一定特征的情景语境中派生出来。译者既可以根据适用于不同情景语境的翻译目的来干预语篇特征，也可以根据所需的语篇特征从语场、语旨、语式三个方面去设定特定的情景语境。在译程中，辜鸿铭也以“虚拟的”教学情景语境为自己译文的基本立足点和出发点。为了能够把“孔夫子”及其“同门师兄弟”的言行、态度等在尽可能保持其原本意义与语言风格的前提下，他在大部分情况下，在高级阶层面尽量减少自己作为译者的介入，仍保持与原文投射小句复合体层面的对应，甚至在相互依存关系的选择上也常保持一致。

投射简单小句级阶在《论语》原文和译文中的对等值明显高于投射短语，稍低于投射小句复合体的对等值，这一点基本是与Halliday（2001）的级阶评估模式一致。我们所分析的数据中绝大部分为投射小句复合体中的言语过程小句，只有一少部分为独立的言语过程小句。投射小句级阶层面较高的对等值一方面说明了英汉两种语言的言语过程小句的高度相似性，另一方面也说明了古代言语过程投射小句与现代语言的言语过程投射小句结构的相似性。《论语》为典型的语录体，绝大部分投射结构都带有投射言语过程小句，这种典型的对话性交际模式，并未因为重构为现代语境而产生太多的变量。可以说投射小句受原语语境与目的语境以及古代语语境与现代语语境的压力较低，因而就出现了较高频率的对等。

在短语级阶的投射动词的对等值远远低于投射小句复合体和投射小句的级阶。相对于其他两个级阶，投射动词受语境影响较大，因而投射动词的级阶对等值低于投射小句等高级阶结构，这与Halliday（2001）提出的一般评估模式是一致的。投射动词的翻译显然受译文文化语境及语篇体裁的影响较大，如果不谈文化语境，很难评估投射动词的对等问题。如“曰”这个投射动词，如果不考虑其语境，单选择与这对等的英文类言说动词，是不可行的，如在论语译文中，所有翻译版本中对“曰”的翻译都无法完全再现“曰”这个投射动词所包含的功能意义，也许在译文语言系统中没有对等的选择项。既然翻译版本无法用古代英语来翻译，“曰”翻译成“say”或“said”被普遍认为是相对较为对等的，这一方面是受目的语读者的接受性影响，具有较大程度的语境的相似性，另外一方面也是因为这两个对应词的词汇语法与语义相似性的程度较高。“曰”的语法功能与“说”和“say”是比较靠近的，一般不接话语对象。“say”作为最常见的投射动词，一般起到投射话语而不带特定的或具体的交际功能效果，所以是无标记的（Tannen, 1986：315）。在译文中，翻译成“say”虽然相对较多，但与其他的级阶对等值比，还是比较低的。不对等的语境因素也与古汉语本身“说”意动词的“蓄词量”小是分不开的。这从另一方面也彰显了《论语》“言近旨远、语约义丰”（聂永华, 2002）的说理特征。对应于现代英语词汇系统的浩如烟海，其中有着丰富的表达“说”的投射动词系统，足够现代英语话语者在感情色彩、语气轻重、音量高低、速度缓急、详略程度、声色等各种潜在系统中的选择。辜鸿铭在翻译原文的投射动词时，一方面，推敲了“曰”背后隐藏的情景语境下的“说–问–答”等功能意义，如“忧曰”被译成了“exclaim”；另一方面，还对“曰”的上下文语境发微掘幽，如被译成“went on to say”，类似的还有“continue”“repeat”等。

总之，从以上在各级阶层面对《论语》原文与译文的主要投射结构的对等评估的讨论，可以看出，高级阶的投射结构相对等值高于低级阶，与“级阶”翻译评估模式并未冲突，从某一方面印证这一评估模式的可行性。

4. 结语

本文运用Halliday（2001）的“级阶”翻译评估模式对《论语》原文与辜鸿铭的译文的主要投射结构进行了级阶层面的分析与探讨。通过分析，初步对投射语言翻译的“级阶”对等结构进行了评估与探讨。本文认为，基于系统功能语言学“级阶”参数的翻译评估模式是有效的，可以揭示与说明译文的相对对等值的“级阶”参数及变量的功能语境对等；同时，也证明了该分析方法与模式对原文与译文的投射级阶的功能结构与功能意义上的相对对等的解释力。需要说明的是，本文只是从级阶层面对《论语》原文与某一译文中投射语言进行了对等分析，这种分析并不能全面对该两种语篇进行对等评估。

参考文献

Baker, M. 1992. *In Other Words: A Coursebook on Translation*. London: Routledge.

Catford, J. C. 1965. *A Linguistic Theory of Translation*. London: Oxford University Press.

Eggins, S. 1994. *An Introduction to Systemic Functional Linguistics*. London: Pinter.

Ku, H. M.（辜鸿铭）1898. *The Discourses and Sayings of Confucius*. Shanghai: Kelly and Walsh.

Halliday, M. A. K. 1962. Linguistics and Machine Translation. Zeitschrift fuer Phonetik, Sprachwissenschaft und Kommunikationsforschung, 15.i/ii.

Halliday, M. A. K. 1994. *An Introduction to Functional Grammar* (2nd edition). London: Arnold.

Halliday, M. A. K. 2001. Towards a Theory of Good Translation. In E. Steiner & C. Yallop (eds.) *Exploring Translation and Multilingual Text Production: Beyond Context*. Berlin: Mouton de Gruyter, 13-18.

Halliday, M. A. K. 2009. The Gloosy Ganoderm: Systemic Functional Linguistics and Translation,《中国翻译》(1): 17-26.

House, J. 1977. *A Model for Translation Quality Assessment*. Tubingen: Gunter Narr.

Martin, J. R. 1992. *English Text: System and Structure*. Amsterdam: Benjamins.

Tannen, D. 1986. Introducing Constructed Dialogue in Greek and American Conversational and Literary Narrative. In F. Coulmas (ed.) *Direct and Indirect Speech*. Berlin: Mouton, 311-32.

黄国文, 2002a, 唐诗英译文中的引述现象分析,《外语学刊》(3): 95-100。

黄国文, 2002b, 功能语言学分析对翻译研究的启示 ——《清明》英译文的经验功能分析,《外语与外语教学》(5): 1-6。

聂永华, 2002, 20世纪《论语》散文艺术研究述评,《孔子研究》(6): 88。

杨伯峻, 2006,《论语译注》(简体字本)。北京: 中华书局。

杨柳, 2006, 西方翻译对等论在中国的接受效果 —— 一个文化的检讨,《中国翻译》(1): 3-9。

曾蕾, 2000, 英汉"投射"小句复合体的功能与语义分析,《现代外语》(2): 163-173。

英汉小说翻译中的去名物化研究

赵 晶

北京科技大学

1. 引言

系统功能语言学认为，名物化是产生语法隐喻最强有力的资源。通过此种方式，小句的过程和特性被隐喻性地措辞为名词（Halliday, 1994：352）。根据表达意义的不同，名物化可分为多种类型，本文仅讨论作为概念语法隐喻同时由动词转变而来的名物化，即动词名物化。

系统功能语言学对英语名物化的探讨已经相对充分，如Halliday & Martin（1993），Halliday & Matthiessen（1999, 2004），Ravelli（1988, 2003），Simon-Vandenberen et al.（2003），Martin（1992, 2008）等。这些研究讨论了名物化的定义、特点、分类和功能，加深了对名物化作为一种语法隐喻的认识。相比之下，汉语的名物化研究存在着更多的争议和疑问，其根本的原因在于汉语词类不能像英语一样截然分清，这就给名物化的翻译研究带来一定的困难。李运兴（2010）认为名物化是一种被冻结了的及物性过程。译者可以选择保留此冻结过程，也可以选择将其解冻为语义与词汇语法相匹配的一致式表达，后者即为“去名物化”（2010：168）的过程。作者讨论了去名物化后与原文意义的不同，但未能结合一定规模的翻译语料进行深入探讨，对其动因以及与译者和翻译策略的关系有待进一步挖掘。

本文以《大卫·科波菲尔》（*David Copperfield*）董秋斯和张谷若两个译本中动词名物化的翻译为例，探究英语小说中的名物化汉译后呈现怎样的形态，表现出哪些规律性的特点，并依循语言系统和语言类型特点对其做出解释，同时结合翻译策略探求它对去名物化程度的制约以及对译文产生的影响。

2. 研究问题和研究语料

为了研究上述问题，本文将围绕以下几个子问题进行展开：

（1）原文的动词名物化在翻译后呈现怎样的形态分布？

（2）英汉语言系统的差异对去名物化有哪些影响？

（3）翻译策略如何制约译文的去名物化程度？主张归化和异化的译者处理名物化时，译文是否呈现显著性差异？

本研究选取狄更斯*David Copperfield*的两个权威中译本：董秋斯的《大卫·科波菲尔》以及张谷若的《大卫·考坡菲》。依据出现频次的高低，从原文中选取一组动词名物化实例（共313例），分别为：consideration(s)（48例），intention(s)（48例），arrangements(s)（33例），observation(s)（29例），admiration（29例），confusion（28例），departure（23例），description（21例），separation(s)（18例），agitation（18例），permission（18例），并找出它们在两译本中对应的译文，共计626例。

在界定汉语的名物化时，本文依据郭锐（2002：165-172）对词项表述功能的论述，参照《现代汉语词典》（第六版），凡词典中仅标注为动词的词语，如果在文中的表述功能为指称时，即认定为汉语的名物化。英语名物化译为汉语后，若译文也使用了名物化，则看作名物化得以保留。若译为动词过程，则意味着去名物化的发生。

3. *David Copperfield*译文中的动词去名物化

动词名物化同其他语法隐喻一样，其产生的根源在于语言是一个可分层的有机系统，其内容层面可分成语义层和词汇语法层。语法隐喻是两个层次之间的再结盟，是语义层到词汇语法层的二次映射，语言不分层，便不存在语法隐喻。（Halliday, 1998/2007：58）当语言表达为一致式时，名词的语义匹配是事物，在词汇语法中做参与者；动词语义匹配是动作或事件，在词汇语法中做及物性过程。动词名物化的使用打破了这种一致式的匹配关系，转而成为过程名化的隐喻式表达。可见，动词名物化的产生正是源于语义同词汇语法表达之间的这种张力。翻译过程中，这种张力的存在，导致名物化翻译的多种可能性。

3.1 名物化翻译在译文中的形态分布

对626例译文逐一考察，发现原文的名物化在译文中对应以下几种形态：

（1）名物化参与者，如“effect a desirable separation”译为“造成一种合意的隔离”；（2）一般名词参与者，如“for any earthly consideration”译为“不拘为了什么人世的理由”；（3）动词过程，如“effect a desirable separation”译为“要把他们两个拆开哪”；（4）定语修饰语，如“in such a state of consternation and agitation”译为“在那样一种又惶恐又激动的境界”；（5）状语修饰语，如“survey it with the greater admiration”译为“好更得意地把它端量”；（6）省略，如“made some hasty but determined arrangements to throw her out of a two pair of stairs' window"译为"甚至鲁莽到想把她抛出三层楼的窗子"；（7）其他（包括代词或介词）。

统计每种形态在译文中出现的频次，从而得到名物化翻译在译文中的形态分布图：

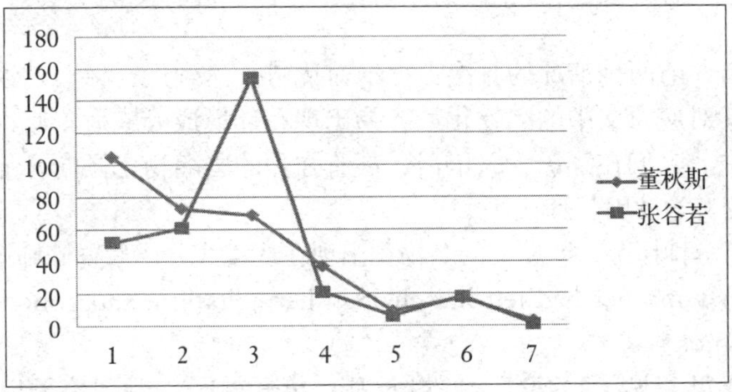

注：横轴1—7为名物化在译文中的七种译法，纵轴为每种译法出现的频次

图1 名物化在两译文中的对应译法形态分布图

可以看出，两译文对动词名物化的译法类型基本相同，且占据前三甲的均为保留名物化、译为名词词组和译为动词过程三种情况；名物化在翻译后表现出多元的形态，并非仅有保留名物化和去名物化两种情况，各种译法之间构成一个连续体；译法1和3出现的频次差异最为显著，分别对应保留名物化和去名物化的译法。结合每类译法的百分比，两译文保留名物化的比例分别为34%（董译）和17%（张译），去名物化的比例分别为22%（董译）和49%（张译），译者在这两种翻译方式的选择上差异悬殊。

3.2 去名物化同语言系统的关系

在选取的313例名物化例句中，译为汉语后发生去名物化的情况董译共69例，张译154例，这表明译文中形成了一定的去名物化趋势。为了探究去名物化与语言系统的关系，下文首先考察原文的名物化有何特点。分析发现，名物化在原文主要出现在以下七种功能域中，两译文每种功能域出现的频次和百分比见表1。

表1 董译、张译中去名物化实例对应原文所在的功能域

功能域	董译	百分比%	张译	百分比%
环境成分或后置修饰语	36	52	87	56
过程范围	12	17	20	13
物质小句参与者	7	10	17	11
关系小句参与者	7	10	15	10
言语小句参与者	4	6	8	5

（续表）

功能域	董译	百分比%	张译	百分比%
心理小句参与者	2	3	6	4
独立小句	1	2	1	1
总计	69	100	154	100

可以看出，前两种情况的频次占据绝对优势，达到近70%。这说明在去名物化的实例中，其对应原文中的名物化最容易出现在环境成分或后置修饰语以及过程范围的功能域中。它们在翻译为汉语后，都有强烈的去名物化倾向。那么，驱使它们进行转换的语言学动因是什么？

先来看第一种情况，即原文的名物化出现在环境成分或后置修饰语的功能域中。

例（1）My mother had left her chair in her agitation, and gone behind it in the corner.（Chapter 1）

张译：我母亲见了我姨婆，心慌意乱，离开椅子，躲到椅子后面的旮旯那儿去了。

原文的"left the chair"和"in her agitation"分别体现不同的功能，前者为小句的核心，后者为表示质量的环境成分[1]，前者通过增加后者的方式进行扩展，从而形成完整的意义配置。前者是该小句唯一的核心成分，后者用来修饰这一核心，对其方式进行说明，充当小句的边缘成分。而在张译中，伴随着"agitation"去名物化的发生，即译为"心慌意乱"，原文的边缘成分变为一个过程小句，充当了另一个核心成分，同"离开椅子"体现相同的小句功能，小句核心通过增加序列的方式加以扩展。再如下面两例：

例（2）Mr. Creakle then caned Tommy Traddles for being discovered in tears, instead of cheers, on account of Mr. Mell's departure.（Chapter 7）

张译：克里克先生于是用手杖揍了特莱得一顿，因为他发现，特莱得不但没欢呼，反倒因为麦尔先生走了，在那儿擦眼泪。

例（3）I returned, after a little consideration.（Chapter 10）

董译：我考虑了一下回答道。

例2和例3中名物化所在的功能域分别为表示原因和时间的环境成分。译文中，动词名物化"departure"和"consideration"分别充当了两个小句中的动词过程，例2为主从式小句复合体中的原因附属小句，例3为并列式小句复合体中的起始小句。系统功能语言学把介词短语看作是次要小句（Halliday, 1994：212），上述三例在翻译中，次要小句均变为主要小句。这一变化基于英汉两种语言系统在构建人类经验时的不同倾向性。

语言的概念功能提供了将外在世界和内在世界的人类经验建构为意义的资源。它有两种实现模式：经验模式和逻辑模式。前者指用意义配置的方式建构人类经验，即在有机的意义配置中，每个成分有不同的功能。小句核心通过增加成分的

1 Halliday 将环境成分分为 9 个大类别，17 个小类，详见 Halliday（1994：151）。

方式扩展，形成结构上的配置。后者指用序列的方式建构人类经验，即在意义序列中，每个成分有相同的功能，它们之间存在一定的逻辑语义关系。小句核心通过增加序列的方式扩展，形成小句复合体。（Matthiessen, Teruya & Lam, 2010：92, 132; Matthiessen, 2004：578）不同语言建构世界经验时如何在两种模式之间分工，存在较大差异。这种分工的不同，体现在概念意义的语言系统中两种语言选择结构配置还是小句序列时的概率不同，而概率又是语言系统的重要特点之一。可见，正是由于英汉语言系统的差异，导致翻译中去名物化趋势的产生。

介词短语译为汉语后由次要小句变为主要小句，正是由于英语的语言系统倾向选择配置的方式扩展小句核心，而汉语则倾向选择逻辑序列的方式。这种选择也导致了不同的语言结构，前者对应单核心语言结构，后者对应多核心语言结构。（参见Martin, 1992：13, 21, 22; Martin, Matthiessen & Painter, 2010：164）。英汉语在表达经验意义时两种模式的分布差异，在翻译中体现得非常明显。英语中用经验方式识解的意义，在汉语中常用逻辑方式加以体现。本研究的数据显示，在九种环境成分中，表示"方式""伴随"和"起因"的环境类型最容易在译文中发生去名物化。

再来看第二种情况，即过程范围结构。Halliday（1966/2006：244）用较大篇幅讨论了名词、名物化的问题。其中，在论述"过程名词"表达语言客观性的作用时，作者指出英语总是倾向于使用"They did a dance"，"They had dinner"，"They made a mistake"，而不是"They danced"，"They dined"，"They erred"。可以看出，英语所倾向的表达正是"过程+范围"结构。这种结构中，虚义动词所体现的过程并没有实际意义，只是充当形式上的过程，而表达过程意义的真正成分是"范围"。正因为如此，Teruya（2007）将此种小句称为"范围过程"（Range Process）。英语对这种范围及物小句有所偏好，如韩礼德（1966/2006：244）所指出的"难怪基础英语仅用18个动词就能运用自如……能被放入名词形式范围的概念是无限的，因为无论完整小句还是部分小句都能被名物化。"相对于英语的这种倾向性，汉语虽然也有"做运动""做调查"等类似的说法，但无论是使用范围还是使用频率都有很大的限制，这就不难理解为什么英译汉后，范围及物小句中的名物化有强烈的去名物化趋势。又如：

例（4）I have an <u>admiration</u> for her character.（Chapter 33）

董译：我<u>羡慕</u>她的品格。

例（5）My poor dear mother, I suppose, had some momentary <u>intention</u> of committing an assault and battery upon my aunt.（Chapter 1）

董译：我想，我那可怜可爱的母亲有一时<u>想</u>打我的姨婆。

除以上两种情况之外，其他几种去名物化所对应的原文中，名物化均充当及物性小句的参与者，且多为物质小句和关系小句中的参与者，这是因为它们是实例化过程中出现概率最高的及物性过程（参见Matthiessen, 1999）。如：

例（6）... effect a desirable <u>separation</u>（Chapter 42）

张译：要把他们两个拆开哪

例（7）It is my intention ... to educate my son for the Church（Chapter 36）

董译：我打算，我的亲爱的科波菲尔，教育我的儿子从事教会工作

做参与者的名物化在翻译中变为过程动词，这是因为动词名物化有重新识解为动词过程的潜力。英文中倾向于用名词性的表达，而汉语倾向于用动词性的表达，这同两种语言类型学上的特点密切相关。不仅如此，上述几种去名物化的情况归根结底均可从类型学上找到根本动因。

3.3 去名物化的类型学动因

上文阐述了去名物化同语言系统的关系，本节从语言类型学的视角出发，进一步挖掘去名物化背后的理据。3.2节提到去名物化的一个主要原因是英汉两种语言在经验模式和逻辑模式的分布上存在差异，其实这种差异有着深刻的语言类型学渊源。刘丹青（2010）指出，汉语是动词型语言或动词突出的语言，英语是名词型语言或名词突出的语言。它们分别代表了在词类的语法优先度上相对立的两种语言类型。具体来说，名词型语言的谓语动词有各种强制性范畴需要表达，动词的形态和句法负担较重，会造成表达的芜繁冗长。为了减少语法负担，常选择用各种非限定形式甚至名词本身来表示事件、命题，乃至单独成句、完成一次交际任务。而动词型语言的谓语动词没有这种强制性重负，随时可以轻装上阵，不必进行非限定性或名词化的操作，增强了动词性成分在语言中的重要性和活跃性。（同上：15）

正是由于上述原因，英汉翻译中才存在着强烈的去名物化趋势。这也解释了为什么英语非限定形式和名物化的使用频率高，而汉语动词的使用频率高，同时还印证了英汉翻译中，非限定小句译为限定小句以及大量去名物化的存在。英语中为了减轻动词句法负担而使用名物化，译为汉语后，该句法负担不复存在，使用名物化的需求降低甚至消失，因而译文更多地选择去名物化为动词过程，以符合汉语表述的习惯。英语对范围及物小句的青睐，同样印证了其名词突出的语言类型学特点。译文的去名物化释放了英语中语义和词汇语法之间的张力，而采用汉语构建世界经验时的一致式选择，即语义事件匹配小句过程。这从根本上也源于汉语是动词型语言的类型学特征。

4. 翻译策略对去名物化程度的制约及对译文特点的影响

上文讨论了由于英汉两种语言类型学上的差异导致语言系统选择的差异，进而产生翻译中的去名物化趋势。本节重点讨论翻译策略对译文去名物化程度的制约作用，以及由此对译文产生的影响。

4.1 翻译策略对译文去名物化程度的制约

为了说明董、张两译文在名物化译法的选择上是否存在差异，可进行卡方独立性检验，结果显示，$p<0.001$，说明两者具有显著性的差异。由此可以假定由于译者的不同，两译文在翻译名物化时差异显著。为了检验译者这一变量同名物化翻译类型之间的相关性，可进行兰姆达系数检验，设定译者为因变量，统计结果显示兰姆达系数为0.275，说明两者有相关性，但相关度不够突出。这是因为3.1节中讨论的（2）、（4）—（6）、（7）五种翻译方法上的差异不如1、3两类明显，一定程度上干扰了相关性的统计结果。为了研究名物化在翻译中选择去名物化还是保留名物化的情况，可只计算1、3两类译法同译者的相关性，结果发现兰姆达系数提升至0.305，表明翻译方法同译者的相关性有了提高。这说明译文保持名物化，还是选择去名物化，同译者密切相关。

两位译者最大的不同体现在翻译策略上。董秋斯是翻译研究科学派的代表，早在20世纪50年代，就从语言学的角度最早肯定了翻译是一门科学。他对鲁迅先生的翻译思想颇为欣赏，认同鲁迅的翻译外国著作是为了“产生中国的新文学”的观点，因而“翻译不仅要输入新的内容，还要输入新的表达法”，应当“装进异样的句法去，古的，外省外府的，外国的，后来便可以据为己有”。（罗新璋, 1984：276）总之，董秋斯身体力行地遵循着翻译的忠实原则进行实践，译文多是依循原文逐字逐句翻译的，主张异化的翻译策略。

相比之下，张谷若（1980）主张“用地道的译文翻译地道的原文”，其译文是归化的代表作。在张先生看来，“译书主要是给不懂原文的人看的”，外国作品译为中文，应“使中国人读起来，觉得通畅明白”，“所得的感受，所起的反应，应该与读原文的人是一样的”（张谷若, 1989：451）。在具体的翻译实践中，如果遇到形式和内容不可兼得的情况，“最好还是以考虑其内容和习惯为主，而不要因单纯为了追求形式相同而损害内容和习惯。”（张谷若, 1980：20）可见，张先生的翻译策略是典型的归化，与董先生的主张有明显的差异。正是翻译策略的不同，限制了译文去名物化程度的高低。董秋斯主张更多的保留原文的名物化，因而对去名物化的限制较高，去名物化程度偏低；张谷若与此相反，去名物化的限制较低，去名物化的程度偏高。

下文结合译例进行说明。

例（8）We had a very pleasant day, though we were all in a tender state about our approaching <u>separation</u>.（Chapter 12）

董译：我们过了很愉快的一天，虽然我们对于行将来到的<u>分别</u>都怀有脆弱的心情。

张译：我们那天很快活，不过因为就要<u>分离</u>了，心里都怀着一种黯然销魂之感。

原文中的名物化“separation”在董译中得以保留，名物化前的修饰语“approaching”在译文中也充当了“分别”的修饰语“行将到来的”。可见，原文的环境成分“about our approaching <u>separation</u>”在译文中对应相同的功能成分。相比之下，张译则把名物化译为过程动词“分离”，把原修饰语“approaching”译为“分离”的过程修饰语“就要”。这一转变使得译文增添了新的小句，原文的经验功能配置变为译文的逻辑序列组合，即小句变为小句复合体。再看另外一例：

例（9）“I thought, at one time,” said Mr. Wickfield, “that you wished to send Maldon abroad to effect a desirable separation.”（Chapter 42）

董译：“我有一度想，”威克菲尔先生说道，“你有意把麦尔顿送去国外，造成一种合意的隔离。”

张译：“我有一阵子，”维克菲先生说，“以为你想要把冒勒顿先生打发到外国去，就为的是要把他们两个拆开哪。”

与例8类似，董译同原文亦步亦趋，既保留了名物化，在结构上也同原文保持一致，唯一的不同是原文的“to effect a desirable separation”为非定式小句，译为汉语后变为定式小句。张译再次选择了去名物化的译法，语言结构上同原文也有较大出入，舍弃了“过程+修饰语+参与者”的配置，转而采用汉语独有的“把”字句。

语料分析结果表明，上述情况在译例中占有相当的比例，两译文在名物化的选择上差异显著，张译的去名物化程度明显高于董译，影响这种差异的因素正是翻译策略。译文去名物化程度不同，也会导致译文呈现不同的语言特点。

4.2 去名物化程度对译文语言特点的影响

董译因追求翻译的科学性和忠实性，同原文的语言结构尽量保持一致，进而大量保留原文的名物化，导致欧化痕迹明显。贺阳（2008）对“五四”以来汉语中的欧化现象做了全面的研究，认为“N的V”“NV”“PP的V”[2]结构都属于现代汉语的欧化语法。我们对董译105例保留名物化的译例进行分析，发现它们所在的结构，如“家庭布置、新生活的安排、对它们的欣赏、对他的品格的赞美”等确属上述欧化语法的内容。可以说，动词名物化的保留是这些结构形成的直接原因。董译受源语结构的影响大量保留名物化，造成译文欧化语法特征明显。进一步分析发现，董译的名物化呈现以下特点：韵律上体现为双音节动词；有一定的抽象义，对应非典型的汉语动词；内部构成关系多为联合式。这是因为双音节的联合式动词，有功能增殖的倾向，且增殖量也最高（详见张国宪, 1994）。董译中的名物化如“赞美、赞叹、布置、准备、观察、钦佩、考虑、羡慕、欣赏、安排、描述、分别”等，进一步证明了这一观点。这些词的大量使用，导致“N的V”“NV”“PP的V”结构的产生，进而使译文呈现欧化语言的特点。

相比之下，张译较少使用名物化，更多地选择去名物化，为一致式的动词表达形式，使得译文小句数量增多，原文表征经验意义的结构配置模式向逻辑序列模式转换。这种转换，符合汉语流水句表达的叙述习惯，体现了张谷若“用地道译文地道翻译”的理念。流水句是最能体现汉语特征的句型之一，简短灵活，富于变化，

2 贺阳讨论的这些结构中的V相当于本文所说的动词名物化。

表面自由松散，内部结构却按照一定的逻辑语义关系铺排。（刘宓庆, 2006：260-262）汉语流水句的使用打破了英语语言严密、精确的句法结构，取之以结构松散、内容流畅的小句群。这种语言特点也符合汉民族有机整体式的思维习惯，使得句子的组织结构呈现“散点透视”的特点，而不同于英语句子“焦点透视”的特点。

5. 小结

本文结合英汉小说翻译中一定规模的动词名物化的翻译实例，探讨了翻译中的去名物化现象及其同语言系统和翻译策略的关系。董、张两译文在名物化的翻译上都有去名物化的趋势，这同语言系统的倾向性密切相关，也体现了英汉两种语言类型学上的差异。英语是一种名词型的语言，汉语是一种动词型的语言，英语的名物化译为汉语后，呈现去名物化的趋势。正是语言系统的差异，导致了翻译中英语构建概念意义的经验模式向逻辑模式转换，以及译文中大量过程动词的增加。同时，翻译策略对去名物化程度具有制约作用，主张异化的董译保留名物化的比例较高，去名物化程度低，欧化语法的特点明显；主张归化的张译保留名物化的比例较低，去名物化程度高，译文呈现散点透视的流水句形态，更符合汉语识解世界经验的方式。

参考文献

Halliday, M. A. K. 1994. *An Introduction to Functional Grammar* (2nd edition). London: Arnold.

Halliday, M. A. K. 1998/2007. Things and Relations: Regrammaticising Experience as Technical Knowledge. In J, Webster (ed.) *The Collected Works of M.A.K. Halliday Vol. 5. The Language of Science*. London: Continuum, 49-101.

Halliday, M. A. K. & C. M. I. M. Matthiessen. 1999. *Construing Experience through Meaning: A Language-based Approach to Cognition*. London: Continuum.

Halliday, M. A. K & C. M. I. M. Matthiessen. 2004. *An Introduction to Functional Grammar* (3rd edition). London: Arnold.

Halliday, M. A. K. & J. R. Martin. 1993. *Writing Science: Literacy and Discursive Power.* London: Falmer Press.

Martin, J. R. 1992. *English Text: System and Structure*. Amsterdam: Benjamins.

Martin, J. R. 2008. Incongruent and Proud: De-vilifying “Nominalization”. *Discourse Society*, 19(6): 801-810.

Martin, J.R., C. M. I. M. Matthiessen & C. Painter. 2010. *Deploying Functional Grammar*. Beijing: The Commercial Press.

Matthiessen, C. M. I. M. 1999. The System of Transitivity: An Exploratory Study of Text-based Profiles. *Functions of Language*, 6(1): 1-51.

Matthiessen, C. M. I. M. 2004. Descriptive Motifs and Generalizations. In A. Caffarel et al. (eds.) *Language Typology: A Functional Perspective*. Amsterdam: Benjamins, 537-673.

Matthiessen, C. M. I. M., K. Teruya & M. Lam. 2010. *Key Terms in Systemic Functional Linguistics*. London: Continuum.

Ravelli, L. 1988. Grammatical Metaphor: An Initial Analysis. In E. Steiner & R. Veltman (eds.) *Pragmatics, Discourse and Text: Some Systemically-inspired Approaches*. London: Pinter, 133-147.

Ravelli, L. 2003. Renewal of Connection: Integrating Theory and Practice in an Understanding of Grammatical Metaphor. In A.-M. Simon-Vamdembergen et al. (eds.) *Grammatical Metaphor: Views from Systemic Functional Linguistics*.Amsterdam: Benjamins, 37-64.

Simon-Vandenbergen, A. M., M. Taverniers & L. Ravelli. 2003. *Grammatical Metaphor: Views from Systemic Functional Linguistics*. Amsterdam: Benjamins.

Teruya, K. 2007. *A Systemic Functional Grammar of Japanese*. London: Continuum.

郭锐, 2002,《现代汉语词类研究》。北京：商务印书馆。

韩礼德著, 李战子、周晓康等译, 1966/2006, 语法、社会和名词, 载《韩礼德语言学文集》。长沙：湖南教育出版社, 224-251。

贺阳, 2008,《现代汉语欧化语法现象研究》。北京：商务印书馆。

李运兴, 2010,《翻译语境描写论纲》。北京：清华大学出版社。

刘丹青, 2010, 汉语是一种动词型语言——试说动词型语言和名词型语言的类型差异,《世界汉语教学》(1)：3-17。

刘宓庆, 2006,《新编汉英对比与翻译》。北京：中国对外翻译出版公司。

罗新璋(编), 1984,《翻译论集》。北京：商务印书馆。

张谷若, 1980, 地道的原文, 地道的译文,《翻译通讯》(1)：19-23。

张谷若, 1989, 谈我的翻译生涯, 载巴金等著, 王寿兰编,《当代文学翻译百家谈》。北京：北京大学出版社, 450-458。

张国宪, 1994, 双音节动词功能增殖, 载邵敬敏主编,《语法研究与语法应用》。北京：北京语言大学出版社, 46-57。

语言的个体发生与隐喻能力的发展[1]

李　杰
汕头大学

1. 引言

语言的隐喻普遍性表明对隐喻的掌握在语言学习中具有十分重要的意义。Halliday（1975）在其著作*Learning How to Mean*一书中就指出，儿童学习语言的目的就是为了很好地表达意义，而要学会表达意义的关键就是要学会使用隐喻表达方式。他认为，个体的语言发展需要经历从原型语言（protolanguage），经历过渡时期，最后才到成人语言（adult language）阶段，而语法隐喻是成人语言的标志，因而学会使用隐喻表达是儿童学习阶段的重要任务。赵彦春（2011：211）认为，“语言水平的提高在很大程度上就是隐喻能力的增强，理想的学习者应能够感悟词汇中蕴含的隐喻信息。”Danesi（1986：9）也曾明确指出，“学习者获得交际水准的真正标记就是以目的语进行隐喻化的能力”。这意味着：语言教育者的首要任务就是想方设法帮助语言学习者获得隐喻能力（赵彦春，2011：211）。本文将从语言个体发生的角度来探索个体语言发展的规律，并揭示语言学习者隐喻能力的发展情况，试图挖掘出在外语教学中培养学习者隐喻能力的参考价值。

2. 对语言个体发生的研究

自从20世纪70年代中期，以Halliday为代表的系统功能语言学派就主张从种系发生、个体发生和语篇发生三个方面来研究语言系统和语言形式的发展演变情况。Halliday & Matthiessen（1999）把种系发生（phylogenesis）看成是“语言的历史”（history of language），把个体发生（ontogenesis）看成是“个人的历史”（history of an individual），把语篇发生（logogenesis）看成是“语篇的历史”（history of a text）。在Halliday等人看来，儿童学习语言的过程是一种学习如何通过语言表达各

1 本文为“教育部人文社科项目”（12YJA740036）部分研究成果。

种社会需要的过程，因此儿童的语言发展体现为学会如何表达意义。在过去的几十年间，系统功能语言学家在个体语言发生方面做了多项个案研究。Halliday（1975, 1980）通过亲自观察、记录和分析他儿子Nigel从出生到18个月的表意方式和语言发展情况，提出了儿童语言发展的三个阶段：原型语言阶段、过渡阶段、成人语言阶段。Halliday发现在原型语言阶段（protolanguage period），儿童的语言只有声音和意义两个层次，声音和意义之间呈现对应的关系，没有词汇语法这个中间层；但到了成人语言阶段（adult language period）儿童开始接受学校的正规教育，除了接触成人日常使用的口语外，还通过阅读书面语学习语言，Halliday称其为“教育语言”（educational language）阶段，其特点是“从具体到抽象”（from concrete to abstract）。Halliday 认为，从小学升入中学是个体语言发展的一个重要转折点，即进入“科技语言”（technical language）阶段，其特点是“从一致式到隐喻式”（from congruent to metaphorical）；儿童学会了通过语言对各种事物和现象进行隐喻化（metaphorization）的过程（朱永生, 2011：63）。

Painter（2003）也在个体语言发展方面做了深入的研究。她分别对自己两个儿子（Hal and Stephen）的语言发展情况进行了长期的观察和研究，取得了令人瞩目的成绩。Painter（2003：154-5）研究发现，儿童使用一个词语构建一个想象的“情景”或表达一个“概念”而不是“事物”，并非就是我们所讲的隐喻，但的确在一定程度上存在向非字面意义或抽象概念转换的情况，这在儿童的语言发展中是非常重要的。儿童早期语言发展时期对词汇意义的过度扩展现象（overextension）就具有明显的隐喻特征。Melissa Bowerman（1978）就发现她15个月大的女儿不仅使用“moon”这个词表示“月亮”，还用它表示“半块西柚”（half a grapefruit），或表示“一片柠檬”（a lemon segment），或“圆形的洗碗机转盘”（the circular dishwasher dial）。Painter（2003：155）认为这样的语言现象是具有隐喻性的, 但属于隐喻性的过度扩展（metaphorical overextension）；儿童并非是掌握了成人语言的表征系统，而是由于他们的表达系统非常有限而不得不扩展他们已有的意义表达方式。Painter进一步分析说，儿童词汇资源的局限使他们不得不使用有限的词汇表达多种意义（ibid）。Painter 发现当她的儿子Hal学会第一个词puss（猫咪）后，便使用这个词表达“猫咪”以外的概念，当然通常是与原本的意义有关联或有相似特征的一些概念。有例为证：

a. Hal approaches collie dog, saying doggy. Then puts hand on dog's coat to stroke, saying 'puss'.

b. Hal occasionally says 'puss' when fondling Mum's or babyminder's hair.

c. Hal meets black dog and says 'doggy, pussy, Katy'.（=this is a dog, soft like a cat, and [?black] like Katy）

d. Hal points at dog and says 'doggy'. Points at its eyes and says 'eyes'. Reaches to its coat and says 'pussy'.

（参见Painter, 2003：155）

在上述语料中，Hal使用“puss”这个词表示类似“软毛的东西”，也可以表示

“抚摸软毛的行为”，而这些概念一定是和他熟悉的猫Katy有联系。由于Hal 还没有词汇来表达 “soft”, “hairy”, “furry”等这些概念，他就只好借助已有的词汇 “puss”的转用（transferred use）方式创造性地表达所想要表达的概念（ibid）。白丽芳（2004）认为，学龄前儿童所创造的许多隐喻是为了满足交际的需要，因为他们所掌握的词汇非常有限，所以不得不借助隐喻方式来表达他们的意思。实际上，类似的情况也发生在学习语言结构的时候。儿童的话语中可以清楚地反映他们具有在不同范畴现象之间发现相似性的能力；如 “chopsticks, they like straws; Mummy hair like a railway” （from Halliday's Nigel）（Halliday, 1975：138）。因此，Painter（2003：156-7）认为，尽管儿童可以创造性地使用一些语言学符号，发现不同范畴之间的一些相似性并进行隐喻性地表达，但通过隐喻形式进行 “意义转移（meaning transfer）” 不是儿童早期语言阶段的主要特征。白丽芳（2004）的研究也表明，儿童天生具有隐喻性思维，学龄前儿童因为思维和语言的贫乏往往会无意识地使用隐喻，但他们的隐喻创造力并不完美，他们的隐喻往往会过于牵强，而且显得不合常理，甚至荒谬；到了小学低年级阶段，儿童能够进行具体的形象思维，他们往往有意识地创造出直观的、拟人化的隐喻；而小学高年级的学生已经具有了抽象思维的能力，随着词汇量的丰富和概念隐喻的逐渐形成，他们的隐喻具有了抽象画和系统化的特征。因此，正如Halliday（1985, 1994/2000）所言语法隐喻是成人语言的标志。只有当语言学习者学会使用语气结构、学会及物性结构，才能算是达到语言使用者的成熟阶段（full status as language users）；而到了这个阶段，大量的隐喻就可能出现，就会用隐喻的方式来表达语法和词汇方面的意义（Painter, 2003：157）。

3. 个体的语言发展与语法隐喻

语法隐喻的概念是Halliday（1985, 1994/2000）在*An Introduction to Functional Grammar*一书中提出的。Halliday（1994：341）认为语法隐喻是一种 “意义表达变异” （variation in the expression of meanings）的语言策略。系统功能语言学家认为，语言系统提供给语言使用者的是一套系统化的意义潜势（meaning potential）。语言使用者为实现某种语义功能必须在这个系统中进行一系列的选择，所选择的结构使意义与其表达之间的关系可能是一致式（congruent），也可能是非一致式或隐喻式（incongruent or metaphorical）。从个体语言发生的角度（ontogenetic perspective）来考察语法隐喻，Halliday（1994：xviii,342）认为儿童逐步学会使用隐喻性语言，使用隐喻表达方式是成人语言的特点，而儿童语言一般不具备这种特点。儿童语言向语法隐喻的过度是儿童语言系统进化发展中重要的一步。掌握语法隐喻并非是不断增加新的语言结构，而是运用现有的结构体现新的功能语法隐喻涉及交叉编码（cross-coding），既涉及 “转意” （transferred meaning），也涉及 “字面意义” （literal meaning）。Halliday把这种现象叫做 “语义融合” （semantic blend）。一致式可以体现 “语义的单一体” （semantic simplex），而隐喻式则体现“语义复合体”（semantic complex）。成人掌握语法隐喻后便可以运用隐喻性结构同时表达语义的复合性。这种交叉编码可以增加语言系统的潜势，因此任何语法隐喻的使用都能够增强语义的复合性（semantic complexity）（Derewianka, 2003：185）。

Beverly Derewianka（2003）对她的儿子Nick从幼儿时期到青少年时期的语言发展情况进行了研究。她搜集了Nick 5到13岁几乎所有的书写文本材料，并通过分析后找出其中的语法隐喻实例。Derewianka（2003：213）研究发现，语料中语法隐喻的使用量随着Nick的年龄呈上升趋势；相对学龄前儿童青少年的语言会出现更多的语法隐喻；这说明在个体语言发展的过程中，直白式先于隐喻式。Painter（2003：159）认为，隐喻表达一般不会出现在儿童早期的话语中，但有可能出现这样的结构，如：have a bath, have a cuddle, do a pee, make a big mess, do a big kick; Painter就发现这些结构出现在她的两个儿子（Hal and Stephen）2岁到2岁半的话语中。很显然，在这些表达式中动词成分并不识解行为，而名词成分指称行为；这些名词成分通过语法的方式将动作行为识解为“事物”（thing）。Derewianka（2003：194）也发现Nick很早就能写出这样的句子：

We also went for a bush WALK and horse RIDING.

如果用一致式的表达，就可能会是：

We also went walking in the bush and we rode horses.

当选择“go + a walk”, “go + a ride”这样的“Process + Range”结构，过程“walk”和过程“ride”都成为名词（“walking” and “riding”），并伴以泛义动词（general verb）“go”；此外，Nick还能够使用类别词修饰名词组（a <u>bush</u> walk and <u>horse</u> riding）。在Derewianka看来，由于词汇语法资源的局限，儿童会不可避免但并非有意识地使用隐喻性的语义表达方式作为一种语言策略（linguistic strategy）。Painter（2003：160）认为这个时期的儿童并不具备使用语法隐喻的能力，而只是学会用一些约定俗成的表达形式（frozen forms）而已，如“死隐喻”（dead metaphor）。

Jane Torr等人（2003：172）也指出，像名词化那样的概念语法隐喻一般不会出现在儿童的话语中，但相类似“死隐喻”的名词化表达形式会出现儿童的话语中。这些“死隐喻”表达形式已经经过长期的使用和约定俗成，通常已经不被看成是隐喻了，如：have dinner, take a bath等。英语中有很多例子可以表明，原来是具备隐喻性的，只是在缓慢的演变过程中失去了其隐喻的特性。Painter（2003：160）认为，尽管儿童要在未来好多年才能真正掌握语法隐喻，但早期这些隐喻现象对儿童的语言发展是很重要的。既然隐喻的本质就是以一事物表示另一事物，那么就不难看出在语言符号系统中隐喻性表达存在的重要原因便是它的指称功能或概念功能，我们也就不难发现在语言系统中存在大量的概念隐喻，在语言使用中也会用到大量的隐喻表达形式。在语言发展过程中，儿童会逐步掌握一些隐喻形式来表征他们的语义系统。

4. 个体的语言发展与隐喻能力

以上研究表明，儿童语言发展的过程就是儿童不断掌握隐喻的过程。儿童在语言学习过程中，习得、产出、理解隐喻的能力是非常重要的，因为在任何一种语言中，隐喻都是一种普遍的现象，生活中处处是隐喻，人们在语言交际中也就会处处使用隐喻。Richards（1936：94）指出，在日常的话语中，我们三句话就会有一个隐喻。因此，隐喻性表达在语言交际中被广泛使用的事实说明，隐喻作为一种语言表达能力，其交际功能和价值是显而易见的。在语言交际中，当人们无法靠一类概念去表达或再现意图时，它们就会借助另一类概念；当人们无法靠使用一种语言形式表达某种意义时，他们就会想办法寻求另一种语言形式。在我们的实际生活中，许多具有普遍意义的主题，如情感、人生、争论等都是用隐喻的手法来表达的。在日常的交际中，许多非比喻性的话语实际上也是隐喻性思维方式的体现，因为它们是对概念隐喻的语言表达，如人们常用“save, waste, run out, spend, invest, borrow, cost”等词和表示时间的结构进行搭配，就体现了“TIME IS MOENY”的概念隐喻。再如，在英语中人们用“UP, DOWN”的概念表示“happy，sad”之意。这些例子说明，隐喻普遍存在于日常的语言交际中。很多语言中都存在诸如“TIME IS MONEY”，“ARGUMENT IS WAR”，“LIFE IS JOURNEY”这样的概念隐喻。因此，隐喻概念的产生和隐喻性的表达形式是人类生存和交际活动的需要。

隐喻不仅可以帮助我们丰富语言表达，更重要的是可以帮助我们进行创新思维。Halliday（1985, 1994/2000）就指出，儿童语法隐喻的习得有助于提高其语言水平，以便使用已有的语言系统进行创新性表达。因此，语言能力的发展同隐喻使用密切相关，语言交际的成功与否与交际者的隐喻能力关系十分密切。儿童语言能力发展的重要标志是能够隐喻性地使用语言表达思想。因此, 我们有理由把隐喻能力看成是语言学习者熟练掌握一种语言的关键性指标。

5. 外语教学与隐喻能力的培养

隐喻的认知本质和语言的隐喻普遍性表明隐喻能力的发展有助于语言学习，特别是有助于语言运用的地道和流利（native-like fluency）。同时，语言学习也可以促进隐喻能力的发展，因为交际活动在很大程度上是基于我们思维和行动的概念系统的语言表达。用隐喻方式说话是讲本族语者的一种基本语言能力特征（Denesi, 1993：493）。外语学习意味着习得目标语中的隐喻机制并学习像本族语者一样能够隐喻式地思维、隐喻性地使用语言。Danesi（1993）认为，隐喻能力对于学习者来说非常重要，如果缺乏隐喻能力就会造成学习者的外语表达没有什么错误，也可以接受，但缺少了母语使用者的地道性，因为学习者往往会依赖其母语的概念基础，将母语概念化过程想当然地映射到目标语的形式上。

有研究表明（如Danesi, 1992, 陈朗，2010），缺乏概念流利和隐喻能力是造成二语学习者语言不地道的主要原因。陈朗（2010）认为，二语习得者缺乏本族语者的流利性的根本原因在于其隐喻意识的缺失，直白表达所占比例过大。外语学习者由于缺乏对外语概念系统的基本认知，常常用母语的概念系统套用外语表达，致使他们产生出生硬的表达或不合规范的表达，即“中文式的英语”（Chinglish）。文秋芳教授曾对我国外语专业学生的语言能力做过调查，她认为，“仅仅追求语言的准确性和流利性而不顾多样性，学生的二语能力长期在低水平上徘徊，没有明显进步”（文秋芳，2001）。造成这种情况可能涉及多方面的原因，但其中肯定与学生的隐喻能力有关。蔡龙权对英语专业三年级本科生和英语专业二年级研究生在理解和使用隐喻表达能力方面进行了抽样比较，其结果显示，很少的被试者能够正确自如地使用和理解隐喻性表达（蔡龙权，2005）。隐喻表达的普遍性及其在语言交际中所发挥的作用，表明在外语教学中教授隐喻表达、进行隐喻思维的培养，提高学习者的隐喻能力具有非常重要的意义。

6. 结语

Halliday 等系统功能语言学家通过对儿童语言发展过程的观察和研究，从而探讨了儿童语言习得过程中隐喻能力的个体发展规律，这对语言教学尤其是外语教学有着重要的启示。在外语教学中需要帮助学生认识和掌握目的语中的隐喻现象，提高学习者的隐喻意识，培养他们的隐喻能力。儿童语言发展的重要标志就是学会使用隐喻的方式表达意义。那么，在外语教学中应注意培养学生的隐喻能力，方能增强学生的语言表达能力。换言之，培养学生的隐喻能力，即是培养学生具备创造性活用语言的能力，增强他们语言表达的丰富性、多样性。这是语言个体发生的路径，也应该是外语教学的方向。Richards（1936：90）就曾强调，唯有隐喻才能帮助我们表达出想要表达的思想。

参考文献

Bowerman, M. 1978. The Acquisition of Word Meaning. In N. Waterson & C. E. Snow (eds.) *The Development of Communication*. New York: Wiley, 263-287.

Danesi, M. 1986. The Role of Metaphor in Second Language Pedagogy. *Rossegan Italiana di Linguistica Aplicata*, (3): 1-10.

Danesi, M. 1992. Metaphor and Classroom Second Language Learning. *Romance Languages Annual*, (3): 189-194.

Danesi, M. 1993. Metaphorical Competence in Second Language Acquisition and Second Language Teaching: The Neglected Dimension. In J. E. Alatis (ed.)

Language, Communication and Social Meaning. Washington D. C.: Georgetown University Press, 489-500.

Derewianka, B. 2003. Grammatical Metaphor in the Transition to Adolescence. In A.-M. Simon-Vamdembergen, M. Taverniers & L. Ravelli (eds.) *Grammatical Metaphor: Views from Systemic-functional Linguistics*. Amsterdam: Benjamins, 185-219.

Halliday, M. A. K. 1975. *Learning How to Mean: Explorations in the Development of Language*. London: Arnold.

Halliday, M. A. K. 1980. Three Aspects of Children's Language Development: Learning Language, Learning through and Learning about Language. In Y. M. Goodman, K. K. Hausser & D. S. Strickland (eds.) *Oral and Written Language Development: Impact on Schools* (Proceedings from the 1979-1980). International Reading Association and National Council of Teachers of English, 7-19.

Halliday, M. A. K. 1985. *An Introduction to Functional Grammar*. London: Arnold.

Halliday, M. A. K. 1994/2000. *Introduction to Functional Grammar* (2nd edition). London: Arnold/ Beijing: Foreign Language Teaching & Research Press.

Painter, C. 2003. The Use of a Metaphorical Mode of Meaning in Early Language Development. In A.-M. Simon-Vamdembergen, M. Taverniers & L. Ravelli (eds.) *Grammatical Metaphor: Views from Systemic-functional Linguistics*. Amsterdam: Benjamins, 151-167.

Richards, I. A. 1936. *The Philosophy of Rhetoric*. Oxford: Oxford University Press.

Torr, J. & A. Simpson. 2003. The Emergence of Grammatical Metaphor: Literacy-oriented Expressions in the Everyday Speech of Young Children. In A.M. Simon-Vamdembergen, M. Taverniers & L. Ravelli (eds.) *Grammatical Metaphor: Views from Systemic-functional Linguistics*. Amsterdam: Benjamins, 169-183.

白丽芳，2004，儿童隐喻性思维的特点及其发展，《外语与外语教学》（4）：53-57。

蔡龙权，2003，隐喻能力在二语习得中的应用，《外国语》（6）：38-45。

陈朗，2010，二语教学中的隐喻能力培养，《外语学刊》（5）：47-49。

文秋芳，2001，从全国英语专业四级口试看口语教学，《外语界》（4）：24-28。

赵彦春，2011，《隐喻形态研究》。北京：外文出版社。

朱永生、严世清，2011，《系统功能语言学在思考》。上海：复旦大学出版社。

Language, Communication, and Social Meaning. Washington, D.C.: Georgetown University Press, 137-160.
Derewianka, B. 2003. Grammatical Metaphor in the Transition to Adolescence. In A.-M. Simon-Vandenbergen, M. Taverniers & L. Ravelli (eds.) *Grammatical Metaphor: Views from Systemic Functional Linguistics*. Amsterdam: Benjamins, 185-219.
Halliday, M. A. K. 1975. *Learning How to Mean: Explorations in the Development of Language*. London: Arnold.
Halliday, M. A. K. 1980. Three Aspects of Children's Language Development: Learning Language, Learning through Language, Learning about Language. In Y. M. Goodman, M. M. Haussler & D. S. Strickland (eds.) *Oral and Written Language Development Research: Impact on the Schools* (Proceedings from the 1979 and 1980 IMPACT Conferences). International Reading Association and National Council of Teachers of English.
Halliday, M. A. K. 1985. *An Introduction to Functional Grammar*. London: Arnold.
Halliday, M. A. K. 1994/2000. *An Introduction to Functional Grammar*. 2nd edition. Beijing: Foreign Language Teaching and Research Press.
Painter, C. 2003. The Use of a Metaphorical Mode of Meaning in Early Language Development. In A.-M. Simon-Vandenbergen, M. Taverniers & L. Ravelli (eds.) *Grammatical Metaphor: Views from Systemic Functional Linguistics*. Amsterdam: Benjamins, 151-167.
Richards, I. A. 1936. *The Philosophy of Rhetoric*. Oxford: Oxford University Press.
Torr, J. & A. Simpson. 2003. The Emergence of Grammatical Metaphor: Literacy-oriented Expressions in the Everyday Speech of Young Children. In A.-M. Simon-Vandenbergen, M. Taverniers & L. Ravelli (eds.) *Grammatical Metaphor: Views from Systemic Functional Linguistics*. Amsterdam: Benjamins, 169-183.
[illegible]
[illegible]
[illegible]
[illegible]
[illegible]
[illegible]

基于语义变化的概念语法隐喻模式与类型

丛迎旭
宁波大学/上海外国语大学
王红阳
宁波大学

1. 引言

语法隐喻（Halliday, 1984, 1998/2005; Halliday & Matthiessen, 1999, 2004）是系统功能语言学的一个重要理论。近年来，语法隐喻理论上有两点重要发展：（1）对“语义同一性”的解读。Halliday（1998/2005：56）提出语法隐喻是“相同的所指，不同的能指”，词汇隐喻是“相同的能指，不同的所指”。然而，系统功能语言学的一条基本原则是不同形式体现不同意义，因此不少学者对“相同的所指”的提法表示异议，如Ravelli（2003）、何伟（2008）、侯建波（2008）。实际上“相同的所指”需要被辩证地解读：隐喻式和一致式之间有相同意义也有不同意义。相同意义主要指相同的词汇意义，这是语法隐喻研究的出发点与基础。不同意义主要指不同的语法意义，以及由此引发的词汇意义改变，这是语法隐喻成立的必要条件和主要研究目的；（2）对语法隐喻与词汇隐喻之间关系的定位。Halliday, Hu & Zhu（2010）指出“词汇隐喻和语法隐喻之间并不存在原则性不同，它们的隐喻性是相同的，只是观察视角不同”。换言之，语法隐喻和词汇隐喻并非相互对立的范畴，常常是一个语言现象的两个属性。总体上看，语法隐喻涉及概念意义的变化，因此必然包含一定程度的词汇隐喻；反过来词汇隐喻却未必涉及语法隐喻。

语法隐喻理论的适用范围较广，因此也引发了许多争议，最突出的问题就是它缺乏严格的界定和清晰的研究对象。朱永生、严世清（2001：126）指出“Halliday引入其理论的方式显得有些随意，甚至有循环论证之嫌”。赵艳芳（2001：170）认为“如果将词汇的选择和语法形式的变异都看作是隐喻，那么（语法）隐喻就有可能成为‘垃圾篓’”。Taverniers（2008：3）也认为“语法隐喻是系统功能语言学最重要的创新之一，但其内部结构却从未被严谨地定义。”

针对这些问题，本文首先以语义变化方式为标准把语法隐喻分为语义删减、语义扩充和语义重组三类，力图使语法隐喻的研究对象更加明晰，并确保理论的内部自洽和研究的系统性。然后，本文从正反两面分析了三类语法隐喻的文体特征和使用限制，特别是借助加的夫语法对语义重组类进行英汉对比，并从象似性和经济性的角度解释了该类语法隐喻在英汉语中的使用差异。下面我们首先对语法隐喻已有的分类模式做一简述。

2. 语法隐喻现有分类模式简述

Halliday（1984）提出语法隐喻包括概念隐喻和人际隐喻两个次类，Martin（1992）增加了语篇隐喻和逻辑隐喻，这样语法隐喻的类型与纯理功能之间呈现了一一对应的关系。当前的语法隐喻研究主要围绕概念隐喻展开，这主要有三个原因：（1）在系统功能语法中概念功能包括了经验功能和逻辑功能，所以逻辑隐喻可以在概念隐喻之下研究而不必单列一类；（2）无论是概念隐喻还是人际隐喻都会涉及语篇层面的改变，或者说都会表现为语篇层面的非自然使用，所以Halliday认为语篇隐喻也没有存在的必要；（3）在三个纯理功能中，概念功能处于最基础的位置，相应地对概念隐喻的研究也最多。Taverniers（2011：1107）指出与语篇功能相比，概念功能和人际功能更为基本。概念功能涉及语言中的实体（content）因素，负责完成对经验世界的建构。人际功能涉及语言中的说话者因素以及说话者和听话者之间的互动。而语篇功能是负责将前两个功能进行整合并组织成语篇，所以语篇功能处于三个纯理功能中的最外层。进一步说，交际是语言使用的根本动因，但人类对其内部和外部经验世界的认知与建构是实现交际活动的前提，因此概念功能又是人际功能的基础。可以看出，语法隐喻主要指概念隐喻有其合理性，所以本文也延续了这一做法。在理论建构之初，Halliday并未论述语法隐喻的内部分类，仅通过例子来说明什么是语法隐喻：

（1）They danced in Hungarian style.

（2）They did a Hungarian dance.

（3）They arrived at the summit on the fifth day.

（4）The fifth day saw them at the summit.

例（2）、例（4）是例（1）、例（3）的隐喻式。例（2）中的名物化现象一直是语法隐喻的主要研究对象。例（4）是非形似类语法隐喻，其中包含着“The fifth day is a man”的词汇隐喻。后来，Halliday & Matthiessen（1999, 2004）把语法隐喻作为系统功能语言学框架下认知研究的主要内容，在术语和研究方法上也借鉴了认知语言学的一些思想。语法隐喻被视为语义域到词汇语法域的非一致式映射，或者说延迟体现（delayed realization），其映射过程如图1[1]所示：

1 笔者对（Halliday & Matthiessen 2004）原图略作调整，用实线箭头标示一致式映射，用虚线箭头标示隐喻式映射。

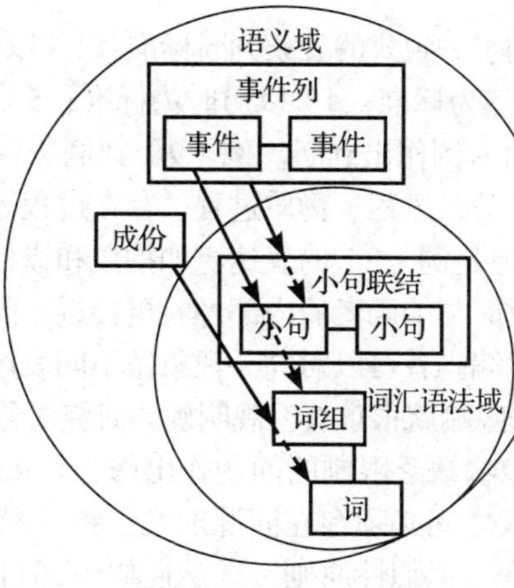

图1 级阶下移语法隐喻图示

Halliday（1998/2005）根据级阶下移中语义和语法之间可能的交叉耦合方式，概括出13种概念隐喻类型，并为每个类型提供了实例。这13类语法隐喻提供了明确的研究对象，但存在两个问题：（1）无法囊括例4那样没有级阶变化的类型和级阶上移的类型；（2）这13类多数是非形似语法隐喻，使研究的主观性较大。朱永生、严世清（2001：123）从发生程序上对语法隐喻加以界定，提出概念隐喻来自说话者的三种非一致式选择：（1）选择过程的类型；（2）选择与该过程有关的功能成分；（3）选择能体现这些功能的词类。每次选择都会导致一致或非一致的体现，如：

（5）I lived in the same room with Jack in college for two years.

（6）I roomed with Jack in college for two years.

（7）The roof has collected a lot of leaves.

（8）A lot of leaves have collected on the roof.

朱永生、严世清（2001）认为例（6）仅涉及词类的非一致选择，例（8）包含功能成分和词类的非一致选择，而上面例（4）的隐喻度最高，因为它的三个选择都是隐喻性的。新研究模式不但使例（4）等语言现象得到了解释，而且为语法隐喻度的量化提供了思路。范文芳（2007）构建了包括词汇语法范畴转移、级转移和语气域转移的语法隐喻综合模式。Martin & White（2008：10）把存在"层间张力"，语义被二次加工的表达变体都归为语法隐喻。上述研究模式都扩大了语法隐喻理论的适用范围，但我们发现在自然语言中同一语义经常存在多个表达方式，有时很难判断哪些是经过了"二次加工"，哪些是一致式，例如：

（9）I love you.

（10）I think of you every moment.

（11）I am fond of you.

（12）You are everything to me.

（13）I fall in love with you.

（14）我心里只有你。

胡壮麟（2000）归纳了一致式的五条判断标准：1）以年龄为标准；2）以难易程度为标准；3）以合乎自然为标准；4）以历时为标准；5）以方式为标准。根据这些标准我们仍然很难对上面六例作出判断。例（9）到例（14）都表示"我爱你"，但编码者可选择心理过程、关系过程、物质过程、存在过程等不同方式体现。直觉上，例（9）较接近一致式，但是例（9）的表达更加抽象和概括，需要经过更多的认知处理，与之相比其他几例反而与编码者的内部经验更接近，因此更符合"合乎自然"的标准。从不同视角出发，编码者可以对同一现象做不同表述，如果完全以语义为标准而没有形式的限制，语法隐喻就很难有客观明确的研究对象，也很难使研究深入。

有学者开始对语法隐喻缺乏限制的问题作出修正。Ravelli（2003：42）指出语法隐喻的隐喻式和一致式之间必须存在同源形式。张德禄、赵静（2008）提出确定隐喻式和一致式应该遵守"形似性原则"。从迎旭（2011）也认为概念语法隐喻的隐喻式必须由一致式直接转类而来。或许，我们可以把缺乏形似性原则限制的语法隐喻研究看作广义模式，而把坚持"形似性原则"的语法隐喻研究看作狭义模式，本文的研究属于后者。

3. 基于语义变化方式的语法隐喻分类模式

语法隐喻被看作是一种"语义发生"的过程，新产生的语义来自于词汇成分在新的句法位置上概念意义与语法意义的互动。对于整个语言系统的发展而言，语法隐喻的使用体现了词汇语法层和语义层之间的多重映射关系，丰富了人类的经验世界，因此属于一种增义过程。但对于具体的隐喻表达式而言，从一致式到隐喻式经过了词汇义与语法义的语义复合，但发生的语义变化却不仅限于语义增加一种类型。我们在形似性原则基础上，从语义变化方式出发将语法隐喻分为：语义删减类、语义扩充类和语义重组类。我们的分类标准参考了认知语言学的转喻理论和意象图式理论。简单说，动词转为名词是整体转指部分，发生了语义删减。名词转为动词是部分转指整体，发生了语义扩充（Langacker, 2008）。另外，依附在名词和动词之上的形容词和副词也会发生互转，在意象图式上它们都表征非过程（nonprocessual）关系，概念意义并没有发生显著的变化，区别是隐喻式和一致式选择了不同的语义组配方式，所以归为语义重组类语法隐喻。从级阶角度看，Halliday提出的13类语法隐喻发生了级阶下移从小句联结或者小句被压缩为小句或者词组，因此属于语义删减类；而名词动词化、名词形容词化等发生了级阶上移，属于语义扩充类；语义重组类涉及非一致的修饰关系，有级阶下移和级阶上移两个次类。

3.1 语义删减类

语义删减类语法隐喻主要包括三个次类：过程→实体，性质→实体，以及过程

→性质。该类型在Halliday经典模式中被看作是意义进化的主要代表，因此以往研究多从其对语言社会功能进化所起的积极作用的角度进行分析。但是，语言的发展同生物体的进化相似，为适应新的需要而产生的新功能常常要以牺牲某些原有功能为代价。下面笔者从语义变化和交际功能损益之间关系角度对语义删减类语法隐喻加以探讨，例如：

（15）The soldiers will execute him on Monday.

（16）His execution is scheduled for Monday.

（17）His execution was disastrous.

（18）His original idea was good, but his execution of the scheme was disastrous.

在一致式例（15）中，动词execute和him存在致使关系，him是动作的目标/受事；在隐喻式例（16）中，动作被隐喻化为实体，相应地，目标/受事转换为实体的拥有者，而且动作者/施事（the soldiers）被删除了。从传递信息和实现交际意图的效率角度出发，名物化现象有收益也有损耗。从收益上说，名物化使动态的、连续的过程或关系属性变成静态的、有界的实体，更容易被量化和修饰，满足了复杂现象被指称和术语化的要求，让语言更具客观性和权威性。因此，科技语篇等正式文体大量使用名物化。

从损耗角度看，当一致式的小句被压缩为词组后，在语义层里与过程自然关联的许多成分，如动作者、目标等参与者成分及时间、地点、方式等环境成分在投射到词汇语法层时都被隐化为修饰成分、甚至被删除。在隐喻式中还删除了与过程相关的时体、语气、情态、语态等信息。虽然这些改变会增加受话者对文本的客观印象，但语义删减引发的一个负面效应就是会导致语义模糊、甚至产生歧义。比如例（17）就存在两种解读：（1）他被行刑这件事太可怕了；（2）他的执行（力）太差了。隐喻式的这两种解读可以通过增加语境信息来确认，如解读1在例（16）中被确认，解读2在例（18）中被确认。例（17）中execution语义不确定的原因就是动作的施动、受动关系不明，导致受话人无法从常规的词汇知识中选择恰当的词义，这是典型的句法与词义之间相互干涉的现象。语义删减类语法隐喻的生成机制可以通过图2说明：

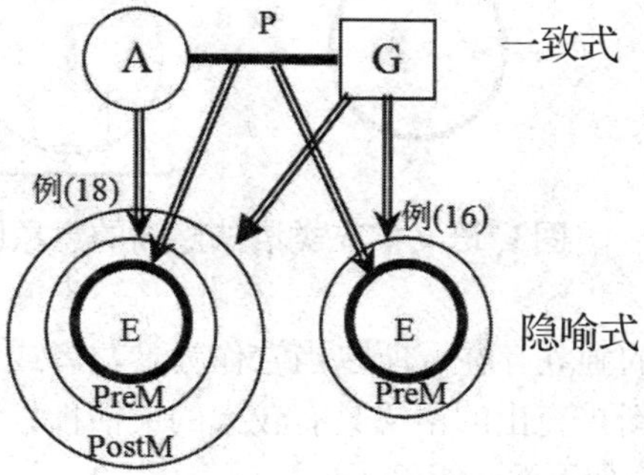

图2 语义删减类语法隐喻图式

通过图2可以看出，一致式的过程（P）转换为隐喻式的实体（E）后，原来的动作者/施事（A）和目标/受事（G）在隐喻式中被体现为修饰语。这样，主谓关系和述宾关系都体现为修饰语和中心语的关系，所以引发了歧义。但英语中当施事与受事同现时，施事一般作前置修饰语（PreM），而受事作后置修饰语（PostM），所以歧义得以消解。语义删减引发的歧义现象在汉语中也存在，如：

（19）对老李的表扬

（20）对报纸的批评

例（19）中的“老李”既可能是“表扬”的动作者，也可能是“表扬”的目标。与之类似，例（20）中“报纸”和“批评”的语义关系也存在两种不同的解读。歧义的消解首先可以借助交际双方共有的背景知识或者增加上下文语境，例如“China's rapid development of information technology”就比“China's rapid development”更加清楚。另一个办法是借助停顿或者重读等副语言手段，由于汉语里只有前置定语，例（19）中当老李是被表扬的对象时，一般会说“对老李的‖表扬”，而当老李是表扬的发出者时，则一般说“对‖老李的表扬”。英语里可以采用不同的介词来消解类似的歧义，相应的表达为：praise of Lao Li和praise from Lao Li。

3.2 语义扩充类[2]

Halliday的分类都是级阶下移的语义删减类，因为语义变化的不对称性语义扩充类语法隐喻过去一直被忽视。小句压缩为词组产生的语义删减是隐性的，语义变化不明显，因此更符合“相同的所指”的要求，而语义扩充类语法隐喻的语义变化是显性的，所以更多被看作是词汇隐喻而忽视了其语法隐喻性。用认知语言学的意象图式来解释，名词体现的是一种名词性述义，在认知域中突显的是一个整体（图3a）。动词体现的是关系性述义，体现为施事、受事、结果、工具或者与事等实体在时间顺序中的关系（图3b）。

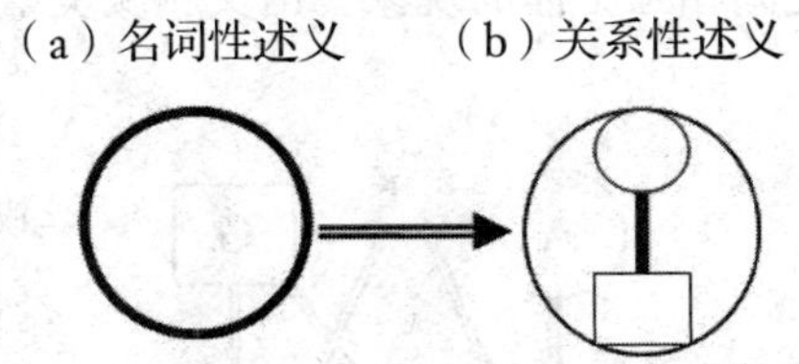

图3 语义扩充类语法隐喻的意象图式

由于实体是离散的独立存在，所以当它作为参与者或者环境成分进入过程中与其他实体发生关系，新扩充出的语义具有较大的灵活性，常需要依赖上下文或者情景语境来确定其词义，如下面一组例子：

2 人际隐喻大部分涉及语义扩充，但因为本文主要讨论概念隐喻，所以对人际隐喻不做论述。

（21）The landscaper seeded the lawn.

（22）The chef seeded the grapes.

（23）勇士入其门，则无人门焉。《公羊传·宣公六年》

（24）晋侯围曹，门焉。《左传·僖公二十八年》

例（21）中的“seed”是“播撒种子”的意思，而例（22）中就变为“去除种子”。同样情况也出现在古汉语中，如例（23）中动词化的“门”是“守门”的意思，而例（24）中的“门”则意为“攻打城门”。因为语义扩充类语法隐喻对语境更为依赖，所以该类型多出现在广告、影视、报纸等现场性更强、语境信息更加突显的文体，例如：

（25）你要是什么都不会，我就把你给微波了。（电影《疯狂的石头》）

（26）记者觉得“丙肝”一词，在季庄已经名转动了。好几个人在解释不能卖血的缘由时，都说“我丙肝了”。（《中国青年报》“探访卖血部落”）

（27）泡吧消化饼，野性你的生活。（广告词）

与语义删减类语法隐喻相比，语义扩充类的使用频率更低，在文体上存在更多的限制，原因在于这两类语法隐喻能满足不同层面的语用需求。语义被删减后，关键信息更突出，动作或属性被静态化更易修饰与量化，这些改变提高了交际效率，更符合信息传递的需求。而语义扩充后，新语义要借助语境来推理、确认，具有现场性、临时性特征，满足了修辞上新奇、生动的需求，但与信息传递中客观、准确、明晰的需求相左。人们运用语言的首要目的是传递信息，然后才是修辞的需要，所以二者相比语义删减类属于优势类型。

3.3 语义重组类

句法研究主要涉及两种关系：（1）动词与其相关名词之间的关系，如主谓、述宾关系；（2）形容词、副词、介词短语等与其中心语之间的修饰关系[3]。从整体上说，对修饰关系的研究要比前一种关系薄弱许多。在语义组配方式上，属性修饰实体、环境修饰过程是一致式的组配，语义重组类语法隐喻研究的是非一致的组配关系。本文讨论的语义重组并不包括前两类语法隐喻的衍生物，即名物化或动词化过程中原来的修饰语同中心语一起发生范畴转移的情况。例如前面提到的“the rapid development”，其中“rapid”虽然由一致式的副词转换为形容词，但在语义上还是修饰“development”，而非小句的过程或者其他成分，因此也不涉及语义重组的情况。我们讨论的语义重组指的是一种错位修饰现象，即本来修饰实体的属性成分在隐喻式中修饰过程，或者本来修饰过程的环境成分在隐喻式中修饰实体。语义重组类语法隐喻在级阶上可分为两个次类：（1）级阶下移类，环境成分（C）下移成为修饰语（M），图4中用向心箭头表示；（2）级阶上移类，修饰语（M）上移成为

3 这里的修饰成分是依据 Halliday（1998/2005：75），但实际上在英汉语中名词和动词都可以作修饰成分，但从语法范畴与语法功能之间的典型关联来说，形容词和副词的典型功能就是作修饰语。

环境成分（C），图4中用离心箭头表示。

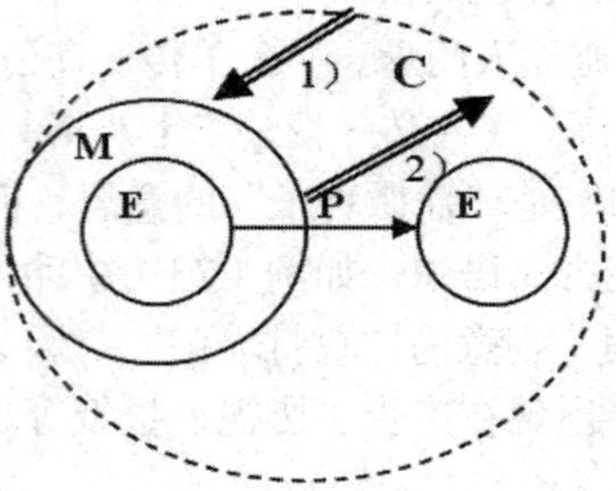

图4 语义重组类语法隐喻的图式

对级阶下移类而言，英汉语中都有大量原本修饰动词的成分转为修饰名词的现象。其中许多用法的修饰语和中心语之间关系较紧密，使用的自由度较高，如“a fast train，an easy book，快马，夜班”等；而有些用法还具有明显的临时性特征，只能出现在一些固定句式中。例如“洗冷水脸”的一致式是“用冷水洗脸”，原来表示方式（方法次类）的环境成分级阶下移后成为属性，但是“冷水脸”的使用并不自由，只能与动词“洗”搭配。再看下面的例子：

（28）I enjoy an occasional drink.

（29）I occasionally enjoy a drink.

（30）Every day ten new people contract AIDS.

（31）Every day ten people newly contract AIDS.

（32）我看了三小时的书。

（33）我看书看了三小时。

（34）他喝了三杯猛酒。

（35）他猛地喝了三杯酒。

按照Halliday语法（亦称为悉尼语法）的分类，例（28）、例（32）和“night shift”、“上夜班”一样，都是本应修饰动词的时间状语级阶下移后成为属性修饰语，区别是例（28）、（29）属于时段（temporal extent）修饰语中的频率，而例（30）、（31）为时点修饰语（temporal location）中的相对近时点。例（34）则是方式状语的转移修饰。事实上，类似现象一直受到语言学界的关注，只是研究视角和侧重点有所不同。修辞学把这类现象称为转移修饰（transferred epithet），传统语法则看作是准定语和准状语现象，在认知语言学中属于语法转喻，计算语言学将之视为一种逻辑转喻（Pustejovsky, 2011），它还属于语义指向研究的一部分。下面介绍级阶上移类：

（36）Alice has cleverly answered the questions.

（37）The senator has been talking foolishly to reporters.

（38）她的面纱长长地在微风中飘动。

（39）一座铁塔高高地矗立在河边。

（40）河边高高地矗立着一座铁塔。

（41）他长长地打了一把刀。

对语义重组类语法隐喻而言，级阶上移指的是修饰名词词组的属性成分上移为修饰动词词组的环境。因为名词词组在小句中的功能是参与者，所以转类后的修饰语被称为参与者指向状语。在形式语言学中，参与者被看作是谓词的论元，所以参与者指向状语被称为指元状语。例（36）中的cleverly与例（37）的foolishly在直接语义关系上都是修饰主语，属于主语指向状语，汉语类似的用法如例（38）、（39）。与英语不同的是，汉语的宾语修饰语也能级阶上移为环境成分，成为宾语指向状语，如例（40）、（41）。在形式上作状语的“长长地”修饰动词“打”，但在语义上的修饰对象是“刀”，其一致式是“打了一把长长的刀”。英语只能通过定语或补语来实现类似意义[4]，如“He made a very long knife”。我们发现属性成分/定语级阶上移为环境成分/状语后，隐喻式的三个纯理功能都发生了改变：在概念功能上，固定的属性义减弱，而临时的状态义增强；在人际功能上，由论元修饰语转为谓词修饰语后，情态意义和评价意义显著增强，具有了更高的言者主观性；在语篇功能上，隐喻式的状语被前景化，成为小句的焦点或次级焦点。

最后，我们用系统功能语法的另一分支——加的夫语法对汉语宾语指向状语作进一步研究。同悉尼语法相比，加的夫语法的一个重要特点是对及物性系统的分类更细，每种过程都被分为几个次类，而且基于语料库统计了各种过程和参与者角色以及环境成分之间的组配百分比。这些变化都提高了加的夫语法研究的客观性和描写的精密度（Fawcett, 2008，2009；黄国文等, 2008）。Dixon（2005：86）从类型学出发认为形容词包括维度、物理属性、颜色、价值、年龄四个核心范畴，它们的典型功能都是修饰具体名词。首先，我们在每个核心范畴中选取10个典型形容词，并变换为复杂形式[5]，如厚厚地、软软地、浓浓地、热乎乎地、黑乎乎地等。然后，在语料库[6]中对它们检索。最后，用加的夫语法对包含宾语指向状语的句子进行统计分析。我们发现四点规律：（1）汉语宾语指向状语主要出现在动作过程和关系过程[7]中。（2）在动作过程中，小句参与者角色包括受事和产物（created），如例（42）、（43）。（3）在关系过程中，宾语指向状语仅能在处所（locational）次类中出现，如例（45）。按照加的夫语法，例（44）、（46）都是关系过程中的趋向次类（directional），所以不能接受。由此可见，参与者角色与过程类型的组配能对环境角色的选择形成限制。进一步说，加的夫语法的及物性分析对悉尼语法构成了有益补充。（4）宾语指向状语主要出现在小说、散文等语体，而在口语和科技语体

4 加的夫语法创始人 Fawcett 提供了例句：“Ivy thickly sliced the potatoes.”，但类似用法在英语中很少。感谢 Robin Fawcett 教授和 Gordon Tucker 博士耐心回答笔者关于加的夫语法对修饰语研究的问题。

5 汉语形容词作状语一般要经过重叠变为复杂形式，主要的重叠方式有 AA 式、ABB 式和 AABB 式，这些形式手段主要是为了满足语法需要，对词汇意义只有程度影响而无本质改变。

6 语料来源包括北京大学现代汉语语料库、中国传媒大学有声媒体语言文本语料库和百度、谷歌搜索结果。

7 加的夫语法的动作过程（action process）与悉尼语法的物质过程（material process）比较接近，但把一部分物质过程划为关系过程。

中很少见。原因是语义重组需要对一致式的语义组配做进一步认知加工，这不符合口语中信息被在线即时处理的要求，而错位修饰体现的言者主观性又不符合科技语体的客观性要求。

（42）这家汤还是蛮香，天冷的时候热热地吃上一大碗很舒服。

（43）把果汁浓浓地泡上一杯，一口咽下。

（44）*他浓浓地端来一杯茶。

（45）石阶上都厚厚地堆满了水沫似的雪。

（46）*他厚厚地给我几本书。

（47）He made a cup of strong tea。

英、汉宾语修饰语的不同体现形式是语言的象似性和经济性两大动因竞争的结果。对宾语修饰语而言，英语是象似性优势语言，汉语是经济性优势语言。象似性体现为形式与意义的直接对应，符合语言解码的需要，是一致式的使用动因。如例（47）所示，英语的宾语修饰语和中心语紧邻，相关语义靠近，因此符合了距离象似性的要求。刘承宇（2005）提出名物化是经济性驱动的。语法隐喻是对一致式的再语法化，原有词汇通过语义与句法之间的互动被赋予了更多的意义，所以使用语法隐喻的基本动因就是经济性。经济性，又称省力原则，符合语言编码的需要。汉语的部分宾语修饰语能够被前置成为小句的信息焦点；前置的焦点信息能被优先处理，体现了经济性的要求。值得注意的是语法隐喻满足了编码的经济性，但同时违背了象似性，因此增加了解码成本，需要在形式上作出补偿。汉语是采用了重读和形态标记两个手段：如例（43）中“浓浓地”需要重读，而无标记小句的重音大多是落在句尾的自然焦点上；与一致式的定中结构相比，隐喻式的状语必须使用形容词的复杂形式，而且必须加形态标记“地”。

4. 结语

语法隐喻研究的重要性至少体现在三点。首先，语法隐喻是系统功能语言学中认知研究的主要内容。其次，语法隐喻是研究一类形义错配现象，而为形义错配提供合理解释是众多语言学理论特别是语法理论的一个核心任务。最后，语法隐喻属于系统功能语言学的界面研究，它既包含了语言结构的词法、句法、语篇界面研究，也包含了语言系统的语义、句法界面研究。

本文从三个方面对语法隐喻理论做了补充。首先，本文以形似性为基础，以语义变化方式为标准对语法隐喻作了分类。新的分类模式明确了语法隐喻的研究对象，保证了语法隐喻理论的自洽性和研究的系统性。其次，本文从收益和损耗两个方面分析了语法隐喻的功能特征，为语法隐喻体现的“语言进化论”哲学观提供了更加全面的认识。“语言进化”是出于特定交际需要产生的“适应性”改变，交际功能获得收益的同时也伴随着损耗，因此常常需要形式手段的补偿。为满足不同的交际需要，不同类型的语法隐喻会有不同的语体选择。最后，通过英汉对比，本文探讨了语法隐喻的跨语言共性与个性。语义删减类和语义扩充类在使用上的不对称体现了跨语言共性。语法隐喻的跨语言个性体现为两种情况：（1）不同语言有相似的语法隐喻类型，但各自的语法隐喻度不同。例如名物化被看作是语法隐喻的典型代表，但名物化在古汉语和现代汉语里都非常普遍，这说明汉语中名物化的语法隐喻度远低于英语。这并不能证明汉语比英语发达，或者汉语的进化程度高于英语，原因可能是英汉语中名词与动词之间的关系存在类型差异（沈家煊, 2012）。（2）相似的语义概念在一种语言中体现为一致式，而在另一语言里有一致式和隐喻式两种形式。宾语修饰语在英汉语中的不同体现便是如此。

参考文献

Dixon, R. M. W. 2005. *A Semantic Approach to English Grammar*. Oxford: Oxford University Press.

Fawcett, R. 2008. *Invitation to Systemic Functional Linguistics through the Cardiff Grammar: An Extension and Simplification of Halliday's Systemic Functional Grammar* (3rd edition). London: Equinox.

Fawcett, R. 2009. *Functional Syntax Handbook: Analyzing English at the Level of Form*. London: Equinox.

Halliday, M. A. K. 1984. Grammatical Metaphor in English and Chinese. In B, Hong (ed.) *New Papers on Chinese Language Use*. Research School of Pacific Studies, the Australian National University.

Halliday, M. A. K. 1998/2005. Things and Relations: Regrammaticizing Experience as Technical Knowledge. In J. J. Webster (ed.) *The Language of Science*. London: Continuum, 49-101.

Halliday, M. A. K. & C. M. I. M. Matthiessen. 1999. *Construing Experience through Meaning: A Language-Based Approach to Cognition*. London: Cassell.

Halliday, M. A. K. & C. M. I. M. Matthiessen. 2004. *An Introduction to Functional Grammar* (3rd edition). London: Arnold.

Halliday, M. A. K., Z. L. Hu & Y. S. Zhu. 2010. Interviewing Professor M.A.K. Halliday by Hu Zhuanglin and Zhu Yongsheng. *Foreign Languages in China*, 6: 17-24.

Martin, J. R. 1992. *English Text: System and Structure*. Amsterdam: Benjamins.

Martin, J. R. & P. R. R.White. 2008. *The Language of Evaluation: Appraisal in English*. Beijing: Foreign Language Teaching and Research Press.

Pustejovsky, J. 2011. Coercion in a General Theory of Argument Selection. *Linguistics*, 49(6): 1401-1431.

Ravelli, L. J. 2003. Renewal of Connection: Integrating Theory and Practice in an Understanding of Grammatical Metaphor. In M, Taverniers & L. J. Ravelli (eds.) *Grammatical Metaphor: Views from Systemic Functional Linguistics*. Amsterdam: Benjamins, 37-64.

Taverniers, M. 2008. Interpersonal Grammatical Metaphor as Double Scoping and Double Grounding. *Word*, 59: 1-31.

Taverniers, M. 2011. The Syntax-semantics Interface in Systemic Functional Grammar: Halliday's Interpretation of the Hjelmslevian Model of Stratification. *Journal of Pragmatics*, 43: 1100-1126.

丛迎旭，2011，概念语法隐喻研究的限制与扩展，《外国语》（5）：46-53。

范文芳，2007，试论语法隐喻的综合模式，《外语教学》（4）：12-15。

何伟，2008，语法隐喻：形式变体和意义变体，《解放军外国语学院学报》（3）：1-6。

侯建波，2008，语法隐喻：新解与反思，《外语教学》（5）：28-32。

胡壮麟，2000，评语法隐喻的韩礼德模式，《外语教学与研究》（2）：88-94。

黄国文、何伟、廖楚燕等，2008，《系统功能语法入门：加的夫模式》。北京：北京大学出版社。

刘承宇，2005，概念隐喻与人际隐喻级转移的逆向性，《外语教学与研究》（4）：289-293。

沈家煊，2012，怎样对比才有说服力——以英汉名动对比为例，《现代外语》（1）：1-13。

张德禄、赵静，2008，论语法概念隐喻中一致式与隐喻式的形似性原则，《外国语》（6）：25-32。

赵艳芳，2001，《认知语言学概论》。上海：上海外语教育出版社。

朱永生、严世清，2001，《系统功能语言学多维思考》。上海：上海外语教育出版社。

国际商务谈判中的语法隐喻

毛凡宇

江西财经大学

1. 引言

随着全球经济一体化的不断深入，区域间的经济贸易日益频繁。国际商务谈判成为经贸领域中一项不可缺少的实践活动。商务谈判是谈判者之间面对面的交流，商品贸易和服务的提供是通过谈判中建立的交易关系而进行的。在商务英语谈判中，双方就会经常运用隐喻进行交流和沟通，而且在谈判中，遇到争辩不休的危急情况或急于解决某个问题时，人们通常会运用隐喻。隐喻在商务谈判中对于人们如何感知目前的状况和对该状况应做出怎样的反应起到核心的作用。我们可以“听”出他们真正想说的是什么，是如何思考的，态度怎样（Schneider，2006）。这些信息也将指导我们如何应对或处理当时的状况。同时我们的谈话中出现的隐喻也会向对方表明我们一些有意识的和无意识的观点和态度。因此隐喻在商务英语谈判中起着举足轻重的作用。要充分注重企业间的商务谈判的措辞和用语，在把握和尊重对方态度的基础上，通过实施相关的语言策略，进而获取谈判的成功。目前，国内外学者对国际商务谈判英语中的语用策略已进行了大量的研究，并取得了丰硕的成果，但对于国际商务谈判英语中的语法隐喻现象研究，却很少见。鉴于此，本文将从系统功能语法的角度对国际商务英语谈判中的语法隐喻现象做一试探性的研究，旨在更好地观察和研究商务谈判英语的相关特点，为外贸企业的商务谈判提供相关借鉴。

2. 语法隐喻

隐喻是语言的根本特性，是人类语言或思维不可或缺的基础。M.A.K. Halliday根据语言中所体现的纯理功能，提出了语法隐喻的概念。它把原来修辞学的隐喻概念运用到语言研究，为隐喻研究开辟了一个新视角。他认为语法隐喻可分为概念隐喻和人际隐喻。概念隐喻指一个过程隐喻另一个过程，隐喻化的小句的功能成分也随之转化；人际隐喻是指情态与语气的隐喻（Halliday，2000）。Martin在此基础上指出语法隐喻还应包含语篇隐喻，即在语篇中相连接的语句之间所存在的语法隐喻。系统功能语言学认为语言的隐喻化过程中词的意义没有发生变化，变化的是它们的语法性状。判断语法隐喻的一对重要的概念是：一致式（congruent form）和隐喻式（metaphorical form）。语法隐喻是对一致式的偏离。语法隐喻作为语言表达的一种特殊形式，是语篇文体特征的具体表现。

3. 商务谈判中的语法隐喻

韩礼德认为语言的运用都是为了在特定的情景下实现一定的功能。商务英语是英语的一种社会功能的变体，是英语在商务活动中的应用，是交易双方通过书信、E-mail等形式进行的双向交流与沟通。受情景语境的制约，商务英语在语言表达形式和谋篇机制上表现出不同于其他文体的语言表达形式——语法隐喻。商务英语中的语法隐喻不仅传递信息，更重要的是通过这种信息传递的过程来影响对方做出相应的反应。

3.1 概念语法隐喻

Halliday把语言的纯理功能分为三种：概念功能、人际功能和语篇功能。概念功能指人们用语言来谈论他们在现实生活中的各种经历，描述周围所发生的事件或情形。作为表现人类活动经验的概念其主要体现形式为“及物性”系统。及物性系统包含三个成分：参与者、过程和环境，过程是及物性系统的核心成分，包括物质过程、心理过程、关系过程、行为过程、言语过程和存在过程。概念隐喻在商务英语中的表现之一是“及物性”系统中的各个过程的隐喻化，随着隐喻化的出现，过程也相应发生了变化，一个过程可以隐喻化为另一个过程。同时，随着过程的变化，过程中的参与者、环境等功能角色也发生相应的变化；随着功能角色的变化，它们在词汇语法层的体现形式也发生相应的变化。如：

（1）a. There is a good market for your T-shirts in the eastern part of our country（存在）

b. Your T shirts can find a ready market in the eastern part of our country（心理）

（2）a. If he wants to make any changes，we can make minor alternations then（行为）

b. If he wants to make any changes，minor alternations can be made then（物质）

概念隐喻在商务英语谈判中的另一个表现是“名物化”。语法隐喻中的名词化隐喻是构建语法隐喻的最有力手段。商务英语谈判中运用了大量的名词化隐喻，在谈判语篇中起着重要的作用。语法隐喻化在语义上是“事物化”，在语法上表现为名物化。Halliday曾指出名物化是创造语法隐喻唯一最有力的方法。通过这种方法，在一致式中作为过程的动词和作为特征的形容词被隐喻转换为名词；它们的作用已不再是在小句中充当过程或属性，而是以名词词组的形式表达“事物性”。如：

（3）a. You are requested to answer immediately without fail.

b. A prompt answer would be highly appreciated.

（4）a. Please ship the goods before August 15 so that we can catch the selling season.

b. Please effect shipment of the goods before August 15 so that we can catch the selling season.

上两例中，a句为一致式，b句为隐喻式，a句中体现事物过程的动词，换做了b句中相对应的名词。随着一致式转化为隐喻式，概念功能词汇语法层中表达经验意义的动词体现为名物化，经验意义被抽象化。b句就事论事，不涉及具体人物，可避免指责读者之嫌，避免有归咎他人之嫌，这样可以保护读者的自尊心，同时帮助说话人委婉地传达不利的信息。过程名词化后，其他句子成分也会相应有所改变，如（4）a中的参与者the goods在b中变成了名词shipment的修饰语。

3.2 人际语法隐喻

语言是社会活动的产物。作为人类交际的工具，它在人类的社会活动中发挥多种功能。功能语法的创始人韩礼德认为，一个小句具有概念、人际、语篇三个元功能，其中，人们使用语言与别人交往，表达自己身份、态度以及他对事物的推断等功能称为人际功能。通过人际功能，讲话者可以使自己参与到某一情景语境中，来表达态度和评价，并试图影响别人的态度和行为；同时表达与情景有关的讲话人和听话人之间的社会关系，即讲话人与听话人在交际过程中所扮演的角色之间的关系。在系统功能语言学的理论框架中，人际隐喻包含语气系统和情态系统的语法隐喻。得体的商务英语交际除了词汇、语法准确无误外，在话语语气、情态的选择与使用上也是十分讲究的。

3.2.1 语气系统的语法隐喻

语气系统的功能是表达人们希望通过讲话所达到的目的。语气系统把英语句子分为陈述句、疑问句和祈使句。这三种语气的基本功能是：陈述语气体现陈述功能，疑问语气体现疑问功能，祈使语气体现提供和命令功能。各种语气与其功能之间表现为“一致的”关系。然而，在实际交际过程中，“语气与言语功能之间并非一一对应的关系。一种言语功能可以由不同的语气来体现，一种语气也可以体现不同的言语功能。”（常晨光，2001）比如说，陈述语气除了体现陈述功能以外，还可以用来表示提问和请求；请求除了用祈使语气表示以外，疑问语气同样可以实现该功能。这类语气变异现象，即从一种语气域向另一种语气域转移，就产生了语气隐喻。

在商务语篇中，一方面，说话者给予受话者关于本公司和产品或服务的信息；另一方面，说话者要求受话者采取行动购买产品或服务。在商务英语交际中，在语气的选择与使用上十分讲究，措辞应谦恭有礼、语气委婉、亲切自然。试比较：

（5）a. Make similar inquiries at your end.

b. We suggest that you make similar inquiries at your end.

c. Meanwhile, may we suggest that you make similar inquiries at your end?

例5中，a句使用了祈使句，口气显得强硬，把自己的想法强加于对方违背了平等合作的商务交际原则；b句虽没有a句的咄咄逼人之势，但仍过于直接；c句为疑问句，通过“询问”方式间接要求对方则显得谦和，避免了过于率直而给人予盛气凌人的架势。

3.2.2 情态系统的语法隐喻

情态表达几乎涉及商业活动的各个领域和交易过程的各个环节。情态系统是表达说话者对事物的判断或评价的语义系统。作为人际意义的重要组成部分之一，情态系统所表达的意义是从说话者本人角度对其命题的成功性和有效性所作的判断，在命令中要求对方承担的义务，或在提议中要表达的个人意愿。韩礼德把情态系统划分为情态化和意态化。情态是说话人对命题的可能性的判断，包括可能性阶（possible、probable、certain）和通常性阶（sometimes、usually、always）。意态是说话人对提议的可希望性的判断，包括责任阶（allowed、supposed、required）和倾向性阶（willing、keen、determine）。但无论是用以交流信息的情态意义，还是用以交流物品和服务的意态意义，都需要通过词汇语法层的小句来实现，表达言语的概率与频率、责任、义务和意愿等功能。此外，情态还可以从主观和客观这两个角度来表达，韩礼德称其为情态的取向：显性主观；隐性主观；显性客观；隐性客观。韩礼德并指出，由小句表达的显性主观和显性客观都是隐喻性的。在国际商务谈判中，情态助动词是表达礼貌、文雅和规则等人际功能的主要手段之一，其传达其情感的功能，有助于实现商务活动的目的。如：

（6）They must have got wet after they arrived in Hong Kong.（可能性）

（7）This offer must be withdrawn if not accepted within five days.（义务）

在情态意义的表达上，还会出现隐喻体现形式，也就是说，情态隐喻可以由小句表达，如例6、例7可以分别改写为：

It is very certain that they had got wet after they arrived in Hong Kong.

It is necessary that we withdraw this offer if it is not accepted within five days.

另外，名词化（如：the possibility/likelihood/probability/certainty of...）是产生情态隐喻的又一个途径。通过名词化将情态意义构建成一个“事物”，这样就掩盖了情态的来源，成为明确的客观取向。英语情态隐喻的存在有着重要的社会文化意义，复杂的情态系统往往是与不同的交际需求、复杂的人际关系或者微妙的社会习俗等直接相关的。为达到某种特殊的目的或效果，说话者有时会故意采用情态的明确主观隐喻形式，强调自己的看法或判断的不确定性，以表示客气或对对方的尊重；有时也会采用明确客观的情态取向，使自己的判断或断言客观化，以隐藏真正的情态来源。

4. 语法隐喻在国际商务谈判中的功能

概念语法隐喻的重要实现手段是名词化。名词化隐喻大量地出现在商务英语谈判的书面语篇中，它使得语篇更加简洁、正式和客观，可以说名词化隐喻使用频率越高，文体的正式程度就越高。黄利民（2011）在韩礼德语法隐喻分类的基础上，发现科技语篇中存在两种特有的语法隐喻形式，即单个形容词和单个名词可以充当环境成分；语法隐喻在科技语篇中具有语篇衔接和语类功能。正因如此，名词化隐喻在商务英语谈判中应用也相当广泛，并具有如下功能：

4.1 概念隐喻的功能

4.1.1 提高商务谈判的简洁性

名词化隐喻的功能之一就是使语篇更具简洁性。通过名词化，原来的小句被"打包"成名词性词组，若干个小句被"打包"成一个小句，语篇的句数减少，但每句的信息量却相对增大。因此名词化隐喻可使语篇更简洁、更紧凑。例如：

a. You fail to pack the goods in the seaworthy cartons. As a result, the goods are damaged during transit.

b. Your failure to pack the goods in the seaworthy cartons results in the damage of the goods during transit.

a句中的动词fail和damaged经过名词化后，合并成b句一个简单句。可见，名词化隐喻能以较少的文字表达更多的内容，从而起到浓缩信息、提高句子信息密度的作用，使文章更加简洁。同时，动词（fail）名词化（failure）后，原来口语化的表达变为抽象的书面语，较少的语言表达出更多的内容，使语篇更具正式性。

4.1.2 加强商务谈判的客观性

名词化有利于表达客观真理和客观事实。名词化把过程变成了参与者，从而省略了逻辑上的参与者，进而使语篇显得更加客观。例如：

a. Only if you execute our order punctually, can we receive the goods on time.

b. Punctual execution of the order will ensure punctual receipt of the goods.

名词化后的b句，省略了主观性较强的参与者"you"和"we"，使句子不受行为人情感因素的影响，语义表达得更客观、真实。

4.2 情态隐喻的功能

在商务谈判中，谈判者之间互动的关键在于双方的言辞与态度。一句话或一种口气，能牵动双方的反应，既微妙又有绝对的影响力。商务谈判英语的使用要求体现礼貌性，更要体现策略和稳妥性。商务英语中情态的使用有利于其交际目的的实现。这就是情态表达在商务英语中的人际功能：

4.2.1 礼貌功能：

由于"语言是表达礼貌的重要手段"（何自然，1997），礼貌策略往往通过语言来实现。情态具有"归一性"，所涵盖的情态意义是在"归一度"之间，是从发话人的角度对其命题的成功性和有效性所作的判断，或在命令中要求对方承担的义务，或在提议中要表达的个人意愿，所以言语交际中恰当地使用情态表达，是为了把话语说得更加含蓄委婉、礼貌客气。Lakoff（1993）认为：在某些类型的言语交际中，礼貌的因素在决定会话的有效性中占上风。Leech（1983）对言语行为中的礼貌现象进行了深入细致的研究以后，在其《语用学原则》一书中提出了"礼貌原则"。如：

a. We cannot make a profit with those numbers.（这样的价格我们赚不了钱。）
b. How can we make a profit with those numbers?（这样的价格我们怎么能赚钱?!）

谈判时虽要坚持原则，但最好不要给人强硬的印象。这两句话中，b是语气隐喻，它用疑问句来表达"We cannot make a profit with those numbers."这一事实，措辞较婉转、礼貌，避免了过于率直而给人盛气凌人的架势，通过"询问"方式间接要求对方则显得谦和，具有更多的磋商余地，更有利达成贸易协议。

在商务谈判中，难免会出现唇枪舌剑的局面，甚至僵局，但是情态表达往往使措辞激烈的命题变得委婉、礼貌得体，让交际对方更易于接受。因此，对于情态表达的礼貌功能的把握，一定要理解其所在的语境，确定其真实的情态意义。

4.2.2 自我保护功能

在商务交际过程中，发话人总要表达自己的观点和态度，或表明自己的立场。为了稳妥全面地实现这一目的，避免绝对化和极端化，发话人可以采用模糊的策略，使言语行为的力度减弱，使之不易被否定。"情态的或模糊的表达只是在对交际不利时才使用"（刘伯茹，2004），这样，既给言语接收者以考虑选择的余地，同时又减轻了发话者对观点和结论所承担的责任，使发话者立于不败之地。情态表达有时以隐喻形式出现，发话者采用客观的情态取向，使自己的判断或断言客观化，以隐藏真正的情态来源。如：

It is required that the stipulations in the relative credit be in exact accordance with the stated in the Sales Confirmation.

通过这个情态隐喻，发话者的个人态度被"非个人化"，模糊了命令的来源。

通过情态的明确客观形式，将情态意义装扮成命题以小句的形式出现，或将情态意义名物化，使个人观点似乎变成了一个固有的特征或无法质疑事实，以便使读者更容易接受其看法（袁娅娅，2007）。发话者借用这种“作者缺席”的隐喻情态手段，最大程度地保护了自己的面子，从而达到发话者自我保护的目的。

在商务英语谈判中，情态表达是一种积极修辞，不仅委婉、礼貌、稳妥地表达交际双方的意愿，明确交际双方的责权义务，而且能缓和紧张的气氛，还能表达愿和对方合作沟通的良好意愿，化险为夷，实现自我保护。

5. 结语

系统功能语言学认为语言是人类进化的产物，意义是人类上层意识的主要方式。 语法隐喻体现了意义进化论的思想，是语言重塑人类经验的一种重要途径（赵霞，2012）。语法隐喻作为一种特殊的语言现象，在国际商务谈判中表现出其自身的一些特点。对国际商务谈判中的概念隐喻和人际隐喻及其特点的分析，有助于我们进一步深刻了解商务英语作为一种重要的功能变体的语法和语用功能。名词化是语法隐喻的一种重要手段，广泛用于书面语体，它使商务谈判语篇更加简洁、正式、客观，同时使语篇衔接得更紧密、合理。人际语法隐喻的使用可以帮助谈判者委婉、礼貌、策略地表明己方观点，可以有效地规定和明确交际双方的责权，有利于谈判双方形成良好的长期合作关系。

通过以上分析，我们发现国际商务谈判中也不乏语法隐喻现象。本文从语法隐喻角度来分析和探讨商务谈判英语的相关特点，为谈判英语的研究展现了一个新的视角，同时也为谈判者提供了相关借鉴。语法隐喻大大丰富了语言体系，掌握名词化隐喻有助于对商务语篇的分析和理解，对商务谈判的翻译和写作也起着重大的指导作用。

参考文献

Halliday, M. A. K. 2000. *An Introduction to Functional Grammar* (2nd edition). Beijing: Foreign Language Teaching and Research Press.

Lakoff, G. 1993. The Contemporary Theory of Metaphor. In Ortony & Andrew (eds.) *Metaphor and Thought* (2nd edition), Cambridge.

Leech, G. H. 1983. *Principles of Pragnlatics*. London: Longrllan.

Schneider, A. 2006. *The Road to Hell is Paved with Metaphors*. Washington, D.C.

常晨光, 2001, 英语中的人际语法隐喻,《外语与外语教学》(7): 6-8。

何自然, 1997,《语用学与英语学习》。上海：上海外语教育出版社。

黄利民, 2011, 语法隐喻在科技语篇中的体现形式及语篇功能,《厦门理工学院学报》

（3）：94-98。
刘伯茹，2004，论大学生英语阅读过程中的词汇附带习得，《重庆交通学院学报（社科版）》（3）：109-112。
袁娅娅，2007，模糊语言在商务英语谈判中的语用功能与表达，《湖北大学成人教育学院学报》（6）：77-78。
赵霞，2012，基于意义进化理论的语法隐喻研究，《内蒙古大学学报（哲学社会科学版）》（7）：94-100。

外向型英汉文化教材话语态度介入策略比较[1]

陈瑜敏

中山大学

1. 引言：跨文化视阈下文化传播的话语方式研究

近年来，汉语国际教育中的文化传播日益受到政府部门和学界的关注，通过比较中外话语体系和文化差异，探索文化传播的方略和路径也逐渐成为共识之一。如许琳（2012：24）指出，“我们所遭遇的种种困难和问题……深层次的原因是中外文化差异和话语体系不同，是跨文化交际能力缺乏”。赵金铭（2011：90）指出，目前汉语国际教育中的文化传播方式“有些急功近利，过于直白，多少带有为介绍中华文化而讲文化的倾向”，并提出研究者应关注“如何与学习者的本土文化相结合，如何克服中外不同话语体系和不同文化差异所带来的障碍，用国外学习者容易接受和理解的方式，来介绍中华文化”。而比较中外话语体系的异同，离不开对文本语料的系统分析。考察其他语种作为第二语言的文化教材，并与汉语文化教材进行系统比较，可为汉语文化教材的编写和研发提供可借鉴的经验（周小兵等，2010：6）。

本文以外向型英汉文化教材为分析对象，比较两类教材态度介入策略的异同。所考察的英语文化教材为英语国家本国人编写的、面向英语作为二语/外语学习者的英美概况教材；汉语文化教材为来华留学生广泛使用的中国概况教材。中国概况课是来华接受学历教育的外国留学生的必修课之一，在汉语国际教育文化课程中具有较强的代表性。以中国概况为代表的文化课程所讲授的文化事实往往涉及态度、视角和价值判断，文化知识包括感情、态度、视角和世界观等主观因素（祖晓梅、陆平舟，2006：122）。

关于汉语文化教材话语态度的研究表明，文化教材中广泛存在表达情感态度的语言资源，叙述体和对话体课文中引起态度类型和倾向变化的因素和方式存在差异，文化教材中态度意义的实现具有显性铭刻与隐形标记两种方式（陈瑜敏，2010：6）。然而，在用语言表达态度时作者是直陈所思还是间接表达，态度介入方式在不同语种文化教材中有何异同，如何有效借鉴留学生本族语言的话语方式，运用各类

1 本文曾发表于《中国外语》2013 年第 4 期。

介入策略，从而使话语方式更容易为学习者理解和接受，是教学资源开发过程中亟待研究的问题。本文试图在功能语篇分析的视阈中对这一问题进行探讨。

2. 文化教材话语态度介入策略分析

本文依据的理论框架为人际意义评价理论的介入系统（Martin, 2000; Martin & White, 2005）。介入系统（Engagement System）是语篇评价系统网络中的一个范畴，借助介入系统，分析者可以考察态度表达时语言来源是否具有对话性，以及对话空间扩展和压缩的具体实现方式。

2.1 介入与话语对话性体现方式

语言使用者在表达态度时，可以直截了当地表达所思所想，也可以采用或明确或隐晦的方式，假借他人的观点或立场来间接表明自己的态度。在功能话语研究中，J. R. Martin及其同事P. R. R. White用自言（monogloss）和借言（heterogloss）两个范畴分析态度表达的具体方式。其中“借言”涉及话语的对话性，常见的借言手段包括投射（projection）、情态（modality）和让步（concession）（Martin & White, 2005：36）。投射将语篇以外的立场、观点引入语篇之中，所提及的观点支持语篇中作者的声音。例如，

（1）... this 24/7 access has a huge impact on leisure time and American's ability to relax. Joe Robinson, in his book *Work to Live: Reclaim Your Life, Health, Family, and Sanity*, states, "The line between work and home has become so blurred that the only way you can tell them apart is that one has a bed."

（see *American Ways*, 225）

（2）中国人常说，“一方水土养一方人”。这是因为中国的饮食文化具有鲜明的地域特色。

（见《中国概况》2011年版［以下简称《中·2011》］, 123）

例（1）介绍了频繁上网的习惯对美国人的业余时间带来了强大的冲击，作者运用投射的语言手段，引用Joe Robinson关于工作和家庭生活的界限越来越模糊的原话来支持自己的观点。例（2）在阐释中国饮食文化具有地域特点时，也运用了投射手段，引用俗谚说明由于每个地区的物候环境不同，人们的生活方式、性格观念也随之不同。与例（1）一样，例（2）中的引述同样支持语篇中作者的观点。

使用情态词也是话语多声的另一种体现方式。例如，

（3）If workers are laid off through no fault of their own, they may be eligible for unemployment compensation.

（see *The U.S.A.*, 205）

（4）应该说中国人对世界的关注度还是很高的。

（见《中·2011》, 137）

例（3）中的情态词“may”表示肯定推测，意为被无故辞职的工人有可能获得失业补偿。“may”表肯定推测，但同时也暗含存在更为确定、不确定甚至否定推测的可能性。例（4）中的情态词“应该说”也表示肯定的推断，但同时也暗含存在其他推测的可能。即使最肯定的情态表达也暗示话语中的立场不只过是众多立场的其中一种（Martin & White, 2005：104-106）。使用情态词的微妙之处在于，作者在主张一种观点的同时，暗示其他声音有可能对所主张的立场持赞同或反对意见。换言之，情态词的使用在一定程度上扩大了语篇对话的空间。

话语多声的实现方式还包括让步词语的使用。譬如，

（5）A view long held by many foreigners is that it takes time to make friends with the English, <u>but</u> that then it becomes something significant and permanent.

（see *Britain — Culture Smart*, 132）

（6）近些年，在国有大中型企业向市场经济过渡的过程中，有许多职工下岗，待业和失业率上升，<u>但</u>国家除了保证下岗职工最低生活收入外，还开辟了许多再就业的渠道。

（见《中国概况》2003年版［以下简称《中·2003》］, 66）

例（5）中“but”表示让步，其语篇功能为“反预期（counter-expectancy）”（Martin & White, 2005：118），用于连接两个关系密切但叙述重点有所变化的命题。经由让步词“but”，前一命题“和英国人交朋友虽然需要一段时间”和后一命题“这种友谊却是持久而有价值的”之间产生了对话。例（6）中让步词语“但”同样具有反预期功能，引出相应的保障措施，话语中前后两种声音存在对话性。

为了更系统地考察话语中体现对话性和实现多声互动的各类语言资源，Martin及其同事从M. Bakhtin（1981, 1986）关于对话（dialogism）和多声（heteroglossia）的理论中得到启发，他们最初从话源（intra/extra-vocalisation）的角度（即对话的声音来源于话语内部还是话语外部）来建构介入系统（White, 1998）。随着研究的深入，近年Martin & White对介入系统中借言范畴的划分标准作了进一步调整，将对话性的扩展和压缩（dialogic expansion/contraction）作为划分借言的主要参数，而话源则作为辅助参考标准（Martin & White, 2005）。以对话性的扩展和压缩作为主要分析框架，其优越性在于能较好地解释为何外部声源也存在不同程度的对话性开放和关闭（王振华、路洋, 2010：55）。下文从对话空间扩展和压缩的角度，分析英汉文化教材中态度介入策略的语言特征。

2.2 扩展与压缩对话空间的策略分析

对话空间的扩展和压缩指的是语言资源在语义功能上是积极地扩展多声互动的空间，还是挑战、限制其他声音和立场（Martin & White, 2005：102）。其中扩展对话空间的策略包括“包容（Entertain）”和“归属（Attribute）”两种方式。英语中“包容”的常见实现方式包括表推测的副词“perhaps”“probably”“possibly”、

情态动词“may/ can/ must/ would（be）”、表推测的小句“It seems that...” “It is probable that...” “Estimates are that...”等。汉语中的“包容”策略可通过语气副词“或许”“恐怕”“大概”、表示必然的副词“会”“应该”等语言手段来体现。上文例（3）和例（4）中的情态词也属于包容。包容之所以扩展了对话的空间，是因为它表明语篇中的声音所暗示的定位只是关于某个论题的其中一种立场，这就为其他可能的定位和立场在不同程度上打开了对话的空间。

“归属”是扩展对话空间的另一种策略。与包容不同的是，它将文本中的命题“归属”为该语篇之外某个声音的立场或看法。根据作者对这一立场的态度不同，归属又可分为“承认（Acknowledge）”和“疏远（Distance）”。“承认”表明作者转述并接受外部声音的观点，常见的实现方式包括表转述的动词和短语，比如例（1）、例（2）中对俗语和名言的投射引用。英汉教材中表“承认”的例子还有“President George W. Bush mentioned in his State of the Union address...” “The Travel Industry of America reports that...”“据调查，……”“据统计，……”等。“疏远”在态度取向方面与承认不同，作者在引述的同时拒绝外部声音的看法。文化教材中疏远策略使用不多，例如

（7）Vince Lombardi, a famous professional football coach, was often criticized for stating that winning is the “only thing” that matters in sports.

（see *American Ways*, 217）

例（7）在引述足球教练Vince Lombardi的“胜利是体育中‘唯一’应追求的事情”观点时，通过“was often criticized for stating that...”明确表示自己并不赞同这一观点。

再来看对话性压缩的实现方式。压缩对话空间的策略包括“声明（Proclaim）”和“否认（Disclaim）”。声明又可分为“赞同（Concur）”、“宣布（Pronounce）”和“认可（Endorse）”三个范畴。“赞同”将命题表述为无可厚非、不可推翻的陈述，其词汇语法体现形式包括表示确认或肯定的“of course”“admittedly”“当然”“……是再贴切不过的”等。“宣布”以强调的方式表明语言使用者的态度，从而排除其他可能性，其体现方式包括“indeed”“really”“确实”“无不……”等。“认可”与“赞同”和“宣布”的差别在于，“认可”借助外部权威的声音来说明文本中命题的真实性，常见体现方式比如“Studies have shown/demonstrated/proven that...”等。

对话性压缩的另一策略为“否认”。否认包括“否定（Deny）”和“反预期（Counter）”。“否定”在引用某一观点的同时否定这一观点，否定词“no”“（did/have）not”“never”“不”“没有”等是常见的体现方式。“反预期”指作者在引用与命题相关但观点不同的外部声音时，通过让步词等语言手段引出事态或观点的另外一面，从而使预期受挫，常见表达包括“but”“surprisingly”“但”“尽管如此”等。

各类介入策略可以用系统网络的方式呈现。根据对话空间是扩展还是压缩（Martin & White, 2005），文化教材中的介入策略可用下图表示：

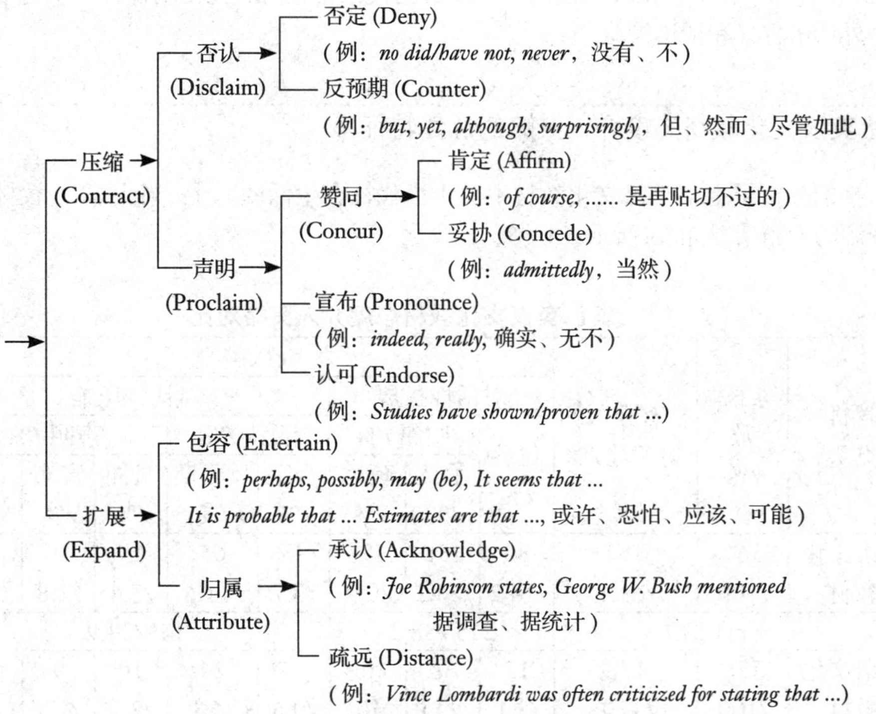

图1　介入系统（图中例子均取自英汉文化教材）

3. 英汉文化教材态度介入策略比较

在比较分析之前，我们先说明英汉教材的选择情况。为保证语料的可比性与研究的效度，我们对所考察教材的教学对象、课文主题、编写者和出版社的情况作了以下限定：均选自近年由所在国出版的外向型文化教材；课文主题为当代社会生活，包括衣食住行、经济生活、文化娱乐、家庭生活、社会交往等方面，共计六十一个语篇，涉及文化教材七部（包括中国概况教材三部、英国概况和美国概况教材各两部），均为纸质书面语篇。用功能语言学的术语来说，交际的语旨（tenor）、语场（field）和语式（mode）（Halliday, 1994; Martin, 1992）三个情景语境因素都得到了界定。

本文选择主题为当代社会生活的课文进行考察，其原因有二。其一、文化教材内容选择的标准之一，是以当代文化还是古代文化为主，以当代文化为主的教材对学习者了解该国当代文化、促进与该国人的交际很有帮助（周小兵等, 2010：3）。所考察的几部英汉文化教材都无一例外地包含当代社会生活这一话题。可见，对当下人们现实生活的介绍和阐释是目前中外文化教材共同关注的重要方面。其二、就第二语言教学中文化的定义而言，“文化是人们的生活方式”（祖晓梅、陆平舟，

2006：121）。在中外比较的视阈下考察对当代社会生活的文化阐释，可以更好地比较中外话语方式和话语策略。

3.1 英汉文化教材态度介入策略的总体特征

我们分析了七部英汉文化教材中关于当代社会生活的六十一个语篇，教材中介入资源的分布情况如表1所示：

表1 英汉文化教材态度介入策略对比

教材类型	句子总数/%	含有介入的句子数/%	介入类型							
			对话性扩展			对话性压缩				
			包容/%	归属/%		否认/%		声明/%		
				承认/%	疏远/%	否定/%	反预期/%	赞同/%	宣布/%	认可/%
英语文化教材	561/100	354/63.1	80/14.2	130/23.1	5/0.9	43/7.7	65/11.6	19/3.4	10/1.8	2/0.4
合计			215/38.2			139/24.9				
汉语文化教材	378/100	178/47.1	12/3.1	86/22.8	0/0	36/9.6	24/6.3	10/2.7	9/2.3	1/0.3
合计			98/25.9			80/21.2				

由表1可以看出，英语文化教材中涉及态度介入的句子数占总数的63.1%，汉语文化教材中态度介入的句子数也占47.1%。可见，富含介入策略的措辞是英汉文化教材的话语特征之一，这在英语文化教材中尤为显著。在向学习者介绍社会文化时，文化教材的编写者常常运用态度介入策略，具体包括援引权威观点、驳斥对立看法、直接表明作者立场、隐晦暗示态度倾向、强调语篇命题的正确性、从正反两面对比论述等。

3.2 对话性扩展策略比较

根据表1的统计可知，英语文化教材扩展对话空间的句子占总数的38.2%，在介入策略中占60.7%（215/354）；汉语文化教材含有对话性扩展策略的句子占句子总数的25.9%，在介入策略中占55.1%（98/178）。换言之，在英汉文化教材中扩展对话空间的语言资源均比压缩对话空间的语言资源使用率高，英语文化教材略为明显。就扩展对话空间的具体方式看，英汉文化教材的主要区别在于包容策略的使用，英语文化教材使用包容的句子数占14.2%，而汉语文化教材使用包容的句子数仅占3.1%。包容策略如“This may still be true.”“It seems to be the case that in many families this is now limited to Sunday lunch or supper.”“Perhaps the greatest change that has come to British sport in the last two decades has been commercialism." 表面上看似乎增加了命题的不确定性，但实际上暗示文本中的定位只是多种可能的定位之一，可协商的对话空间增加了。文化教材中包容策略的运用可使语篇的表述避免过于绝对，在某种程度上给予了读者思考和判断的空间。

下面考察扩展对话空间的另一策略——归属，根据对所引述内容的态度倾向不同，归属分为承认和疏远两类。疏远在汉语文化教材中很少使用，在英语文化教材中也仅为5例（占句子总数0.9%），如 "About two-thirds of adults claim to take part in some kind of activity, ..." "One of the great ironies about Britain is that..." 。如上文所述，疏远策略表明作者不同意所引述的观点，可增强语篇的批判性。

承认包括明确和非明确两种实现方式。教材中明确承认的例句有：

（8）Those who find themselves short of cash open their houses（the "stately homes of England", as they were famously described by Noel Coward）to the public and charge a fee for entry, ...

（see *Britain — Culture Smart*, 144）

（9）根据2010年9月中国政府公布的《留学中国计划》，到2020年，中国将成为亚洲最大的留学目的地国家，……

（见《中・2011》, 66）

非明确承认的例句包括：

（10）Cricket, for example, has always been primarily an English sport rather than a British one, ...hence the famous putdown of ungentlemanly behavior: "It's just not cricket".

（see *Contemporary Britain*, 199）

（11）据统计，城乡居民家庭每百户电视机拥有量超过100%,已经高于世界平均水平。

（《中国概况》2009年版［以下简称《中・2009》］, 148）

我们对英汉文化教材中明确承认和非明确承认的使用情况进行了比较（见表2）。

表2 英汉文化教材承认策略对比

教材类型	含有承认的句子数 /%	明确承认的句子数 /%	非明确承认的句子数 /%
英语文化教材	130 /100	44 /33.8	86 / 66.2
汉语文化教材	86 /100	13 /15.1	73 /84.9

由表2可知，汉语文化教材中明确承认所占比例较低（占15.1%），英语文化教材中虽然非明确承认仍占优势，但明确/非明确的比率较为平衡（分别占33.8%和66.2%）。明确承认提供了所引述观点的确切来源，使命题得到可查证依据的支持，可增强论述的信服力。

3.3 对话性压缩策略比较

如表1所示，在英汉文化教材中对话性压缩策略的使用率均低于对话性扩展策略。换言之，英汉文化教材在态度介入方面的主要话语特征为扩展对话空间，文化教材更多地以增加语篇协商空间（即包容）和引述语篇外的观点（即归属）的方式来增强对话和多声。

虽然对话性压缩并非英汉文化教材实现态度介入的最主要策略，但是在教材话语中仍具有其存在的必要性。就压缩对话空间的具体手段而言，英汉文化教材的主要区别在于反预期的使用情况不同。汉语文化教材中反预期策略的使用率为6.3%，英语文化教材中反预期策略的使用率则较高，为11.6%。反预期策略首先提出与话语中的命题相关但立场不同的前命题，再通过让步词引出真正的命题意图。前后命题表述的是关于某个问题或事态的两个方面，两个命题之间存在协商和对话。

4. 结语

有学者指出，“借鉴其他国家和民族文化走出去的策略”研究分为两个层次，“第一个层次是知己，第二个层次是知彼”（崔希亮, 2012：27）。本文尝试在这两个层面进行探索。比较英汉文化教材的态度介入策略，研究表明：

第一、富含介入策略的措辞是文化教材的话语特征之一。文化教材中对话性扩展策略的使用率高于对话性压缩策略，英汉文化教材均更多地以增加语篇协商空间和引述语篇外观点的方式来增强对话和多声。英语文化教材更为明显。

第二、就扩展对话空间的具体方式而言，英语文化教材中包容策略和明确承认策略的使用率较汉语文化教材高。包容策略可增强协商和对话，有助于给予读者思考和判断的空间。明确承认使命题有据可依，有助于增强语篇论述的理据和信服力。

第三、就压缩对话空间的具体手段看，英语文化教材中反预期策略的使用率较汉语文化教材高。反预期策略将相关而不相同的两个命题相联系，使论述更为全面客观。

本文从话语态度介入策略的角度比较了英汉文化教材话语方式的异同，全面考察中外教学话语方式和话语体系的异同需要从不同角度、采用多种方法进行分析。期待今后有更多研究采用不同视角、在多种教学语境中进行更为深入的探讨。

注：

本文研究的语料来自以下英汉文化教材：

Datesman, M.K., Crandall, J. & Kearny, E.N. 2005. *American Ways: An Introduction to American Culture* (3rd Edition). New York：Pearson Education.

McCormick, J. 2007. *Contemporary Britain* (2nd Edition). Hampshire: Macmillan.

Norbury, P. 2006. *Britain — Culture Smart: A Quick Guide to Customs & Etiquette*. London: Kuperard,.

Tiersky, E. & Tiersky, M. 2001. *The U.S.A.: Customs and Institutions* (4th Edition). New York: Pearson Education.

郭鹏、程龙、姜西良, 2011,《中国概况》。北京：高等教育出版社。

王顺洪, 2003,《中国概况》。北京：北京大学出版社。

肖立, 2009,《中国概况教程》。北京：北京大学出版社。

参考文献

Bakhtin, M. 1981. *The Dialogic Imagination: Four Essays*. M. Holquist (ed.) C. Emerson & M. Holquist (trans.). Austin: University of Texas Press.

Bakhtin, M. 1986. The Problem of Speech Genres. In C. Emerson & M. Holquist. (eds.) V. W. McGee. (trans.) *Speech Genres and Other Late Essays*. Austin: University of Texas Press.

Halliday, M. A. K. *An Introduction to Functional Grammar* (2nd edition). London: Arnold, 1994.

Martin, J. R. 1992. *English Text: System and Structure*. Amsterdam: Benjamins.

Martin, J. R. 2000. Beyond Exchange: Appraisal Systems in English. In S Hunston & G Thompson (eds.) *Evaluation in Text: Authorial Stance and the Construction of Discourse*. Oxford: Oxford University Press.

Martin, J. R. & P. R. R. White. 2005. *The Language of Evaluation: Appraisal in English*. London: Palgrave.

White, P. R. R. 1998. Telling Media Tales: The News Story as Rhetorics. Unpublished PhD thesis, University of Sydney.

陈瑜敏, 2010, 对外汉语文化教材话语态度资源分析,《语言教学与研究》(6): 1-7。

崔希亮, 2012, 汉语国际教育与中国文化走出去,《语言文字应用》(2): 25-27。

王振华、路洋, 2010, "介入系统"嬗变,《外语学刊》(3): 51-56。

许琳, 2012, 我们从哪里来，要到哪里去,《语言文字应用》(2): 23-25。

赵金铭, 2011, 国际汉语教育研究的现状与拓展,《语言教学与研究》(4): 86-90。

周小兵、罗宇、张丽, 2010, 基于中外对比的汉语文化教材系统考察,《语言教学与研究》(5): 1-7。

祖晓梅、陆平舟, 2006, 中国文化课的改革与建设——以《中国概况》为例,《世界汉语教学》(3): 121-127。

态度系统视角下小说《手斧男孩》的评价意义研究[1]

杨汝福 曲春玲

河南工业大学

1. 引言

Gary Paulsen（2007）凭借《手斧男孩》获得美国1988年纽伯瑞儿童文学奖；《手斧男孩》被评为美国100年来最优秀的50部青少年图书之一。作者以主人公Brian的野外生存经历为背景，用写实描述与史诗般的结构造就了这部超越一般冒险小说的传奇故事。该小说也受到中国读者欢迎，并受到学术界的关注，如毛新耕（2009a, 2009b）从文学批评的视角，围绕身份认同这个主线，探讨主人公Brian“孤单旅行，亲近自然，探寻成长人生主题”的历程，恰如作家Paulsen自身成长经历的写照和再现。文献表明，这两篇文章对小说作品情节的讲述和主题的阐述都很到位，但美中不足的是，该研究对作品的语言特色以及语言使用所体现的意义和功能用力不够。鉴于此，我们尝试以系统功能语言学理论为基础对该小说进行多维度的语篇分析。通过对该语篇的及物性系统和衔接系统的探讨（参见杨汝福、曲春玲, 2013a, 2013b），我们能更好地了解小说的主题如何在语篇中借由语言形式体现的经验纯理功能和语篇纯理功能来体现。系统功能语言学认为，语言形式体现三大纯理功能，即语篇功能、经验功能和人际功能。前两者已经分析过（杨汝福、曲春玲, 2013a, 2013b），该语篇的人际功能分析尚是空白，因此，下文将从态度系统的三个子系统，即情感系统、判断系统和鉴赏系统对所选语篇进行词汇层面的分析（参见Martin, 2000, Martin & Rose, 2003, Martin & White, 2008：42），来考察小说语篇中的语言形式对协商和结盟的人际功能的体现及其评价意义。

1 本文是国家社会科学基金项目（08CWWW002）、河南省哲学社会科学规划项目（2013BYY013）、江西省社会科学研究规划课题（08WX14）和河南工业大学科学研究基金研究生教育创新计划项目——“儿童小说的功能语篇分析”（11YJCX86）的阶段性研究成果。

2. 态度系统理论简介

评价理论是对人际功能研究的拓展，由Martin于20世纪90年代提出，是“关于评价的，即语篇中所协商的各种态度、所涉及的情感的强度以及表明价值和联盟读者的各种方式”（胡壮麟等, 2008：74）。按照语义划分，评价理论包含三个方面的子系统：态度系统（attitude）、介入系统（engagement）和级差系统（graduation）（杨汝福, 2006; Halliday, 2008：320; 王振华, 2012, 2013），而态度系统又有三个子系统，即情感系统、判断系统和鉴赏系统（彭宣维, 2012; 刘世铸, 2012）。如图1（Martin & White, 2008：45）所示，态度系统是评价理论的中心，其又细化为有正负两种含义的三个子系统：即对人的情感的表达——属心理学范畴的情感（affect）系统、对人的性格和行为的评价——属伦理学范畴的判断（judgement）系统以及对事物的价值的评价——属美学范畴的鉴赏（appreciation）系统。

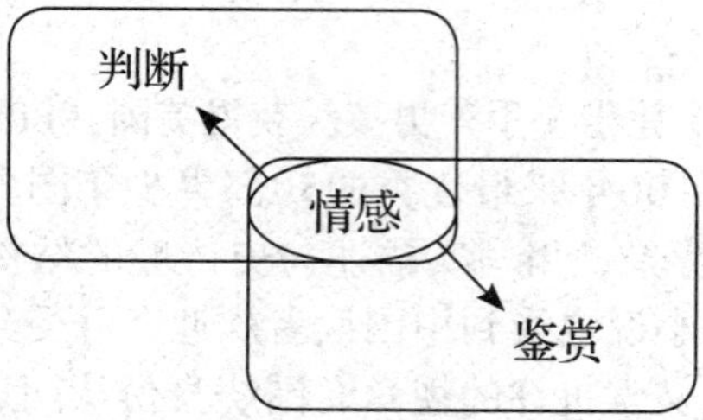

图1 态度系统简图

2.1 情感系统

情感系统位于态度系统的中心，它是解释语言使用者对行为、语篇/过程及现象作出感情反应的评价资源，由它导出判断系统和鉴赏系统（Martin & White, 2008：45; 王振华, 2001：15）。关涉的情感反应具体包含三个方面，即心灵的感受（是否幸福）、社会生存状态的感受（是否安全）以及对目标达成的感受（是否满意）。如图2（王振华, 2004：32）所示，情感系统也包含三个子系统，即品质情感（affect as quality）、过程情感（affect as process）和评注情感（affect as comment）。情感表达可以通过表达品质的形容词或副词、表达感情的心理过程和关系过程动词以及表达评注的情态状语等实现，通过名词化、名词也可以实现情感表达（Martin & Rose, 2003; 胡壮麟等, 2008：321）。情感表达有积极和消极两种含义。

2.2 判断系统

判断系统是解释语言使用者根据伦理道德标准和规范对某种行为作出评判的评价资源，包含两个子系统：社会认同（social esteem）和社会制裁

（social sanction）。前者考察一个人是否具有做事才干（capacity）、坚忍不拔（tenacity），其行为是否符合社会规范（normality），用来判断一个人的所作所为是否能够得到社会的尊重，而后者主要考察一个人是否诚实可靠（veracity），行为是否得当（propriety），用来评价此人的行为是否受到社会的制裁（王振华, 2010：8）。

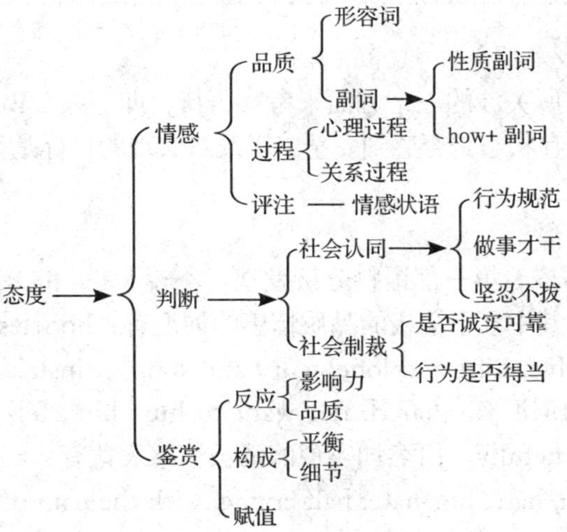

图2 态度系统详图

2.3 鉴赏系统

鉴赏系统是解释语言使用者对行为、语篇/过程及现象的美学品格欣赏的评价资源，其同样有积极和消极两种含义（王振华, 2010：8）。其由三个子系统组成：反应（reaction）表示情感反应，它包含影响力（impact）和品质（quality），其分别指语篇 / 过程对言者吸引力的程度和对感情的影响力；构成（composition）包含平衡（balance）与细节（detail），其分别指语篇 / 过程是否相称和是否因为复杂而难以理解；赋值（valuation）则表示用社会标准来衡量语篇 / 过程时，判断其是否重要和有价值。

3. 语料简介

《手斧男孩》第一部讲述的主人公Brian是一个13岁的都市男孩，在去加拿大探望父亲的途中，Brian的情感变化由坠机前忧心忡忡，满心怨恨到积极面对父母离异的现实，走向心灵成长之路。小说的态度系统分析主要围绕以下三个部分展开：（1）Brian在独自去见父亲的飞机上心事重重。（2）飞机中途失事，Brian落到荒野丛林里却侥幸幸存，他从惊恐不安中镇定下来，积极采取行动融入自然，以至成功获救。（3）Brian在大自然中重获新生，获得心灵成长。

4.《手斧男孩》的态度系统分析

4.1 情感系统分析

本文从情感反应所关涉的三个方面来考察语料，即主人公Brian的心灵感受是否幸福、在荒野中的生存状态是否感到安全，以及对实现的目标是否感到满意。

4.1.1 幸福/不幸福

通过对《手斧男孩》第一部语料分析发现，小说（1）和（2）前半部分中以消极的情感词汇居多，其中表示消极的品质情感的词汇有：hopeless, tight and aching, wet and cold, miserable, hurt and lonely, dry and snug, painstaking, nearly mad。表示消极的过程情感的词汇有：hated, not want to hurt him, felt his frustration and anger rise, looking ruefully。由名词实现的消极情感表达有：tears, crying, the cry, frustration, sobs, pain, hate, hot-hate, half crying, with the pain of movement, in pain, all-over pain, hurt, new aches and pains, agony, hot little jets of hate, in disgust, a strange new twinge, self-pity, long tears, self-pity tears, wasted tears, disgust, with the pain and fear, pointed injury pain, the pain filled his leg, new waves of self-pity, his leg aching, sore leg。这些消极情感词汇主要体现了Brian坠机前的心事重重，曾目睹母亲外遇的秘密和父母最终离异让他内心十分痛苦，而Brian坠机后落到荒野丛林中，面临艰难的生存环境，他虽幸存但伤痕累累、疼痛难忍，因此主人公心灵的感受以“憎恨”“疼痛”“哭喊”“沮丧”“痛苦”“自怜自艾”等消极情感为主。

而表示积极的情感词汇则是出现在（2）的后半部分语篇中，Brian渐渐从惊恐不安中镇定下来，积极采取行动融入自然，表示品质情感的词汇有：形容词interesting and exciting，pleased, 表示过程情感的词汇有：动词smiled, grinned, laughed, almost laughed, nodded and smiled, 由名词实现的积极情感包括：名词短语initial excitement, the smile half on his face, the happy crackle of the dry wood, a good laugh, no pain, with the pain almost all gone, the stiffnesses also gone。由此可见Brian的情感变化随着在自然中渐渐适应生存而由消极转向积极，他开始感到“高兴”“微笑”“疼痛消失”，甚至与狼群“点头微笑”等。

4.1.2 安全/不安全

关于Brian在荒野中生存状态的感受，在（2）的前半部分语篇中仍以消极情感为主，其中表示消极的品质情感的词汇由形容词embarrassed, afraid, panic, hopeless, trembling, too dark, too hard dark 等体现。表示消极的过程情感的词汇有：动词及短语scream, frightened, terrified, his heart hammered in his throat, put his head down on his arms across his knees, cried until he was cried out, crying in the corner of the dark cave, felt afraid。由名词体现的消极情感的表达有：horror, terror, panic, fear and pain, half crying, disbelief, worry, shame, thought of bear, thought of Bigfoot, every monster, fright movie, sitting alone in the dark, alone with no fire, the fear。“害怕”“颤抖”“恐惧”“忧虑”“哭喊”等消极词汇表达了Brian在坠机后，独自在荒野中生存所经历的害怕和恐惧，内心极度缺少安全感。

积极的情感表达则出现在小说（2）的后半部分，表示品质情感的有形容词safe, safer, livable, 表示积极的过程情感由动词短语no move to hurt you, to threaten you, not want to cause you harm, no danger here that he could sense, could feel等体现。在经历了与体型硕大的熊和狼相遇后，Brian发现动物们并没有意图伤害自己，竟然可以和它们和平相处，Brian的情感变化由消极转向积极，不再“害怕”“恐惧”而是感到在自然界中更“安全”。

4.1.3 满意/不满意

语篇中对目标达成的感受出现的情感词汇明显较少，主要由名词anger, disappointment和形容词not satisfied等实现的消极情感表达，而积极情感表达仅有较少名词satisfaction等实现，由于篇幅有限，本文不做重点讨论。

4.2 判断系统分析

通过对《手斧男孩》第一部语料进行分析（见表1），社会制裁作为判断系统的子系统很少出现在语篇中，而另一个子系统，即社会认同则较多地出现在（2）的语篇中。在社会认同的三个子系统中，表达Brian的做事才干和坚忍不拔的评价词汇多于行为规范。同样在（2）的前半部分主要体现了Brian消极的做事才干，坠机受伤的Brian经历了“虚弱”“疲惫”“饥饿”“恶心”“想死”，然而置之死地而后生的Brian最终决定采取积极行动，勇敢克服重重磨难，他展现了积极的做事才干，即在自然中获得“敏锐的听觉、视觉”和顽强的生存能力以及Brian“认真”“小心翼翼”“轻轻地”“耐心地”用手斧凿出了唯一的“火”伴。

4.3 鉴赏系统分析

反应、构成和赋值作为鉴赏系统的三个子系统（见表2），在小说（1）和（2）的语篇中以表示情感反应的情感词汇居多，构成和赋值所占比例较少。Brian曾目睹母亲外遇，随后遭遇父母离婚，这让他内心十分痛苦，作者用形容词“丑陋的”“撕裂的”来评价Brian对父母离异产生消极抵触的心理反应。他也因此怪罪母亲，认为把母亲送他的手斧挂在腰间是“荒唐可笑的”。

表1 语料中的判断系统统计情况

判断		积极	消极
社会认同	行为规范	lucky, good luck, new Brian	strange, vague, surprised, back to normal, old Brian
	做事才干	full, a good taste in his mouth, slightly heavy with a little extra weight, hear differently, truly see that thing, felt full	weak, puffy, swollen, awfully tired, dizziness, unbelievably, viciously thirsty, cracked, bleeding, foul and sticky, sick, hunger, emptiness, too weak, weak from hunger, deeply tired, aching, sickness, vomiting and with terrible diarrhea, so empty, a hissing madness, wishing for death, wishing for an end, lay and hated and wished for an end, wanting all his clouds to come down, wanted to die
	坚忍不拔	carefully, with great caution, gently, struck harder, careful blowing, brushed the top off gently, carefully kept scraping and digging, carefully peeled the bark, carefully used the hatchet, patiently, breathing gently	
社会制裁	诚实可靠		
	行为得当	stay positive, get motivated, right, so right	bad, wrong, incorrect

语篇中Brian多次将城市与自然相比，对城市的评价是消极的，“灰蒙蒙的”和“吵闹和喧嚣的”，而“美丽的”“郁郁葱葱”和“安静的”等则用来积极评价Brian落到荒野中，经过痛苦挣扎后，他开始认识和融入自然，欣赏自然的美景。Brian对在湖中看到狼狈不堪的自己的倒影评价是“难看的”“脏乱的”，在荒野中艰难生存, Brian经常“饥肠辘辘的”，在他饥饿难耐、狼吞虎咽地吃过“酸涩的”浆果后，他终于在丛林中找到了“美味”和“甜甜的”黑莓。经历了诸多苦难，作者用“简单的”“容易的”“平衡的”等形容词来评价Brian已经显示出在自然中努力生存下去的决心和意志。而形容词“最好的”“最有价值的”“最重要的”“非常珍贵的”则体现了Brian在困境中不断用Perpich老师的话语激励自己，他深知在布满荆棘的成长道路中，最重要的是相信并依靠自己，充分发挥自己的主观能动性，积极乐观地勇于克服困难，以收获身心的丰盈。

表2 语料中鉴赏系统的统计情况

鉴赏	积极	消极
反应	beautiful, pretty, green and blue blur, good, unbelievable, wet with juice, rich, sweetness, full and ripe, sweet, so good, so sweet, sweet juice, a beautiful white with bark, wonderful discovery, beauty of the scenery, incredibly beautiful, absolutely, perfectly still, great noise, silent	tearing, ugly, ridiculous, hokey, gray and black of the city, bitter, tart flavor, dry feeling, hard to chew, very ugly, dirty, starving, bitten, greasy, almost oily taste, awful night, hum and whine of the city
构成	simple, easy, flammable, dry and nearly powdery, easier, have good balance	hard, impossible, surprisingly tough
赋值	valuable, best, the most important rule of survival, so important, his only tool, the key to it all, so precious, so close and sweet, effective	hollow

5. 结语

通过对小说《手斧男孩》第一部进行语料分析，研究发现态度系统对展现主人公的情感世界以及揭示小说心灵成长的主题有着积极的语篇建构意义。作者运用情感系统着重揭示了主人公Brian从消极到积极的情感变化。通过运用判断系统，作者向我们展示了主人公如何在荒野中历经重重磨难，心灵因知晓母亲外遇的秘密及父母离异而倍受折磨，身体遭受来自自然环境的种种考验，而经历了绝望的Brian如何不断激励自己，最终通过积极认识自然、融入自然到由衷地热爱自然，成功生存到救援人员的到来。语篇中作者运用鉴赏系统，让我们看到Brian在自然中历经磨难后，心灵得到了成长和丰盈，从而认同了自身的重要价值。作者通过这部小说倡导人们回归自然，尤其是青少年读者，从小培育他们亲近自然，热爱自然，积极构建人与人、人与动物、人与自然和谐相处的生态价值观（杨汝福、曲春玲，2013c）。正如辛志英、黄国文所言（2013），生态意识是系统功能语言学者的社会责任之一，也是21世纪不可避免的核心议题。

参考文献

Eggins, S. 1994. *An introduction to Systemic Functional Linguistics*. London: Printer.

Paulsen, G. 2007. *Hatchet*. New York: Simon & Schuster.

Halliday, M. A. K. & C. M. I. M. Matthiessen. 2004. An *Introduction to Functional Grammar* (3rd edition). London: Arnold.

Halliday, M. A. K. 2008. *An Introduction to Functional Grammar* (3rd edition). Beijing: Foreign Language Teaching and Research Press.

Martin, J. R. 2000. Beyond Exchange: Appraisal Systems in English. In S. Hunston, & G. Thompson. (eds.) *Evaluation in Text: Authorial Stance and the Construction of Discourse*. Oxford: Oxford University Press.

Martin, J. R. & D. Rose. 2003. *Working with Discourse: Meaning Beyond the Clause*. London: Continuum.

Martin, J. R. & P. R. R. White. 2008. *The Language of Evaluation: Appraisal in English*. Beijing: Foreign Language Teaching and Research Press.

Matthiessen, C. M. I. M. & M. A. K. Halliday. 2009. *Systemic Functional Grammar: A First Step into the Theory*. G. W. Huang & H. Y. Wang (trans.) Beijing: Higher Education Press.

Thompson, G. 2008. *Introducing Functional Grammar*. London: Arnold.

胡壮麟、朱永生、张德禄、李战子，2008，《系统功能语言学概论》。北京：北京大学出版社。

刘世铸，2012，评价理论观照下的翻译过程模型，《山东外语教学》（4）：24-28。

毛新耕，2009a，主人公的成长人生作者的生活写照，《云梦学刊》（2）：117-119。

毛新耕，2009b，孤单旅行成长人生，《湖南科技学院学报》（5）：25-27。

彭宣维，2012，从评价理论反观亚里士多德有关思想，《山东外语教学》（1）：16-20。

王振华，2001，评价系统及其运作——系统功能语言学的新发展，《外国语》（6）：13-20。

王振华，2004，“物质过程”的评价价值——以分析小说人物形象为例，《外国语》（5）：41-47。

王振华，2010，从态度系统考量奥巴马获 2009 年度诺贝尔和平奖引发的争议，《当代外语研究》（3）：7-11, 46, 61。

王振华，2012，评价理论研究在中国，载黄国文、辛志英（编），《系统功能语言学研究现状和发展趋势》。北京：外语教学与研究出版社，210-238。

王振华、刘成博，2013，从态度视角看人际和谐，载黄国文、朱永生、张德禄、杨信彰（编），《功能语言学与语篇分析研究（第 5 辑）》。北京：高等教育出版社，168-183。

辛志英、黄国文，2013，系统功能语言学与生态话语分析，《外语教学》（3）：7-10, 31。

杨汝福，2006，从态度系统看喜剧小品的评价意义，《外语教学》（6）：10-13。

杨汝福、曲春玲，2013a，回归自然心灵成长——儿童小说《手斧男孩》的积极话语分析，《安阳师范学院学报》（4）：74-77。

杨汝福、曲春玲，2013b，《手斧男孩》及其汉译本的词汇衔接手段对比研究，《漯河职业技术学院学报》（5）：155-157。

杨汝福、曲春玲，2013c，《少年 Pi 的奇幻漂流》的生态话语分析，《现代语文》（8）：117-119。

语篇中的篇章连贯问题

王　璐

首都师范大学

1. 引言

目前，有关篇章连贯的系统研究比较少，且研究者大多集中于影响篇章连贯的某一层面。譬如，张德禄和刘洪民（1994）在研究主位结构与语篇连贯的关系之后指出，选择合适的主位是保持语篇连贯的重要条件之一，研究主位结构与语篇连贯的关系可以从主位选择的过程和主位选择的结果两方面进行。苗兴伟（2003）从信息传递的角度研究语篇连贯，认为语篇是信息流不断推进的动态过程，发话者在语篇的信息流中发挥着积极的作用。以往研究者主要针对连贯的语篇，从理论上笼统地讨论连贯语篇所应具备的条件或具有的特征。

本文以欠连贯语篇为主要研究对象，所用语料选自国内某学术期刊收集的投稿语料，均为学术话语，采用质性分析的路径，对引起篇章意义欠连贯的诸种因素加以系统地探讨。

2. 理论基础

本文的理论基础是程晓堂（2005）根据语言的三个纯理功能提出的语篇连贯框架。在这一框架中，语篇的连贯性包括三大方面，即概念连贯、人际连贯和篇章连贯，其中每个方面又包含若干具体的连贯特征。为使讨论更具针对性，本研究只涉及篇章连贯。

在程晓堂（2005）的语篇连贯框架中，篇章连贯是指语篇为了有效地组织内容信息而体现出的连贯性。为了使语篇显得有组织、有条理，语篇必须充分利用多种微观和宏观的语篇组织结构，如主位结构、信息结构、命题结构和语类结构。

主位“是信息的起点，是小句中受关注的成分”。在很多情况下，主位往往是小句的话题所在，代表小句谈论的主题。主位与连贯的关系是：（1）从局部上讲，主位的选择可保证句际（句与句之间的）连贯；（2）从整体上讲，主位的选择可在信息组织方式上，使语篇形成一个有机整体；（3）有助于语篇与情景联系起来。主位以外的其余部分是述位；述位是围绕主题所说的话，是对主位做出叙述、描写、解释和说明。与主位结构相同，信息结构也限定语篇连贯的微观结构。然而，信息结构与主位结构有着明显的区别，主位是从讲话者的角度出发，关注的是讨论的话题；新信息是从听话者的角度出发，关注的则是信息的焦点。通常情况下，二者是一致的，即主位表达已知信息，述位传达新信息，但在某些特殊情况下，主位也可以是新信息，述位相应的也可以是已知信息。每个小句都有自己的主位结构和信息结构，主位结构之间和信息结构之间都不是孤立的。随着语篇内容的逐步展开，各个小句的主位以相同或不同的模式向前推进，新旧信息在语篇再现过程中前后交错、相互作用；前者帮助说话者或作者传递信息，引导读者接受信息，而后者在便于听话者或读者对信息的理解和储存的基础上，通过信息重组来更有效地传达信息。从语用的角度讲，二者都是影响语篇连贯的重要因素。

主位结构和信息结构属于微观结构，而命题结构和语类结构属于宏观结构。Van Dijk（1977）将宏观结构定义为“宏观语义结构”，这一定义隶属于命题宏观结构。根据这一定义，连贯篇章通常包括一个宏观语义结构。该宏观结构是由一些宏观命题按照层级关系构成的。篇章中的宏观命题是由微观命题衍生出来的。宏观结构是语篇中“话题”或“主位”的重组。宏观结构从整体上再现语篇中重要的、突出的语义信息。语篇宏观结构决定语篇宏观连贯。宏观结构包括命题宏观结构和语类宏观结构。命题宏观结构建立语篇命题的层级关系，由逐个的微观命题渐渐引出宏观命题。语类宏观结构对语篇各个组成部分加以归类和排序，从宏观角度探讨语篇成分的布局，其重要作用在于它决定篇章的构成因素，从而实现篇章的完整和连贯。

如果语篇生产者不能合理、有效地使用这些结构，语篇就可能出现欠连贯的现象。然而，值得指出的是，语篇中的篇章结构体系是多层次、多维度的。多层次是指篇章结构既包括微观结构又包括宏观结构，两者之间没有明显分界。微观结构和宏观结构是相对的，因为结构划分的标准取决于其在语篇中的位置和功能。多维度是指篇章结构既包括语篇的内容，又包括语篇的形式。尽管主位结构和语类宏观结构含有语义因素，但是二者基本上还是属于语篇的形式范畴。信息结构和命题宏观结构属于语篇的内容范畴。

本文所选语篇均属非面对面的书面交际语料，作者与读者之间的交流完全依赖于他所创作的语篇，其篇章意义的表达主要是通过主位结构、信息结构、命题宏观结构和语类宏观结构实现的，语篇无论在以上四种结构中哪一方面出现问题，都会导致语篇的连贯性遭到破坏，形成不连贯或欠连贯的语篇。

3. 研究结果

本研究语料语篇在篇章意义表达中出现的问题主要表现为：主位结构不明（正）确、信息分布不合理和命题宏观结构缺失，下面我们将通过实例分析说明这些问题对语篇连贯性产生的不良影响。

3.1主位结构不明（正）确

在完整的语篇中，句子前后的主位与主位、述位与述位之间会发生某种联系和变化，这种联系和变化就叫推进。有关主位推进模式，各家说法不一，其中最常见的四种模式为：主位一致型（亦称平行型，特点为主位相同，述位不同）；述位一致型（亦称集中型，特点为主位不同，述位相同）；延续型（亦称梯型，特点为前一句的述位或述位的一部分成为后一句的主位）；交叉型（特点为前一句的主位是后一句的述位）。实际上，大多数语篇的主位推进并非是采用单一的模式，而是几种形式结合使用。两种或两种以上基本模式放在一起使用的情形叫做复合模式（朱永生、严世清, 2001）。主位推进体现出篇章结构的框架，随着主位的向前推进，整个语篇内容也逐步展开，其篇章功能在于主位包含的信息构成了小句的主题，在限制语篇的微观结构的同时，也会影响语篇意义的连贯性和局部或整体结构的紧凑程度。如果小句之间的主、述位选择不合适，就会导致语篇的篇章意义欠连贯或不连贯。例如：

（1）通过任务型评价，学生可以充分展示出他们所具有的语言知识与能力，可以全面地衡量学生在多大程度上达到了课程标准所设定的各项目标。

（2）学生对任务难度的看法是最直接和最真实的，对教师和任务设计者针对学生的感受、结合所教内容设计任务有一定的参考价值。

在例（1）中，“通过任务型评价”是主位，是句子的话题；其后部分是述位，是对前面话题的内容展开说明。例句中的述位部分可做进一步的划分，其中“学生”是主位，其后两个分句内容则被视为两个并列的述位。该例句中的主位结构问题主要出现在全句述位部分的主、述位划分上。具体地讲，“学生”和“可以充分展示出他们所具有的语言知识与能力”构成的主、述位关系是不容质疑的。然而，“可以全面地衡量学生在多大程度上达到了课程标准所设定的各项目标”从逻辑上却不能和“学生”构成合理的主、述位关系。“可以全面地衡量学生在多大程度上达到了课程标准所设定的各项目标”的主位应该是“教师”；只有如此它才能和“学生可以充分展示出他们所具有的语言知识与能力”这个小句一起与“通过任务型评价”构成正确的主、述位关系。

与例（1）不同，例（2）中的主位结构不存在正确或不正确的问题，只是在某些地方不够明确或得当，使读者易对其篇章意义产生误解。首先，句子的主位既可以是“学生对任务难度的看法是最直接和最真实的”，也可以是“学生对任务难度的看法”。如果是前者，后面的述位则应加上代词“这”来指代前面的句项主位；如果是后者，需在“对教师和任务设计者……有一定的参考价值”前面加上“而且”这样的连词，使之与“是最直接和最真实的”一起构成句子的述位。例（2）除了整个句子的主、述位关系不明确外，其述位部分也存在同样的问题。在“对教师和任务……参考价值”这一述位中，主位既可以是“对教师和任务设计者”，也可以是“对教师和任务设计者针对学生的感受、结合所教内容设计任务”。无论是哪一种，都在结构上使主位与述位之间失去平衡，这不仅会导致头重脚轻或者脚重头轻的现象出现，在篇章意义的表达上也不够流畅，于无形中为读者对语篇意义的理解设置障碍。如果将其改为“对教师和任务设计者有一定的参考价值，使其在设计任务上可以更好地针对学生的感受、结合所教内容”，就可以避免此类现象的发生。

一个完整的句子有自己的主位（T）和述位（R）。然而，语篇往往是由若干句子组成的。如果在一长段语篇中，句子的主位和述位在形式上和意义上缺乏关联性，那么这段语篇就难以上下连贯。试看下面的例子：（为了方便分析，我们将该语篇中的小句按顺序进行了数字编号；如果主位相同的小句属于一个句子，则将小句中的主位以句子为单位进行一次性编号，而不对其进行单独编号。）

（3）①阅读是人类获取知识的重要途径，也是一个有着深厚文化内涵的人类素质要求。②古人强调博览群书，通晓古今中外，也说明阅读不是短期行为，更非功利的应试教育所能习得。而且，③阅读品质的好坏和阅读质量的高下，与阅读者个人的兴趣、志向、意志等非智力因素有着千丝万缕的联系，而④这些品质的形成并非靠单一的强化训练就能达成。一直以来，⑤高中教师在教学中更注重于开发学生的智力因素，对学生的非智力因素重视不足；⑥而学生在阅读时也抱着应付、应试的心态，不能养成良好的阅读习惯，⑦其阅读的质量和阅读效果就自然会大打折扣。

例（3）的内容主要与阅读有关。“阅读”是该语篇的话题；在对“阅读”作了具体的定义之后，话题转向古人对阅读的态度，阅读品质的好坏和阅读质量的高下，以及这些品质的形成。从T5到T7分别叙说了高中教师在教学中的偏重和学生的阅读态度，对其阅读的质量和阅读效果的影响。在这段语篇中，各小句主位之间虽然都在某种程度上和阅读有关，但却很难被认为是存在着某种必然的语义联系。除了T3和T4的模式是主位同一型外，其他主位涉及的话题都可视为一个全新的话题，这样的话题在下文中没有通过任何主位推进模式得以展开，如R1中“也是一个有着深厚文化内涵的人类素质要求”，而下文中提到的内容也无法和上文内容在语义上有所联系，如R2“也说明阅读不是短期行为，更非功利的应试教育所能习得”和R5“对学生的非智力因素重视不足”。主位推进中产生的这些问题中断了语篇内各个句子之间的内在关系，使其无法组合成一个有机的整体。

3.2 信息分布不合理

信息结构和主位结构一样可以帮助读者理解语篇，但是方式不同。主位结构通过提供信息传递的出发点，帮助读者理解语篇，也就是说，主位展示给读者语篇的主题。然而，信息结构采用不同的方式。已知信息提供必要的背景知识，在此基础上，读者可以更好地解读新信息。从信息结构的角度讲，如果新信息出现的顺序反映篇章意义发展的顺序，新信息的总和反映语篇总的信息重点，语篇就可以是连贯的。语篇信息结构之间的关系对语篇连贯性的影响可通过下面的例子得以体现：

（4）在任务型语言评价中，任务设计及任务难度是我们首要考虑的问题。

（5）因此，如何让教师省时省力同时又能保质保量地开展教学，是笔者在教学实践中不断探索研究的一个问题。

（6）英语学习者对学习资源的获取、选择和运用能力，作为自主学习能力的重要表现之一，应该受到更多的重视。

上述例句不存在任何语法问题，但通过对其信息结构加以分析，我们可以看出，两个小句中的已知信息都位于句末，新信息则位于句首。根据汉语表达的惯例，新信息作为信息的焦点，通常都出现在句子的末尾。如果不是为了取得某种特殊效果，如对比或强调，新信息置于句首的做法是不可取的，这样做虽然不会影响语篇意义的表达，却使句子的结构头重脚轻，也使读者难以识别语篇的主要信息和组织脉络。下面我们将选取几个层次在小句之上的语篇，并结合其中问题小句的主位结构分析对此做进一步的阐释。

（7）主张从认知的角度确定任务的难度的Robinson（2001），Long（1985），Long & Robinson（1998），Skehan（1998），Skehan & Foster（2001）以及 Doughty（2001）等认为，按认知难度排列教育任务并以这样的排序作为设计教学大纲有助于设计语言新知识的学习顺序，可以据此重新建构第二语言的教学目标并有效地促进第二语言教学的发展。

（8）在课堂教学中，传授知识、培养能力、发展智力是教学的主干，这必须通过系统讲授来实现。

（9）在听力训练中，他们力图听懂每个词，却往往顾此失彼，抓不住重点，即使听力材料不带任何新词。

在例（7）中，“主张从认知的角度……认为”的主位结构和信息结构是一致的，即主位是已知信息，述位是新信息。然而，由于该小句的主位过长，即便小句从顺序上讲符合汉语中信息传递的惯例，但结构上的失衡却不便于读者对该小句意义的理解及主题的把握。针对该小句主位结构上的问题，如果将其改为“Robinson（2001），Long（1985），Long & Robinson（1998），Skehan（1998），Skehan & Foster（2001）及 Doughty（2001）等主张，从认知的角度确定任务的难度，他们认为……”，那么小句所传递的信息就容易为读者理解和接受。

在例（8）中，“传授知识、培养能力、发展智力是教学的主干”的主位结构和信息结构并不一致，其中主位是新信息，述位是已知信息。信息在小句内的顺序对小句本身在语义的表达上并没有不利之处，问题的关键在于这样的顺序影响了这个小句与下个小句之间的衔接。在下个小句中，“这必须通过系统讲授来实现”中的“这”指代的是“传授知识、培养能力、发展智力”。如果按小句现在的顺序，代词“这”是不必要的，整个句子可以改为“在课堂教学中，传授知识、培养能力、发展智力是教学的主干，（都）必须通过系统讲授来实现”；只有在将问题小句的顺序颠倒过来，即将已知信息置于主位，新信息置于述位时，才需要“这”来指代前面的“传授知识、培养能力、发展智力”。那么，整个句子修改后应该是“在课堂教学中，教学的主干是传授知识、培养能力、发展智力，这都必须通过系统讲授来实现”。

在例（9）中，小句“即使听力材料不带任何新词”作为新信息被放在句子的末尾加以强调和突出，这种做法明显体现了语篇生产者的英语学习对母语表达产生的负面影响。在英语中，从句既可以置于主句前面，他可以放在主句后面；汉语却不同，作为从句的小句通常只放在主句的前面。例（9）中这种将从句置于主句之后的做法，不仅违反了汉语表达的习惯，也使该小句与其他小句之间的逻辑关系显得过于牵强。如果将该小句单独置于另一句中，与适合它的主句搭配，并在前后两句之间选择适当的连接词，用以理顺逻辑关系，那么，整个句子不仅在语法上是正确的，在语义上也是连贯的，如：“在听力训练中，他们力图听懂每个词，却往往顾此失彼，抓不住重点。因此，即使听力材料不带任何新词，他们也未必能完全领会。”

通过以上语料分析，我们可以清楚地看出，与主位结构一样，信息结构都是语篇连贯中不可缺少的重要因素。如果二者不能相辅相成，语篇的连贯就会受影响，不仅使语义不能得以有效传达，读者也不易理解语篇的内容，难以掌握语篇的发展动态。

3.3 命题宏观结构缺失

宏观结构分为语类结构和命题结构。语类结构是一个语篇的最高层次的宏观结构，对整个语篇的连贯都起到限定作用；命题结构则在微观上限定局部语篇的连贯，并最终使局部连贯与整个语篇产生联系，从而在宏观上影响语篇的整体连贯。根据程晓堂（2005），连贯的语篇通常围绕一个宏观话题展开，这个宏观话题在语篇内部可扩展为若干微观话题，微观话题不能与语篇的宏观话题背道而驰，且微观话题的转换必须通过语义、语用等手段直接或间接地在语篇中体现。因此，如果语篇中的宏观结构缺失，容易产生两方面的问题：（1）语类结构的问题，（2）话题断裂的问题。在宏观结构上，语篇的缺陷使语篇缺乏整体性、系统性，没有层次感，直接导致语篇的连贯性下降，不利于其篇章意义的表达。

本文所用语篇在语类结构上没有太大的出入，基本上能反映出科研论文所必备的语类结构特点，语篇中出现的问题主要是由于命题宏观结构缺失引起的话题断裂，如：

（10）有了阅读能力和良好的阅读习惯，学生不仅能够主动获取知识、提高自学能力，也能扩大视野、提高文化修养、增强理解力和判断力。对今后发展和成长具有关键作用。英语阅读促使学生了解英语国家的风土人情、文化艺术，生活习惯等，帮助学生了解中西文化的差异，培养爱国主义精神和世界意识，提高跨文化交际的能力。

（11）一次偶然的机会，我在学院期刊阅览室无意间拿起了一本《基础英语教育》。没有想到，随便浏览了一下，却被几篇文章吸引住了。其中有一篇刘莹老师的论文《对我国儿童英语单词读写教育的初步构想》引起了我很大的兴趣。很长时间以来，我也一直在思考这个问题，寻找着和自己有相同研究兴趣的同伴，现在她就出现在面前的期刊中——真是踏破铁鞋无觅处，得来全不费功夫。我为找到了这位志同道合的伙伴而高兴。让我更为欣喜的是，我找到了阐述自己英语教学观点的一个好平台——《基础英语教育》。多年来，《基础英语教育》一直陪我成长、进步。我与《基础英语教育》结下了深厚的友情。

例（10）是由三个句子组成的。第一个句子的话题是阅读能力和良好的阅读习惯，第三个句子的话题是英语阅读；虽然这两个句子的话题都与阅读有关，但涉及的却是阅读的不同方面。如果要保持语篇连贯，一、三两句间的第二句须在二者之间产生有效的联系。但是，第二句显然并没有发挥这方面的作用，所以导致该语篇在意义上不连贯。一、三句之间的话题产生偏差，主要是因为其间的话题转换缺乏过渡，并且其所在的段落缺乏中心话题。

在连贯的语篇中，通常每个段落都有各自的中心话题，缺乏中心话题的段落讨论的内容往往比较零散。例（11）中有七个小句，第一小句的话题是《基础英语教育》，第二小句的话题是其中的几篇文章，第三小句的话题是其中的一篇（刘莹老师的论文），第四小句的话题是刘莹老师，第五小句的话题是志同道合的伙伴，第六和七小句的话题是《基础英语教育》，因而其中心话题应围绕《基础英语教育》展开，而第三、四、五小句都是关于刘莹老师及其论文的，不属于中心话题要讨论的内容。第二小句虽然提到了《基础英语教育》中的几篇文章，但接下来的小句并没有对此话题展开。这个段落中的第一、第六和第七小句虽然都提到《基础英语教育》，但只有第六小句“多年来，《基础英语教育》一直陪我成长、进步”可以作为中心话题，其他小句都是对这一中心话题的详细论述和展开。

例（10）和例（11）是从不同投稿论文中节选出来的两个小段落，对其所在语篇连贯性的影响只是局部的。如果欠连贯或不连贯部分基本构成语篇主体，它对所在语篇连贯性的影响就会范围更大一些，有时甚至有可能波及整个语篇，如：

（12）学生对任务型测试这种形式持肯定的态度，并对英语学习提出了建设性的意见。总结起来有以下几点（表九）：（表九：学生对英语学习的看法）

例（12）的问题出现在第二个句子中“表九”的标题上。“表九”是对前一句中提到的学生对任务型测试的态度，以及对英语学习的意见总结。然而，在表格的标题中，却只提到了英语学习一个方面的内容，并未提及学生对任务型测试的态度。原则上，“表九”的标题在宏观上为语篇的发展提供了线索，如若有所缺失，必将影响下文中要讨论的内容。

4. 结语

判断语篇连贯的最基本依据是看语篇是否有效地传达了作者希望传达的意义。根据系统功能语言学的思想，语篇应同时传达三重意义，即概念意义、人际意义和篇章意义。因此，我们可以通过分析语篇是否有效地传达了这三重意义来考察语篇的连贯性。

本文从篇章意义的角度，探讨了语篇的连贯性。根据程晓堂（2005）提出的语篇在篇章连贯方面应满足的四个组织条件，本文通过对欠连贯语料语篇的分析，讨论了这些语篇组织结构中出现的具体问题和其对语篇连贯性产生的负面影响。研究结果表明，欠连贯语篇各有各的问题，研究这些语篇的连贯问题具有极大的现实意义，不仅有助于了解产生问题的原因，而且能够更加清楚地认识连贯的本质。

参考文献

Danes, F. 1974. Functional Sentence Perspective and the Organization of the Text. In F. Danes (ed.) *Papers on Functional Sentence Perspective*. The Hague: Mouton, 114.

Halliday, M. A. K. 1985. Dimension of Discourse Analysis: Grammar. In T. A. van Dijk (ed.) *Handbook of Discourse Analysis, Vol 2: Dimensions of Discourse*. London: Academic Press, 29-56.

Hasan, R. 1989. Part B. In M. A. K. Halliday & R. Hasan, *Language, Context, and Text: Aspects of Language in a Social-semiotic Perspective*. London: Oxford University Press, 63-66.

Van Dijk, T. A. 1977. *Text and Context: Explorations in the Semantics and Pragmatics of Discourse*. London: Longman.

Van Dijk, T. A. 1985. Semantic Discourse Analysis. In T. A. van Dijk (ed.) *Handbook of Discourse Analysis*, Vol 2: Dimensions of Discourse. London: Academic Press, 115.

程晓堂, 2005,《基于功能语言学的语篇连贯研究》。北京：外语教学与研究出版。

苗兴伟, 2003, 语篇的信息连贯,《外语教学》(2)：17-20。

张德禄、刘洪民, 1994, 主位结构与语篇连贯,《外语研究》(3)：27-33。

朱永生、严世清, 2001,《系统功能语言学多维思考》。上海：上海外语教育出版社, 105。

国际通用英语本土化语篇实证研究[1]

——以新闻评论语篇为例

孙红梅

浙江科技学院

1. 引言

国外对世界英语的研究始于1982年，Kachru（1992）提出三个同心圈模型，指出世界英语是不同文化背景中所使用英语的模式或变体。Kachru（1992）坚持英语标准的多元化，引发了与坚持标准化的Quirk的争论，更多的学者从社会、历史、意识形态等方面对“国际英语”和“各体新英语”的语言特征进行描述。“很多英国学者包括Quirk开始从80年代谨慎的立场转向多元化和独特性”（McArthur, 1997：67）。对世界英语的本质、特征、分类进行描述的有Smith（1976），Butler（1997），Schneider（2003），Mufwene（2003）等。Crystal（1999）指出语言的通用功能与本土化功能应该互补。Alptekin（2002）对以英语本族语的文化、语用、语篇为标准的单一交际能力提出质疑。综观以上，国外学者从各自的本土化视角对英语的本土化与国际化进行研究，但对本土化语篇模式特征的研究为数不多。

国内对世界英语的研究首先表现在中国英语标准之争方面，谢之君（1995），邱立中（2008），徐晓晴（ 2005）等反对中国英语变体说，主张英语本族语标准；汪榕培（1991），李少华、王万平（2002），李文中（1993），姜亚军、杜瑞清（2003）等肯定中国英语有广阔发展前景。其他研究涉及中国英语的概念、本质、可理解度，中国英语的词汇、语音、句式、语篇修辞特征、功能、思维方式等。俞希、文秋芳（2010）分析了英语报章中评价性形容词搭配的本土化特征，提出双层英语的假设，并指出本土化英语层与英语共核层和谐相处的关键在于可理解度。俞希（2006）和高超（2007）分析中国语境下英语搭配的惯例化，体现规律性的差异正在形成。综观国内对英语国际化与本土化的研究，可以发现，大多数研究集中于世界英语的概念和标准的争论，中国英语词汇、句式的例举，世界英语的述评及对

1 本文为浙江省教育科学规划研究课题“大学英语课堂教学多模态语篇能力培养研究”（2013 SCG 063）部分研究成果；浙江科技学院科研基金项目“国际通用语背景下的英语本土化研究”研究成果，项目编号 2011XJYB10。

教学的启示。仅有的实证研究也限于句式和语块，不涉及语篇。涉及语篇的研究则从文化、修辞或思维与语篇的辩证关系上进行论述。“中国英语的研究不管从已发表的论文数量上，还是从研究的深度和广度上看都还处在初级阶段。人们还只是停留在对一些概念的争论上”（潘章仙, 2002：26），“从20世纪80年代起，大量研究都围绕国际语境中英语的本土化展开……考察语篇和语用模块的研究较少”（俞希、文秋芳, 2011：38）。笔者在国际通用语背景下，对英语本土化语篇模式的规律性特征展开实证研究。

2. 研究设计

本研究从《中国日报》（*China Daily*）、人民网英文版等国内权威网站搜集本土化新闻评论语篇10篇，涉及经济、外交、医疗、教育、囚徒虐待、工作等话题，并从《洛杉矶时报》《纽约时报》《华尔街日报》搜集相对应话题的新闻评论10篇，长度相当，从而保证本土化语篇和本族语篇在语场、语式、语旨上相近似，增强同类语篇的可比性。

确定本土化的研究区域为本族与本土化英语的语篇模块，子模块为中外报纸评论性英文语篇，研究参数为语类结构潜势GSP、主位推进程序和非结构性衔接。作为语篇宏观结构，GSP是某种特定语篇类型的原型，它表现同一语篇类型中结构实现的最典型的组织模式。因为文化语境决定人们根据交际目的的不同而采用的不同交际阶段和步骤，即语篇类型结构，因此语类结构分析可以揭示文化语境差异。主位模式从整体上讲可以在组织方式上使语篇形成一个有机整体。对主位推进程序的追踪可以明晰语篇的发展进程。非结构性衔接手段出现频数多寡可以影响语篇的整体连贯效应。该研究比照本族语篇分析本土化语篇以上三个参数的本土化程度，表现在量化与质化两方面的差异。

该研究要回答的问题是，本土化语篇和本族语篇在以上三项参数上是否有差异？如果存在差异，本土化语篇的差异是否呈现规律性？这些差异的根源是什么？

3. 分析过程与结果

研究分两步进行，首先对比分析本土化语篇和本族语篇中的结构性衔接和非结构性衔接，计算其在语料中的使用频率，找出本土化语篇和本族语篇在衔接上的异同。然后，对比分析两类语篇的语篇类型结构的异同，找出其深层的差异。

3.1 结构性衔接对比

首先对比分析本族和本土化语篇在结构性衔接即主位推进程序上的差异。本研究主要采用黄国文（1988）的六类型主位推进程序。平行型以第一句的主位为出发点，其余各句都以此句的主位为主位，各自引出不同的述位，从不同的角度对同一个主位加以揭示、阐发。延续型是第一句的述位或述位的一部分作为第二句的主位，这个主位又引出另一个述位，这个述位又成为下一句的主位，这样延续下去，不断带出新信息，推动思想内容的表达。集中型是第一句的主位、述位做了基本叙述以后，以后各句分别以新的主位开始，各句不同的主位都集中归结为同一述位或述位的一部分。交叉型是第一句的主位成为第二句的述位，第二句的主位成为第三句的述位，第三句的主位又成为第四句的述位，如此交叉发展下去。并列型是第一、三、五、七等句的主位相同，二、四、六、八等句的主位相同。这一模式多用于表达对比比较。派生型是第一句的主位、述位作了叙述后，随后各句的主句都从第一句的述位的某一部分派生出来。

从本土化语篇、本族语篇中分别随机抽取20个段落，分析其主位推进程序的类型（表1）及出现频数（表2）。本土化英文语篇由C表示，本族英文语篇由N表示。

表1 主位推进程序的种类在语料中的分布情况

本土化语篇段落	推进模式	本族语篇段落	推进模式
Para4 C1	平行型	Para2 N1	平行型
Para5 C1	延续型→平行型	Para6 N1	延续型→集中型
Para4 C2	延续型	Para1 N2	延续型→派生型
Para6 C2	延续型	Para5 N2	集中型
Para3 C3	集中型	Para2 N3	平行型
Para7 C3	平行型→延续型	Para4 N3	平行型→延续型→交叉型
Para4 C4	延续型	Para3 N4	集中型
Para6 C4	平行型	Para4 N4	延续型
Para2 C5	延续型	Para4 N5	集中型→延续型→交叉型
Para6 C5	平行型	Para5 N5	延续型→平行型→集中型
Para6 C6	平行型	Para3 N6	集中型
Para17C6	集中型	Para6 N6	集中型
Para5 C7	平行型	Para4 N7	派生型
Para11C7	派生型	Para8 N7	集中型
Para5 C8	平行型	Para3 N8	派生型
Para6 C8	集中型	Para6 N8	派生型
Para6 C9	平行型	Para6 N9	派生型
Para3C10	平行型	Para4 N10	派生型
Para4C10	延续型→集中型	Para5 N10	平行型
Para6C10	延续型	Para9 N10	延续型

表2 主位推进模式在语料中出现次数统计

主位推进程序	本土语段落	本族语段落
平行型	10	5
延续型	8	7
集中型	4	8
派生型	1	6
交叉型	0	2
并列型	0	0
总计	23	28

表1显示本土化语料、本族语料中出现的主位推进程序类型在有些段落并不是单一的，本族语料显示更为混合的主位推进程序。表2显示本土化语段，平行型用得较多，句间关系相对单一；本族语段前四种主位类型应用比较均衡，句间关系相对丰富。两类语料的交叉型和并列型主位推进程序应用都不多，交叉型是对不断出现的两种事物进行循环表述，而并列型限于两种事物之间的细致比较，多出现于论述文。交叉型和并列型的缺乏体现了新闻评论的时事性，即不局限于两个事物间的详尽长篇评述。

3.2 非结构性衔接对比

非结构性衔接的种类来自于Halliday & Hasan（1985）在1985年出版的《语言·语境·语篇》一书中划分的四种非结构性衔接成分：指代、替代、省略和词汇衔接。指代可以进一步划分为指示指代、人称指代、比较指代，替代可以划分为名词性替代、动词性替代、小句性替代，省略可以分为名词性省略、动词性省略、小句性省略，词汇衔接分为两大类，即复现与搭配。

对比分析两类语料中的非结构衔接成分的出现频次。表3和表4分别显示非结构衔接在本土化和本族语料中的分布，表5统计了非结构衔接在两类语料中出现的次数。

表3 语义衔接小类在本土化语料中的分布

衔接手段	C1	C2	C3	C4	C5	C6	C7	C8	C9	C10
指示指代	7	7	5	5	12	9	6	2	1	11
人称指代	3	6	6	5	3	5	3	21	4	13
比较指代	2	2	3	2	1	0	2	0	1	8
名词性替代	0	0	0	0	0	0	0	0	0	1
动词性替代	0	0	0	0	0	0	0	0	0	0
小句性替代	0	0	0	0	0	0	0	1	0	0
名词性省略	1	0	1	1	1	0	0	0	5	1
动词性省略	0	0	0	0	0	0	0	0	0	0

（续表）

衔接手段	C1	C2	C3	C4	C5	C6	C7	C8	C9	C10
小句性省略	0	0	1	1	0	0	0	0	0	0
词汇：复现	1	7	4	0	5	2	12	7	0	9
词汇：搭配	0	7	2	2	4	1	7	0	3	3

表4 语义衔接小类在本族语料中的分布

衔接手段	N1	N2	N3	N4	N5	N6	N7	N8	N9	N10
指示指代	16	14	12	12	14	9	15	6	2	1
人称指代	14	4	5	7	6	9	3	11	6	2
比较指代	4	2	4	2	3	3	3	3	1	1
名词性替代	0	0	0	0	0	0	0	1	1	0
动词性替代	1	0	0	1	0	0	0	0	0	0
小句性替代	2	0	1	0	1	0	0	0	0	0
名词性省略	0	1	0	2	2	0	2	1	0	2
动词性省略	0	0	0	0	0	0	0	3	0	0
小句性省略	1	0	0	0	0	0	1	0	0	2
词汇：复现	9	11	3	4	9	15	5	2	5	9
词汇：搭配	2	2	0	7	2	1	1	1	1	2

表5 本族本土化语料中各类衔接出现次数统计

语义衔接手段		C1—C10	N1—N10
指代	指示指代	65	101
	人称指代	69	67
	比较指代	20	26
替代	名词性替代	1	2
	动词性替代	0	2
	小句性替代	1	4
省略	名词性省略	10	10
	动词性省略	0	3
	小句性省略	2	4
词汇衔接	复现	47	72
	搭配	29	19

3.3 语篇类型结构对比

Hasan（1985）认为语篇的语类结构成分（包括必要成分和非必要成分）是由语境配置（contextual configuration）来实现的，也就是语域的三个变量：语场、语旨和语式。语境配置的三个变量在很大程度上决定了“语类结构”（generic structure）成分。本研究所选语料在语场上相互对应，即本土化语料和本族语料在某一主题上相互对应，在语旨、语式上都是正式书面新闻评论语篇，以此来考察语域相似的本族和本土化语篇在类型结构上是否存在明显差异。

Bolivar（1994）认为，英语本族语社论有“三段式”的宏观结构，导语、主体和评价分别具有开篇、接续和对前两者进行评价的功能。英语社论在导语部分多直接提出论点。范荣康（1985）指出新闻评论的结构为引论、正论和结论。引论部分可以摆论点，摆情况，摆问题，摆驳论，摆结论等。郭可（1993）认为社论的结构分为三部分，即陈述（statement）、论证（argument）、结论（conclusion），社论开头多是对事件的陈述和介绍，主体是论证分析，结尾提出论点。本研究综合中外新闻评论语篇结构模式，把新闻评论语篇的主体结构概括为论点、论证、结论，以此分析比较本族和本土化新闻评论语篇在语篇类型结构上的异同。表6统计了两类语料中语篇类型结构的种类及各类型下语篇数量。表7显示了论点出现的位置。

表6 本族、本土化语料语篇类型结构对比

本族语料语篇类型结构	本土化语料语篇类型结构
论点—背景—论证—结论5	论点—背景—论证—结论3
论点—论证—背景—结论1	论点—论证—背景—结论1
背景—论点—论证—结论2	背景—论点—论证—结论1
背景—论点—论证1	论点—论证—结论3
论题—背景—论证—论点1	论题—论证—论点2

表7 本族、本土化语料中论点的安排

	开头	中间	结尾	总数
本族语料	6	3	1	10
本土语料	7	1	2	10

4. 讨论

首先，两类语篇随机抽取的段落中出现的主位推进程序在有些段落并不是单一类型，本族语篇表现出更为混合的主位推进程序，本土化语篇则相对单一。这表明本族语篇在语段结构、句间关系上更为复杂、丰富、多变。本族和本土化语料在主位推进程序上差别较大的是平行型、集中型和派生型。本土化语料平行型使用较多，平行型是从不同角度对同一主位加以揭示、阐发，即对已知信息的罗列、阐明，句间关系是平行、发散的；本族语料的集中型和派生型较多，集中型与派生型都是对述位即未知信息的阐释，是进一步论证，具有深层结构性与论证归一性特点，在论证上更为严密和有说服力。

在非结构衔接方面，本土化语料除了在词汇衔接手段的搭配上使用较多，其他非结构衔接类型数量都不如本族语料，而且没有动词性替代和动词性省略，这与英语和汉语的语法习惯有关。汉语是意合语言，离不开表达核心意义的动词，又缺少形式连接手段，因而本土化语篇很少有省略动词的情形；英语是形合语言，语法关系严谨，较多使用语义衔接手段，因而本族语篇有动词省略和替代的出现。本土化语篇中小句的省略与替代较少也因意合的语言思维习惯倾向于保留意义核心的动词，又缺乏形式连接手段，从而保留了小句。本土化语篇中词汇衔接的词汇复现频率远低于本族语篇，说明词汇量的匮乏和本土化语篇思维倾向于重复主位的习惯，而本族语篇倾向于变换主位。本土化语篇中发散性的平行型主位结构的高频使用决定大量词汇搭配的出现，而本族语篇中归结性的主位结构则减少大量发散性的词汇搭配的出现。

在语篇类型结构上，本土化和本族语篇都表现出论说语篇的类型结构特征，都包括必要成分，即论点、论证、结论，非必要成分为背景、现状、历史。Kaplan（1996）认为汉语语篇结构为“螺旋型”的。Hinds（1990）认为汉语语篇结构特征是“起—承—转—合”。他认为英语文章是作者负责型，作者应该把文章讲清楚，所以论点通常放在文章的开始部分；汉语篇章是读者责任型，主题思想大多是含蓄的，是通过文章描述反映出来的，所以汉语文章强调读者在语篇中的责任。Scollon（1995）等认为，汉英语篇组织结构的不同来自两种语言推理模式的不同。汉语语篇主要采用归纳式推理而英语语篇主要是演绎式推理。在以上文献背景下，本研究发现本族和本土化语篇在论点提出方式上没有表现出较大差异，即都倾向于开门见山提出论点。本族语料似乎更倾向于迂回曲折的先表述背景现状再进入论点的语篇模式，并且也有类似汉语传统修辞“起—承—转—合”归纳论点的情形。本土化的新闻评论语篇在类型结构上表现出与本族语篇一致的倾向。本土化语篇和本族语篇在语境配置即语域上相近，即语场上都是相关领域话题，语旨上都是提供信息、论证、说服，语式上都是正式书面新闻语体。文化语境决定了人们为了不同交际目的而采取的不同阶段和步骤，表现在语篇上为类型结构。本土化和本族新闻评论语篇类型结构的相似性说明在新闻论说这一交际目的上，汉英采取的阶段和步骤相近，其深层文化语境趋同。

5. 结论

本族语篇呈现出更为混合复杂的主位推进程序，段落内句间关系超越了单一模式，呈现出多样化关系，表明本族语篇的语段结构和句间关系更为丰富多变，表现手法更为灵活多样。本土化语篇中平行型的高频使用说明本土化语篇的句间关系和语段结构较为简单划一，缺乏多样性变化，表达方式单调性罗列。本族语篇集中型和派生型的高频出现说明其在句间结构上有层级递进性深入论证和论点归一性论证的特点。本土化语篇倾向于固定主位，同一主位贯穿始终，说明结构性衔接的手段还较为单一，而作为意合的语言思维方式，非结构性衔接的手段也相对缺乏，综合造成本土化语篇简单刻板，论证不够深入。动词为核心的意合的语法习惯使本土化语篇的非结构性衔接也不够多样，造成符合汉语语法习惯的语义衔接手段较多使用而不符合的则较少，甚至没有使用。本土化与本族新闻评论语篇在宏观语篇类型结构上的相似性说明汉英在评论上的文化趋同，这为丰富本土化语篇的句间结构关系提供了文化语境的支持。

综观以上结论，得出以下几点教学启示。首先，要加强本土化与本族语篇的句间结构关系对比，冲破汉语思维的藩篱，克制同一主位到底的现象，挖掘本土化语篇更丰富的句间结构方式。其次，加强丰富的词汇输入，注重词汇在语篇中的具体应用。再次，本土化语篇在宏观结构上与本族语篇的趋同性，说明丰富本土化语篇的句间结构方式具有共同的心理基础。

本研究的结论基于所选取的小范围样本，期待今后能在更大规模语料基础上进行更深入研究。

参考文献

Alptekin, C. 2002. Towards Intercultural Communicative Competence in ELT. *ELT Journal*, 56(1): 57-64.

Bolivar, A. 1994. The Structure of Newspaper Editorials. In R. M. Counlthard (ed.) *Advances in Written Text Analysis*. London: Routledge, 276-294.

Butler, S. 1997. Corpus of English in Southeast Asia: Implications for a Regional Dictionary. In M. L. S. Bautista (ed.) *English Is an Asian Language: The Philippine Context*. Manila: Macquarie Library.

David, C. 2001. *English as a Global Language*. Beijing: Foreign Language Teaching and Research Press.

Halliday, M. A. K. & Hasan, R.1985. *Language, Context and Text*. Victoria: Deakin University Press.

Hinds, J. 1990. Inductive, Deductive, Quasi-inductive: Expository Writing in Japanese, Korean, Chinese, and Thai. In U. M. Connor & A. Johns. (eds.) *Coherence in Writing: Research and Pedagogical Perspectives*. Alexandria, VA: TESOL,87-109.

Kachru, B. B. 1992. Models for Non-native Englishes. In B. B. Kachru (ed.) *The Other Tongue: English Across Cultures*. Urbana, IL: University of Illinois Press.

Kaplan, Robert B.1996. Cultural Thought Patterns in Intercultural Education. *Language Learning*, (16): 1-20.

McArthur, T. 1997. The Printed Word in the English Speaking World. *English Today*, 13 (1).

Mufwene, S. S. 2003. Approaches to Change in American English. *World Englishes*, 22 (4): 347-349.

Schneider, E. W. 2003. The Dynamics of New Englishes: From Identity Construction to Dialect Birth. *Language*, 79 (2): 233-281.

Scollon, R. & S. Scollon. 1995. *Intercultural Communication: A Discourse Approach*. Oxford, UK: Blackwell Publishers.

Smith, L. E. 1976. English Is an International Auxiliary Language. *RELC* (Regional English Language Center) *Journal*, 17.

Yu, X. A. 2006. Corpus-based Study on the Nativized Use of Evaluative Adjectives in China's English Newspapers. Ph. D Dissertation. Nanjing: Nanjing University.

范荣康，1985，新闻评论的结构，《新闻实践》（11）：29。

高超，2007，《中国语境中的英语报章变革动词研究》。南京：南京大学。

郭可，1993，试析英语社论的写作结构及语言特色，《外国语》（2）：26。

黄国文，1988，《语篇分析概要》。长沙：湖南教育出版社。

姜亚军、杜瑞清，2003，有关"中国英语"的问题——对"'中国英语'质疑"一文的回应，《外语教学》（1）。

李少华、王万平，2002，中国英语和中国英语教学，《广东外语外贸大学学报》（2）：33-37。

李文中，1993，中国英语与中国式英语，《外语教学与研究》（4）。

潘章仙，2002，中国英语变体的研究——回顾与展望，《外语研究》（6）：26。

邱立中，2008，离析还是向心：英语本土化的误区，《四川外语学院学报》（5）：91。

汪榕培，1991，中国英语是客观存在，《解放军外语学院学报》（1）。

谢之君，1995，中国英语：跨文化语言交际中的干扰性变体，《现代汉语》（4）：10。

徐晓晴，2005，世界英语的发展与中国英语变体，《苏州大学学报》（哲学社会科学版）（1）。

俞希、文秋芳，2010，中国英语报章中评价性形容词搭配的本土化特征，《外语与外语教学》（5）。

俞希、文秋芳，2011，构建英语本土化特征的描述框架，《外语教学》（2）：38。

Schneider, E. W. 2003. The dynamics of New Englishes: From identity construction to dialect birth. *Language* 79(2): 233-281.

[illegible]

[illegible] 1976. [illegible] international auxiliary language. [illegible]

[illegible]

[illegible]

语篇中的衔接与语篇主旨大意的关系研究[1]

李元科

华南师范大学

1. 衔接研究综述：现状与不足

衔接（cohesion）指的是语篇中语言成分之间的语义联系（胡壮麟等, 2005：179）。Halliday & Hasan（1976）《英语的衔接》（*Cohesion in English*）被普遍认为是研究衔接的奠基之作。他们在书中给衔接下了定义，阐述衔接的本质，对衔接的方式做了全面和细致的分类，详细讨论实现各种衔接方式的语法和词汇手段，并且探讨了衔接在语篇谋篇方面的作用。该书出版后研究衔接的文献大量涌现，它们的侧重点涵盖以下5个方面：（i）发展和完善《英语的衔接》的理论框架，主要表现在拓宽衔接的范畴（Halliday & Hasan, 1985；张德禄，2000/2001）；（ii）研究英汉语篇衔接手段的异同（朱永生、郑立信、苗兴伟, 2001）；（iii）分析英语学习者作文中的衔接现象，旨在对比不同类型或不同层次的学生在作文中使用各种衔接类型概率的差异（Yang & Sun, 2012）或分析学生使用衔接的类型与数量和作文得分的关系（Chiang, 2003; Liu & Braine, 2005）；（iv）探讨衔接理论在各领域的应用，如翻译（王东风, 2009）、文体学（Gutwinski, 1976）和外语教学（刘辰诞, 1999; 张德禄, 2012）；（v）研究衔接与语篇某方面属性的关系，其中研究衔接和语篇连贯关系的文献居多（Hasan, 1984; Halliday & Hasan, 1985; 胡壮麟, 1994; 朱永生、严世清, 2001; 张德禄、刘汝山, 2003）。然而，学界至今未充分关注衔接与语篇主旨大意的关系这一具有广泛和重要研究意义与价值的课题。

现有研究主要从以下两个视角来探索衔接与语篇大意的关系。（1）分析语篇中显著词汇或短语模式的表意功能。近年来语料库语言学的研究表明关键词（Scott & Tribble, 2006; Stubbs, 2010）、关键语义域（Rayson, 2008）、关键词与搭配词的语义联系（Bondi, 2010; Phillips, 1989; Sinclair, 2005; 吕桂、何安平, 2013）以及关键短语（Warren, 2010）都具有凸显语篇大意的功能。（2）分析语篇的小句、句子或段落之间的逻辑关系，探讨各种关系的语用功能（Mann & Thompson, 1988a, 1988b;

1 本研究受华南师范大学青年教师科研培育基金项目（13SK05）资助，谨此致谢。

Matthiessen & Thompson, 1988）。

然而上述研究在以下方面仍存在不足：（1）较少关注语篇中词汇或短语的重复出现对读者解读语篇大意的影响。（2）较少研究语篇中词汇或短词的频率与它们对于语篇大意重要程度的关系。此外，少有文献研究虚词（如连词）的表意功能。（3）现有研究短语功能的文献主要采用语料库驱动的方法，基于其他理论框架的研究并不多见。

鉴于现有研究的不足，本文应用系统功能语言学的衔接理论（Halliday & Hasan, 1976, 1985; Hasan, 1984; Halliday & Matthiessen, 1999, 2004, 2013; Hoey, 1991）在命题意义重复的视角下研究硬新闻（hard news）语篇中的衔接与它们主旨大意的关系（语篇的大意由读者撰写的摘要来体现）。本文将探讨以下三个问题。问题1研究新闻命题的重复出现对读者解读语篇大意的影响。问题2和3从两方面探索连词的表意功能。

（1）硬新闻命题的频率与它们对于语篇大意的重要程度是否成正比关系?

（2）当新闻的两个或以上命题被收录到摘要时，它们之间的逻辑关系是否也被收录?

（3）出现在新闻导言（即首段落）从句（secondary clauses）或内嵌句（embedded clauses）的命题通常在什么情形下被收录到摘要。

2. 研究设计

2.1 分析的文本

作者从Document Understanding Conferences获取了80篇硬新闻和从事信息提取研究的专家们为它们撰写的摘要。Document Understanding Conferences是由美国国家标准与技术研究所（National Institute of Standards and Technology）组织的旨在促进文本摘要自动化（automatic text summarization）技术发展的年会。每年该会议邀请全球从事文本摘要自动化研究的科研机构或团队参加其举办的大型文本摘要比赛，要求与会者用他们开发的系统为组委会统一发放的文本自动生成摘要，然后组委会用从事信息提取研究的专家们为这些文本撰写的摘要来评估与会者摘要的质量。该会议的介绍见http://duc.nist.gov/。本实验的每篇新闻都有3个摘要，分别由3位专家独立撰写，每个摘要包含大约10个词。

2.2 命题的定义和表征形式

语料库研究表明自然语言输出的单位不是单个单词，而是短语（即两个或以上单词的组合）（见Sinclair, 2004, 2008）。近年来短语的功能是语料库研究的焦点。然而系统功能语言学界至今尚未关注短语。本文在系统功能语言学衔接理论的框架下研究一种形态的短语——命题的表意功能。

下面我们来明确命题的定义和表征形式。命题由事件的过程（process）和过程所涉及的事物来组成（Brown & Yule, 1983; Kintsch & Keenan, 1974; Kintsch & Van Dijk, 1978）。Halliday认为命题在词汇语法层一致式的表达方式是小句（clause），而小句的核心（nucleus）是过程和它的承载体（medium）两者的组合（见Halliday, 1994：163; Halliday & Matthiessen, 1999：154）。Halliday把过程的承载体定义为过程实现的载体（the participant through which the process is actualized, Halliday, 1994：163）。各种类型过程的承载体是：

物质过程：动作者（中动语态）、目标（非中动语态）
行为过程：行为者
心理过程：感知者
言语过程：讲话者（中动语态）、对象（非中动语态）
归属类关系过程：载体
识别类关系过程：被识别者
存在过程：存在物

（Halliday, 1994：165）

由于过程和其承载体组成小句的核心，因此本文用这两者的组合来简略地表征小句表述的命题。例如，例一中小句表述的命题可以简略地用它的核心captured the trophy来表征。

例一：

Switzerland's tennis legend Roger Federer captured the trophy for the fourth time in six years on Sunday.

3. 问题1的研究方法和结果

3.1 问题1的研究方法

问题1研究硬新闻命题的频率与它们对于语篇大意的重要程度是否成正比关系。研究方法如下：

第一步分析新闻的任意两个命题的意义是否存在重复关系。由于命题由过程和其承载体的组合来表征，因此，如果两个命题的过程和承载体都分别存在重复关系，那么这两个命题的意义就构成重复关系，即它们表述相同或同类的经验意义（experiential meanings）。本文按照Hoey（1991）的方法来分析两个命题的过程是否存在重复关系。Hoey（1991）把语篇中的词汇重复（lexical cohesion）分为四种类型：简单重复（simple repetition）、复杂重复（complex repetition）、简单释义

（simple paraphrase）和复杂释义（complex paraphrase）。表1给出了它们的定义和例子。

表1 Hoey（1991）阐述的词汇重复关系的定义和例子

词汇重复的类型	定义和例子
简单重复	某词项被另一词项重复时两者的差异仅仅是语法变体。例如 kill，kills，killed 和 killing（做动词用时）中的任意两个都构成简单重复关系。
复杂重复	包括以下两种情形： （1）两个词项具有相同的词素但形式不同。例如 kill, kills，killed 和 killing（做动词用时）中的任意一个都是 killer（s）的复杂重复。 （2）它们的形式相同但语法功能不同。Human（做名词用时，如 a *human* being）和 human（做形容词用时，如 *human* frailty）构成复杂重复关系。
简单释义	两个词项在形式上既不相同也不相似，但在语篇的语境中一个被另一个替代时它们所在句子的经验意义没有发生变化。简单释义允许一个词项在替代另一个词项时做语法上的词形变化。例如在 The joint investigation team felt the need to question Chong because when Kim killed Pak he was nearby 这一句子中，用 assassinate 替代该句中的 killed 时需要把它转变为过去式形式。Killed 和 assassinate 构成简单释义关系。
复杂释义	包括以下三种情形： （1）反义词，如 happy—unhappy; wet—dry （2）语篇出现词项 a, b 和 c, 如果 a 与 b 构成复杂重复关系，同时 a 是 c 的简单释义（或反义词），那么 b 和 c 构成复杂释义关系。例如，kill 和 killer 构成复杂重复关系，kill 是 assassinate 的简单释义，因此 killer 和 assassinate 构成复杂释义关系。 （3）该情形是第二种情形的复杂化。如果第二种情形描述的三个词项中的一个（比如 c）没有出现在语篇中，但是在语篇的语境中 c 是 a 的简单 / 复杂释义，c 也是 b 的简单 / 复杂重复，那么 a 和 b 构成复杂释义关系。

Hoey（1991：51-68）对这四种关系进行了界定，即给出两个词项构成这些关系需要满足的条件。由于篇幅限制在这里不详细说明。两个过程的承载体存在重复关系的条件是它们在语篇的语境指代相同事物（co-referentiality）或同类事物（co-classification, 见Halliday & Hasan, 1985：74）。

第二步把新闻中的重复命题分在同一组。这样表述相同或同类经验意义的命题被分在同一组，而表述不同类经验意义的命题被分在不同组。

第三步统计新闻所有命题的频率。

第四步分析新闻哪些重复出现的命题的意义出现在读者撰写的摘要。新闻中被分在同一组的任意两个命题都存在重复关系，因此如果小组的任意一个命题和摘要的某个命题存在重复关系，那么该组的其他命题和摘要的那个命题也都存在重复关系（Hoey, 1991：57）。如果新闻某命题的过程和承载体与摘要某命题的过程和承载体分别存在重复关系，那么新闻那个命题（的意义）就被收录到那个摘要。本文采用Li & Hoey（2014）阐述的方法（见图1）分析新闻命题的过程是否与摘要命题的过程构成重复关系以及它们的重复关系的类型。该图的问题8、9、10和11都询问新闻某命题的过程X和摘要的过程是否有相同的语境或两者的语境是否在某方面有关联。当下述任何一个条件满足时，它们的答案是肯定的（Hoey, 1991：57）：

a. 它们的语境是否有词项指代相同事物？

b. 它们的语境是否有词项指代同类事物？

c. 它们语境的结构是否相似？

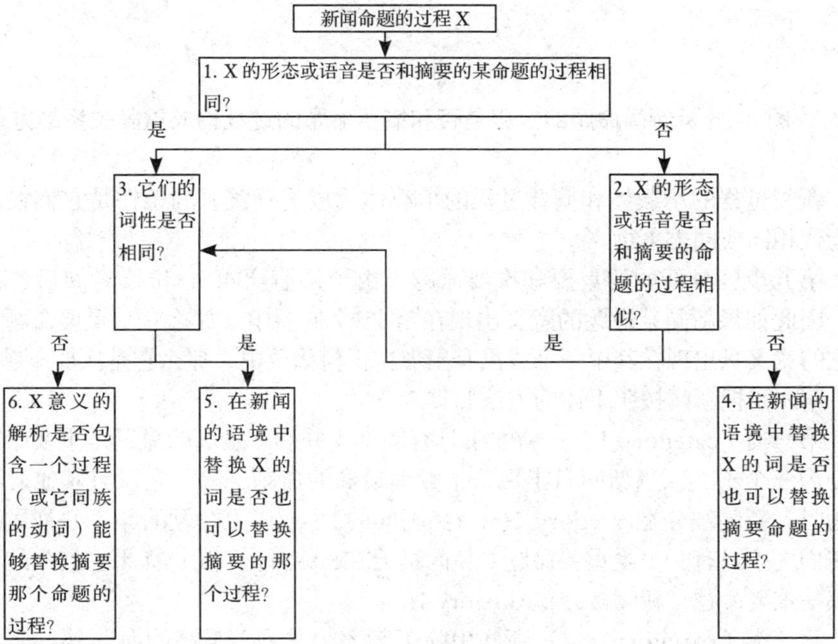

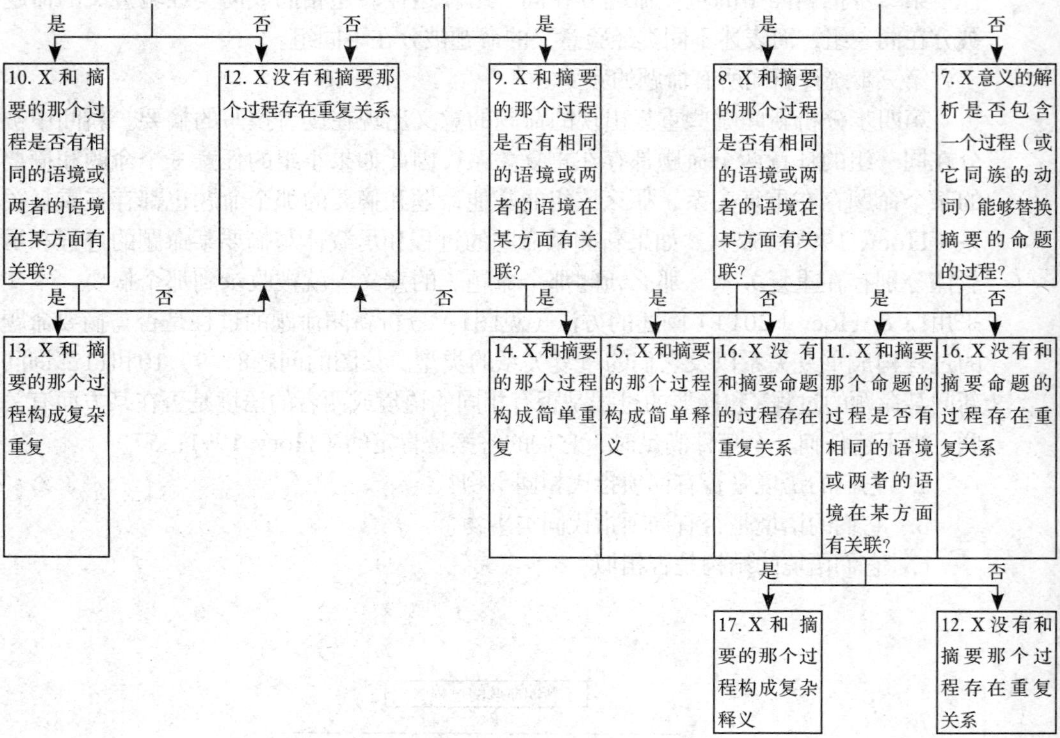

图 1 分析新闻命题的过程是否和摘要命题的过程构成重复关系的方法

新闻过程的承载体和摘要过程的承载体构成重复关系的条件是它们在新闻的语境指代相同或同类事物。

第五步区分新闻的重要和次要命题。由于每篇新闻由3位读者阅后各自撰写摘要，因此如果新闻某命题的意义出现在至少2个摘要中，那么它是重要命题。相反如果它的意义只出现在其中一个或没有出现在任何摘要中，那么它是次要命题。

第六步把新闻按照下述的方法归类：

第一类（category 1）：新闻中只有频率（并列）最高的命题是重要命题。它被细分为三个子类。当新闻只出现一个频率最高的命题，除了它没有其他命题是重要命题时，新闻被分在category 1(a)。当新闻的2个或以上命题的频率并列最高时，如果它们之中只有一个是重要命题，新闻被分在category 1(b)；如果它们中的两个或以上都是重要命题，新闻被分在category 1(c)。

第二类（category 2）：新闻中除了频率（并列）最高的命题外，还有其他命题也是重要命题。它被细分为两个子类。如果新闻只出现一个频率最高的命题，除了它还有其他命题也是重要命题，新闻被分在category 2(a)；如果新闻的2个或以上命题的频率并列最高，它们之中至少有一个和其他命题都是重要命题，新闻被分在category 2(b)。

第三类（category 3）：新闻中（并列）最高频率的命题不是而其他命题是重要命题。它也被细分为两个子类。如果只有一个不是最高频的命题是重要命题，新闻被分在category 3(a)；如果两个或以上不是最高频的命题是重要命题，新闻被分在category 3(b)。

第四类（category 4）：新闻中没有一个重复出现的命题是重要命题。也就是说，表述原文主旨大意的重要命题在新闻中只出现一次。

3.2 问题1的结果和讨论

图2给出各类别包含新闻的数量及占总数的比例（C代表Category）。

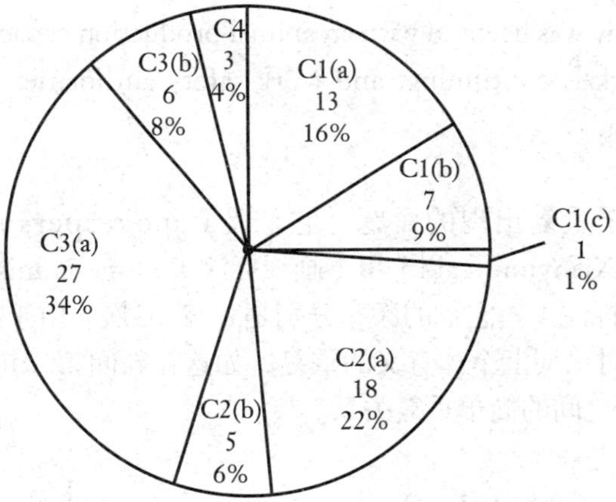

图2 各类别包含的原文数量以及占总数的比例

图2显示categories 1和2的每一篇新闻都至少有一个（并列）最高频的命题被读者认为是所在语篇的重要命题。这两类共有44篇新闻，占总数的54%。因此，硬新闻的频率最高的命题大约有54%的概率是所在文本的重要命题。然而，categories 2、3和4的每一篇新闻都至少有一个不是最高频的命题是重要命题。这三类共有59篇新闻，占总数的74%。因此，硬新闻非最高频的命题大约有74%的概率是所在语篇的重要命题。对比这两个百分比可以看到，这类体裁语篇的非最高频的命题比最高频的命题有更高的概率被读者认为是重要命题，表明硬新闻命题的频率与它们对于所在语篇大意的重要程度不成正比关系。Category 3的新闻为这个结论提供了实证，因为在这些语篇中频率最高的命题都不被读者认为是重要命题。此外，categories 2和3共有32个命题在所在新闻中只出现两次，但它们都被读者认为是重要命题；同样category 4的每一篇新闻的重要命题在原文只出现一次。这些也都证明了上述结论。例二给出频率最高的命题不被读者认为是重要命题的一篇新闻。

例二：

YUXIAN, Shanxi — (1) At least **10 people died** and one is missing after a coal mine gas explosion Tuesday in north China's Shanxi Province, a spokesperson for work safety authorities said on Wednesday.

(2) The accident occurred at around 4:50 p.m. Tuesday when 41 miners were working in the shaft of Chentong Coal Industry Co., Ltd., in YuXian county.

(3) Twenty-seven people escaped from the scene unhurt and 14 were trapped underground, said Liu Xianyun, of the work safety committee of Yangquan City, which administers YuXian county.

(4) Three of the trapped had been rescued, while **10 died** and *one is missing*, Liu said at a press conference.

(5) The company was licensed with an animal production capacity of 600,000 tonnes.

(6) Rescue work is continuing, and work safety authorities are investigating the cause of the accident.

这篇新闻有3个重复出现的命题，它们是a spokesperson for work safety authorities（即Liu Xianyun）said（用下画线标注），one is missing（用斜体标注）和10 died（用粗体标注）。它们的频率分别是3、2和2次。由于本文分析的是命题意义的重复，因此不讨论词汇个体意义的重复，如这篇新闻第二句开头的accident和第六句结尾的accident之间的简单重复关系。

本文的3个摘要是：

(a) At least **10 were killed** and *one was missing* in an explosion.

(b) **10 died** and *one was missing* in a coal mine explosion.

(c) **10 died** and *one was missing* in a mine explosion in north China.

这则新闻频率最高的命题Liu Xianyun said的意义并没有出现在任何摘要。然而，另外两个命题one is missing和10 died的意义都出现在这3个摘要中。

硬新闻命题的频率与它们对于语篇大意的重要程度不成正比关系，这个结论表明，在分析语篇大意时，除了命题出现的频率外也需要考虑其他因素。在研究问题1时有两个因素没有被考虑。一是命题在新闻出现的位置。李元科（2012）发现大多数被收录到新闻摘要的命题都出现在导言；新闻导言的命题比没有出现在导言的命题有更高的概率被收录到摘要。这和Bell（1991）、Van Dijk（1988）和 White（1997）等人认为硬新闻的标题和导言通常概括它们的主旨大意的观点是相符的。另外一个没有被考虑的因素是不同命题之间的逻辑关系。William Mann、Sandra Thompson和Christian Matthiessen的修辞结构理论（Mann & Thompson, 1988a, 1988b; Matthiessen & Thompson, 1988）认为语篇的结构是层级性的，每级层面的两个或以上的文本节段（text span）以某种修辞关系连接起来组成高一级层面的节段，并和该级的其他节段再以某种修辞关系连接，以此类推。他们发现出现频率较高的修辞关系大约有20多种。他们把这些修辞关系分为两类：多核心类（multi-nuclei）

和核心–辅助类（nucleus-satellite）。如果各节段的地位同等，连接它们的修辞关系属于多核心类;如果它们的地位不同等，它们的修辞关系属于核心–辅助类，核心节段表述作者的中心意思或主要的交际意图，是语篇不可或缺的部分，而辅助节段从属于核心节段，并通过某种修辞关系帮助核心节段实现其交际功能。大多数的修辞关系属于核心–辅助类，只有少数几种属于多核心类。Mann & Thompson（1988a, 1988b）指出如果把语篇的辅助节段删除只保留核心节段，那么由核心节段组成的短文通常能够概括原文的主旨大意。因此，分析语篇的主旨大意时也需要分析节段之间的逻辑关系。下文探讨问题2和3时将详细讨论这些因素。

4. 问题2的结果和讨论

问题2探讨当新闻的两个或以上命题被收录到摘要时，它们之间的逻辑关系是否也被收录。图2中categories 1(c)，2和3(b)的每篇新闻都有两个或以上命题被收录到摘要。以下关联词出现在这些新闻的导言连接两个或以上命题：因果关系的关联词有due to, in hopes of, in an effort to和to（in order to的缩略）；时间关系的关联词有and（then缺省），after和while（=at the same time）；以及并列关系的关联词and。问题2的分析结果显示当新闻的两个或以上命题被收录到摘要时，导言中连接它们关联词的意义也经常被收录（下文把这种现象称为连接复制）。例如例三给出一篇新闻的导言和三位读者为这篇新闻撰写的摘要。

例三：

Beijing — Police in a county of North China's Hebei province issued fake warrants to detain six villagers in a land dispute for bail money, the *Beijing News* reported on Wednesday.（导言）

导言所在新闻的摘要：

(a) Police issued fake warrants to detain six villagers for money.
(b) Police used fake warrants to detain six villagers for bail.
(c) Police in Hebei issued fake warrants to detain six villagers.

该导言的命题issued fake warrants被收录在摘要(a)和(c)，另外一个命题detain six villagers被收录在这三个摘要中。在导言这两个命题由表示目的关系的关联词to（in order to的缩略）来连接，它们之间的这种逻辑关系也被复制到摘要(a)和(c)。

Li & Hoey（2014）与李元科、邓飞（2015）讨论本实验的读者为硬新闻撰写摘要采用的策略以及各种策略涉及的词汇语法知识。表2显示读者在摘要中建构新闻命题的方式和它们在每100个摘要的频率。

表2 本实验的摘要撰写人建构新闻命题的方式与标准频率
（李元科、邓飞，2015）

读者在摘要中建构新闻单个命题的方式	读者在摘要中建构新闻两个或以上命题方式
简单释义（35%）	复制导言的连接（30%）
复杂释义（25%）	创建连接（10%）
复杂重复（16%）	
简单重复（13%）	

复制导言的连接是读者在摘要中建构有关新闻两个或以上命题时最经常采用的方式。另外一种方式创建连接指，新闻没有明确说明两个或以上命题的关系，但读者在摘要中用关联词明确标示它们的关系。例如例四给出一篇新闻的导言和它的三个摘要。

例四：

Police in Beijing's Chaoyang district on Tuesday discovered 557 hostesses providing paid services, which is against the law, in four luxury night clubs, and suspended the clubs' business for six months, the *Beijing Times* reported Thursday.（导言）

三位读者阅读这篇新闻后各自撰写的摘要是：

(a) Four night clubs were suspended for providing paid hostesses services.

(b) Four night clubs were suspended due to provision of paid services.

(c) Four night clubs were suspended for paid services.

该导言的providing paid services的意义出现在（a）和（b）两个摘要。这个导言有两种分析方式。557 hostesses providing paid services可视为被心理过程Police in Beijing's Chaoyang district on Tuesday discovered投射。Providing paid services也可视为内嵌句（embedded clause）修饰前面的557 hostesses。但无论采纳哪种分析方式，在导言providing paid services和suspended the clubs' business不存在任何语义关系。但（a）和（b）两个摘要分别用表示因果关系的关联词for和due to来连接这两个命题。读者在创建连接时需要推测（infer）命题之间的关系，这是语言能力层次较高的读者才具备的能力（Brown & Day, 1983; Keck, 2010; Shi, 2012）。

读者在摘要中复制和创建连接表明把握命题之间的逻辑关系是读者分析文本连贯的重要手段。这一点修辞结构理论和Li & Hoey（2014：99-100）都有论述，在这里由于篇幅限制不做详细说明。

5. 问题3的结果和讨论

上文提到被收录到摘要的新闻命题趋向于出现在导言，确切地说是趋向于出现在导言的主句（primary clauses）或独立句（independent clauses）（见李元科，2012）。当导言由主从关系（hypotactic）的两个小句（或句簇clause complex，下同）组成时，被依附的小句是主句，而依附于主句的小句是从句。当导言只包含单个小句或由两个或以上并列（paratactic）句组成时，它们都是独立句。学界较少探讨从句和内嵌句的命题在什么情形下被读者认为是语篇的重要命题。这是这一小节要探讨的问题。

本文采用Halliday & Matthiessen（2004：363-395）分析小句的框架分析这80篇新闻导言的重要命题所在小句类型，然后观察出现在从句或内嵌句的重要命题被收录到摘要的条件。分析结果表明，导言的从句和内嵌句的命题通常不会单独成为重要命题，它们在摘要中以某种逻辑关系依附导言主句或独立句的命题。下文具体描述它们被收录到摘要的条件。

当导言从句的命题被读者认为是重要命题时，它们所依附的主句的命题也被认为是重要命题，而且读者在撰写摘要时复制它们在导言的关系（即上文描述的复制导言的连接）。例如，例三导言的被投射（projected）部分是主从复合句，主句是Police in a county of North China's Hebei province issued fake warrants，从句是detain six villagers in a land dispute for bail money。issued fake warrants和detain six villagers是该导言所在新闻的重要命题，因为它们分别被收录在两个或以上摘要，但前者出现在导言的主句而后者出现在从句。后者依附前者的方式也被复制到同时收录它们的摘要。

当导言内嵌句的命题被读者认为是重要命题时，主句或独立句的命题也被读者认为是重要命题，而且读者在摘要中用关联词标示它们的关系（即创建连接）。例如，例四导言的被投射部分由一个主从复合句（i.e. Police in Beijing's Chaoyang district on Tuesday discovered 557 hostesses providing paid services, which is against the law, in four luxury night clubs）和一个小句（i.e. suspended the clubs' business for six months）组成。Providing paid services和suspended the clubs' business是这篇新闻的重要命题，因为它们都被收录到两个或以上摘要。前者可视为后置修饰557 hostesses的内嵌句，而后者出现在与主从复合句并列的小句。如前文所言，在导言中它们不存在任何逻辑关系，但本实验的摘要撰写人在摘要（a）和（b）中用因果关系的关联词连接它们。

6. 结束语

本文在命题意义重复的视角下研究硬新闻语篇的衔接与语篇主旨大意的关系，着重探讨命题在新闻出现的频率对读者解读语篇大意的影响及连词的表意功能。研究结果表明，命题的频率与它们对于语篇主旨大意的重要程度不成正比关系；复制导言的连接是读者在摘要中建构新闻两个或以上命题时最经常采用的方式。导言的从句和内嵌句的命题通常不会单独成为重要命题，它们在摘要中以某种逻辑关系依附导言主句或独立句的命题。

目前学界研究短语主要采用语料库驱动的方法，本文阐述的基于系统功能语言学衔接理论的方法为研究短语提供了新的方法和手段。此方法具有广阔的应用前景，如Li & Hoey（2014）与李元科、邓飞（2015）讨论它在研究摘要写作策略方面的应用。

参考文献

Bell, A. 1991. *The Language of News Media*. Oxford: Blackwell.

Bondi, M. 2010. Perspectives on Keywords and Keyness. In M. Bondi & M. Scott, (eds.), *Keyness in Texts*. Amsterdam: Benjamins. 1-18.

Bondi, M. & M. Scott. 2010. *Keyness in Texts*. Amsterdam: Benjamins.

Brown, A. L. & J. D. Day. 1983. Macrorules for Summarizing Texts: The Development of Expertise. *Journal of Verbal Learning and Verbal Behavior*, 22: 1-14.

Brown, G. & G. Yule. 1983. *Discourse Analysis*. Cambridge: Cambridge University Press.

Chiang, S. Y. 2003. The Importance of Cohesive Conditions to Perceptions of Writing Quality at the Early Stages of Foreign Language Learning. *System*, 31: 471-484.

Gutwinski, W. 1976. *Cohesion in Literary Texts*. The Hague: Mouton.

Halliday, M. A. K. 1994. *An Introduction to Functional Grammar*. Beijing: Foreign Language Teaching and Research Press.

Halliday, M. A. K. & R. Hasan. 1976. *Cohesion in English*. London: Longman.

Halliday, M. A. K. & R. Hasan. 1985. *Language, Context, and Text: Aspects of Language in a Social Semiotic Perspective* (2nd edition). Oxford: Oxford University Press.

Halliday, M. A. K. & C. M. I. M. Matthiessen. 1999. *Construing Experience through Meaning: A Language-Based Approach to Cognition*. London: Continuum.

Halliday, M. A. K. & C. M. I. M. Matthiessen. 2004. *An Introduction to Functional Grammar* (3rd edition). London: Arnold.

Halliday, M. A. K. & C. M. I. M. Matthiessen. 2013. *Halliday's Introduction to Functional Grammar* (4th edition). London: Routledge.

Hasan, R. 1984. Coherence and Cohesive Harmony. In J. Flood (ed.). *Understanding Reading Comprehension*. Delaware: International Reading Association, 181-219.

Hoey, M. 1991. *Patterns of Lexis in Text*. Oxford: Oxford University Press.

Keck C. 2010. How Do University Students Attempt to Avoid Plagiarism? A

Grammatical Analysis of Undergraduate Paraphrasing Strategies. *Writing & Pedagogy*, 2: 193-222.

Kintsch, W. & J. M. Keenan. 1974. Recall of Propositions as Function of Their Position in the Hierarchical Structure. In W. Kintsch (ed.). *The Representation of Meaning in Memory*, Hillsdale, New York: Lawrence Erlbaum Associates, 137-140.

Kintsch, W. & T. A. van Dijk. 1978. Toward a Model of Text Comprehension and Production. *Psychology Review*, 85: 363-394.

Liu, M. & G. Braine. 2005. Cohesive Features in Argumentative Writing Produced by Chinese Undergraduates. *System*, 33: 623-636.

Li, Y. K.（李元科）& M. Hoey. 2014. Strategies of Writing Summaries for Hard News Texts: A Text Analysis Approach. *Discourse Studies*, 16(1): 89-105.

Mann, W. & S. Thompson. 1988a. Rhetorical Structure Theory: A Theory of Text Organization. In L. Polanyi (ed.) *The Structure of Discourse*. Norwood, N.J.: Ablex. Also available as ISI/RR, 87-100.

Mann, W. & S. Thompson. 1988b. Rhetorical Structure Theory: Toward a Functional Theory of Text Organization. *Text*, 8(3): 243-281.

Matthiessen, C. M. I. M. & S. A. Thompson. 1988. The Structure of Discourse And 'Subordination'. In J. Haiman & S.A. Thompson (eds.) *Clause Combining in Grammar and Discourse*. Amsterdam: Benjamins, 275-329.

Phillips, M. 1989. *Lexical Structures of Text*. Birmingham: ELR, University of Birmingham.

Rayson, P. 2008. From Key Words to Key Semantic Domains. *International Journal of Corpus Linguistics*, 13(4): 519-549.

Scott, M. & C. Tribble. 2006. *Textual Patterns: Key Words and Corpus Analysis in Language Education*. Amsterdam: Benjamins.

Shi, L. 2012. Originality of Expressions and Formal Citation Practices. *Writing & Pedagogy*, 4(1).

Sinclair, J. McH. 2005. Document Relativity. Ms, Tuscan Word Centre, Italy.

Sinclair, J. McH. 2004. *Trust the Text: Language, Corpus and Discourse*. London: Routledge.

Sinclair, J. McH. 2008. The Phrase, the Whole Phrase, and Nothing but the Phrase. In Granger & Meunier (eds.) *Phraseology: An Interdisciplinary Perspective*. Amsterdam/ Philadelphia: John Benjamins, 407-410.

Stubbs, M. 2010. Three Concepts of Keywords. In M. Bondi & M. Scott. (eds.), *Keyness in Texts*. Amsterdam: Benjamins. 21-42.

Van Dijk, T. A. 1988. *News as Discourse*. Hillsdale, NJ: Lawrence Erlbaum Associates.

Warren, M. 2010. Identifying Aboutgrams in Engineering Text. In M. Bondi & M. Scott (eds.), *Keyness in Texts*. Amsterdam: Benjamins. 113-126.

White, P. R. R. 1997. Death, Disruption and the Moral Order: The Narrative Impulse in Mass-Media "Hard News" Reporting. In M. Toolan (ed.) *Critical Discourse Analysis: Critical Concepts in Linguistics*, Vol. 3. London and New York: Routledge, 390-424.

Yang, W. X. & Y. Sun. 2012. The Use of Cohesive Devices in Argumentative Writing by Chinese EFL Learners at Different Proficiency Levels. *Linguistics and Education*, 23: 31-48.

胡壮麟 , 1994,《语篇的衔接与连贯》, 上海 : 上海外语教育出版社。

胡壮麟、朱永生、张德禄、李战子 , 2005,《系统功能语言学概论》, 北京 : 北京大学出版社。

李元科 , 2012,《语篇中的衔接和语篇主旨大意的关系》, 广州 : 中山大学出版社。

李元科、邓飞 , 2015, 命题意义重复视角下的语篇衔接与语篇主旨大意的关系及应用研究 ,《外语与外语教学》(3): 79-86。

刘辰诞 , 1999,《教学篇章语言学》。上海 : 上海外语教育出版社。

吕桂、何安平 , 2013, 医学英语关键词的语义关系探究 ,《语料库的短语理念及其教学加工》: 97-105。

王东风 , 2009,《连贯与翻译》。上海 : 上海外语教育出版社。

张德禄 , 2000, 论语篇连贯 ,《外语教学与研究》(2) : 103-109。

张德禄 , 2001, 论衔接 ,《外国语》(2) : 23-28。

张德禄、刘汝山 , 2003,《语篇连贯与衔接理论的发展及应用》。上海 : 上海外语教育出版社。

张德禄 , 2012,《语篇分析理论的发展及应用》。北京 : 外语教学与研究出版社。

朱永生、严世清 , 2001,《系统功能语言学多维思考》。上海 : 上海外语教育出版社。

朱永生、郑立信、苗兴伟 , 2001,《英汉语篇衔接手段对比研究》。上海 : 上海外语教育出版社。

评价资源的语篇组织功能

——以丘吉尔就职演说《热血、辛劳、眼泪和汗水》为例

张冉冉

北京师范大学

1. 引言

Halliday曾提出“语言文体学”的概念，把语言学理论和方法应用于语篇分析。系统功能语言学从创立之初便与语篇研究结下了不解之缘。无论是及物性结构、语气结构以及主位结构，还是后来作为小句语法的补充而提出的衔接理论等，都为语篇分析提供了重要的理论支持。衔接理论主要是关注词汇概念意义的衔接关系，忽略了语篇中人际意义资源的衔接作用。本文将基于Martin的语言评价系统，以英国前首相丘吉尔的就职演说《热血、辛劳、眼泪和汗水》为例探究语篇中评价资源的组篇功能，包括评价资源形成衔接链的条件，态度链间以及态度链与介入链、级差链间的相互作用，尤其是态度链之间的互动方式。

2. 语言评价系统简介

语言评价系统是J.R. Martin在人际意义方面对系统功能理论的进一步发展，并与协商系统、参与系统一起构成语篇语义层的三大人际意义系统。语言评价系统通过对语篇语言形式的分析关注作者或说话人在语篇中的主观投入，分为态度、介入和级差三个子系统，彼此间为合取关系（Martin & White, 2005）。

首先，态度是情感表达的方法，由情感、判断和鉴赏三个范畴构成。情感处于中心地位，包括意愿性、愉悦性、满意性和安全性；判断和鉴赏是体现化的情感，前者是对行为的评判，表示人或行为的态势性、能力性、可靠性、真诚性和恰当性，后者是对事物或现象的评估，由反应性、构成性和估价性构成。其次，介入指示态度的来源，按对话空间大小可分为收缩性介入和扩展性介入：收缩性介入包括否定、对立、认同、宣告和引证；扩展性介入则包括接纳、宣称和疏离。最后，级差调节态度或介入的强弱，依据等级性分为语势和聚焦，前者又进一步包括数量、体积、跨度、质量和过程等子范畴[1]。

语言评价系统作为一个语篇语义系统，在词汇–语法层具有不同的体现形式。尽管语言评价系统依然存在不足之处，但它包含了对社会符号资源更系统和全面的描述，是对Halliday系统功能语言学人际意义研究的补充（张德禄、刘世铸, 2006）。随着在语篇分析中的广泛应用，语言评价系统自身也获得了长足发展，尤其是在评价组篇方面，如评价意义的韵律结构（Martin, 2000）、评价意义与语篇周期性的关系（Marin, 2004; Hood, 2009）、评价语篇性和评价隐喻等重要观点的提出（彭宣维, 2009, 2010）等。

3. 语言评价系统在语篇分析中的具体应用

3.1 语篇评价资源的整体分布

《热血、辛劳、眼泪和汗水》是丘吉尔于1940年5月13日在下院发表的首相就职演讲，由4段构成，共计938个词，共有156个评价单元[2]，这些评价单元在整个语篇中的分布密度为0.166。评价单元在演讲各段的分布情况如表1所示：

表1 评价单元在语篇中的分布

段	一	二	三	四
评价单元（个）	36	19	37	64
词（个）	242	163	246	287
分布密度	0.149	0.117	0.150	0.223

由表1可知，评价单元在各段落中的分布密度由高到低依次为四、三、一、二，只有第四段的分布密度0.223高于平均密度0.166。此外，图1为我们展示了演讲中出现最多的词：

1 为便于阐述，本文将用数字 (1—26) 表示整个语言评价系统的 26 个范畴。其中：
态度意义，情感：意愿性 (1)、愉悦性 (2)、满意性 (3)、安全性 (4)；判断：态势性 (5)、能力性 (6)、可靠性 (7)、真诚性 (8)、恰当性 (9)；鉴赏：反应性 (10)、构成性 (11)、估价性 (12)；并用 "+/-" 表示态度意义的极性："+" 表示积极态度，"-" 表示消极态度。
介入意义，收缩性：否定 (13)、对立 (14)、认同 (15)、宣告 (16)、引证 (17)；扩展性：接纳 (18)、宣称 (19) 和疏离 (20)。
级差意义，语势：数量 (21)、体积 (22)、跨度 (23)、质量 (24) 和过程 (25)；聚焦 (26)。

2 同一个评价单元可同时体现不同的评价意义，如 can 既有态度意义又有介入意义。

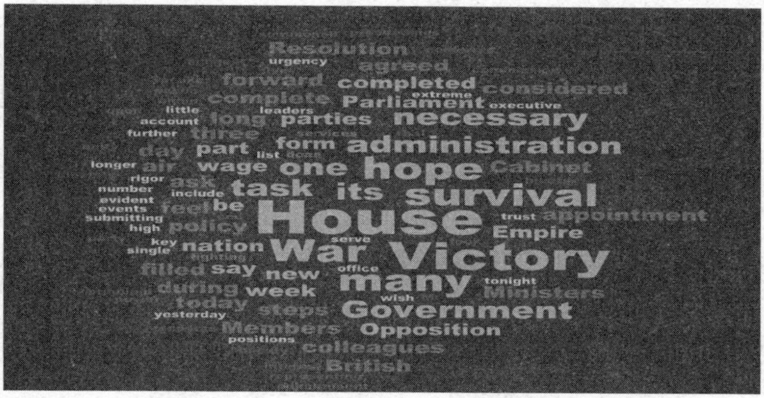

图1 《热血、辛劳、眼泪和汗水》词云

其中，出现频次由高到低分别为House、victory、survival、hope、war、many、government、administration和necessary；具有评价意义的为victory（+12）、survival（+12）、hope（+1）、necessary（+12，+7，18，16）、many（21）。由这几个词，我们可获得演讲的大概主题：胜利与生存的重要性。

本研究将从评价对象、评价范畴和评价者等方面具体考察评价资源的语篇组织功能，关注它们的互动方式。

3.2 语篇中的评价资源及其互动关系

首先，该文第一段的态度资源较多（61%），共有22个，其中判断资源11个，占50%，鉴赏资源7个，占32%，情感资源4个，占18%。分析发现，第一段的评价对象大多与组阁即组织新政府有关，可分为两类：（一）组阁任务本身或一部分，如$this_1$、part of $this_1$ task、$this_2$、$this_3$ part of my task。这里重复出现指示代词this，但其具体所指并不相同（图2），只有$this_1$是指整个组阁任务。

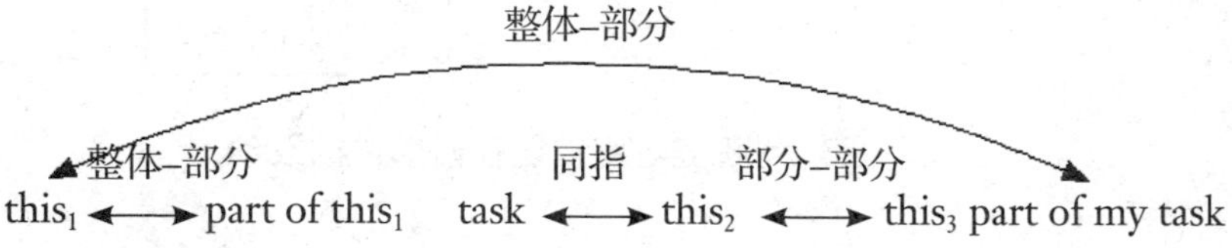

图2 语义关系

（二）组阁任务中的具体行为，如a War Cabinet、the three party leaders、the three fighting services、a number of other key positions、the appointment of the principal Ministers等。这些行为实际是图1中part of $this_1$ task（$this_2$）所包含的具体内容。然而上述一些与组阁有关的名词性结构并不是评价的直接评价对象，而是

组阁具体行为的对象，只不过在被动语态中处于主语位置；由及物性系统看，它们又是物质过程的目标（Goal），如A War Cabinet has been formed of five Members, representing、The three fighting services have been filled等。这些物质过程在语篇中可引发态度意义，体现积极可靠性（+7），由于动作者（Actor）“我”通过被动形式隐藏，这里便会突出“过程+目标”这一行为本身的可靠，也就是说评价对象变为与组阁有关的具体行为本身。

这样，基于评价对象（组阁或与组阁相关）和评价范畴，评价资源随语篇的动态发展可形成两条人际意义衔接链。

判断链：should（+9）—has been formed（+7）—have agreed（+7）—have been filled（+7）—necessary（+7）—should（+7）—be done（+7）—were filled（+7）—to complete（+7）—be completed（+7）

鉴赏链：important（+12）—urgency（-10）—rigor（-10）—key（+12）—principal（+12）—complete（+11）

它们在语篇中的互动关系如图3所示：

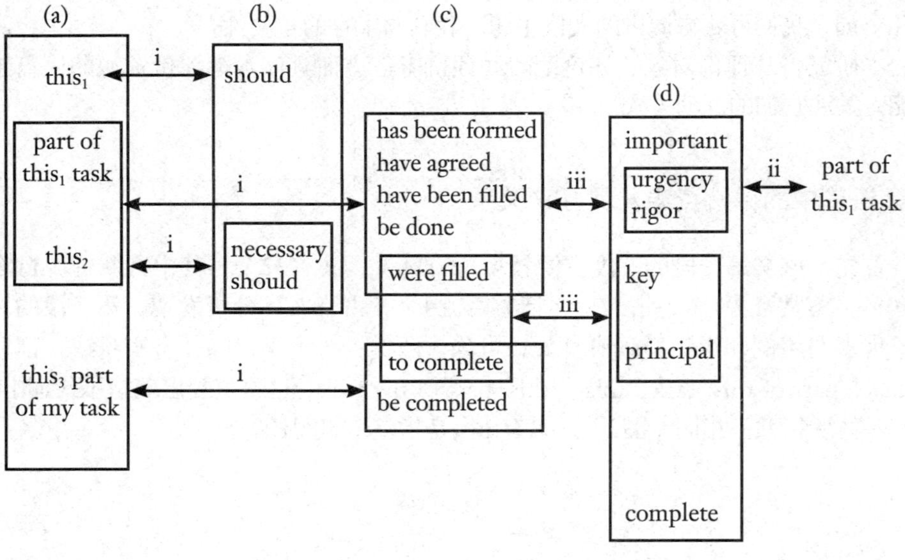

图3 判断链与鉴赏链在语篇中的互动

图3方框代表一条衔接链或衔接链的一部分。其中，（a）链是由评价对象构成的语义衔接，与组阁任务有关，属于经验意义链；（b）链由情态资源构成，既有态度意义，又有介入意义，这里与宣告意义（16）有关，用于调节语篇中的态度意义；（c）链是由判断资源构成的判断链，判断意义（+7）由及物性过程引发，主要是物质过程；（d）链则是由鉴赏范畴构成的鉴赏链，important、urgency和rigor的评价对象为组阁任务的一部分，key与principal的评价对象则是相关物质过程的目标，与组阁行为有关。箭头表示衔接链间的关系为：

i　判断意义的评价对象；

ii　鉴赏意义的评价对象；

iii　原因（消极或积极鉴赏资源为及物性过程引发积极态度意义提供依据）。

鉴赏链的最后一个成分complete没有与其他衔接链发生交互作用，它却是整个第一段评价意义的落脚点：是对组阁后新政府的积极评价（+11）。换句话说，组阁任务的重要性和迫切性为组阁（具体）行为的必要性和可靠性提供支持，而组阁任务的完美落幕也就预示着新政府在各个方面都将是完整无缺的。

其次，第二段与第一段的明显不同在于介入资源的变化：由单声转向多声，由收缩性介入转向扩展性介入。该段介入意义的体现形式有I considered、suggest、will、of course、if、need、will、I invite等。这些资源都是内部声源，除of course外均属于接纳范畴（18），在构成语篇多声背景的过程中开放对话的空间，使潜在听话者能够最大限度地就某一态度或观点达成一致。此外，尽管of course属于收缩性介入，但这里它是指让步性认同，其修辞效果在于承认并认同可能存在其他不同意见。这将进一步增大了说话者与潜在听话者结盟的可能。

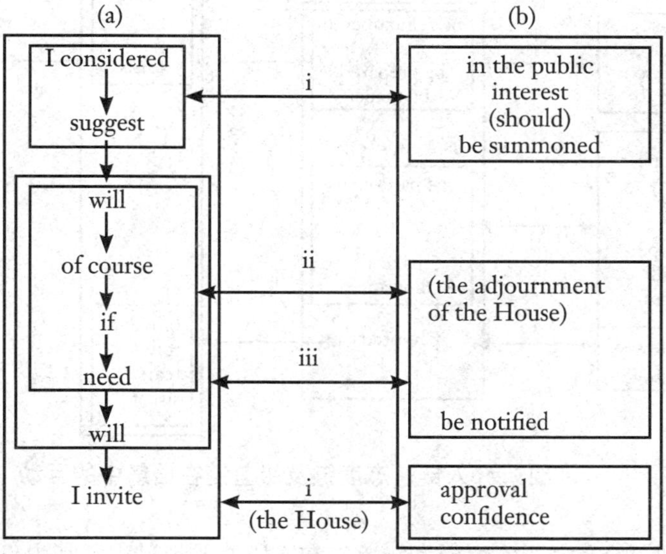

图4　介入链与态度链在语篇中的互动

图4的（a）链由表示内部声源的介入资源资源组成；（b）链则是说话者的相关态度或观点。这两条人际意义衔接链在语篇中的交互关系包括：

i　态度来源；

ii　多个介入资源调节某一观点；

iii　命题或观点来源。

值得注意的是，（b）链最后两个成分approval与confidence表面上是对下院的情感评价，分别属于积极愉悦性（+2）和积极安全性（+4），实际暗示说话者对新政府的行为评判，即认为新政府是可靠的，令人信任的（+7）。

总之，上述两段的评价资源随语篇动态发展呈现出不同评价特征：第一段的态度意义比较明显，尤其是判断意义和鉴赏意义；说话者“我”在很多情况下通过被动形式隐藏。第二段则突出说话者的内部声源，多为接纳意义；相比第一段而言，语篇的多声对话背景更加突出。两段的相同之处在于，评价意义最终都聚焦于新政府，由第一段的积极鉴赏意义发展到第二段的积极判断意义。

再次，第三段评价资源的一个典型特征是级差资源引发态度意义，如preliminary、greatest、continuous、many等可突出形势的危急，暗含消极鉴赏意义（-10）。另一个评价特征是内部声源由“我们”（we）到“我”（I）的转化。面临紧迫形势，说话者先使用第一人称复数通过介入系统的宣告资源（16）向听话者喊话，缩小对话空间的同时使相关态度立场不容质疑，如must、have to；之后又以第一人称单数的形式运用相应的接纳资源（18），展现自己对听话者的愿望或期盼，如I hope、may、if 、will等。

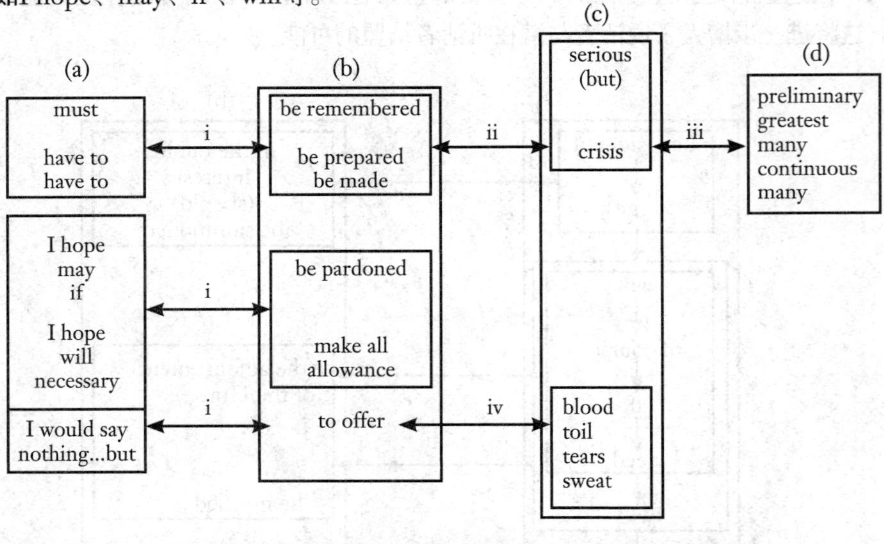

图5 介入链、态度链及级差链在语篇中的互动

图5呈现了介入链、态度链和级差链在本段的互动过程。其中，（a）链由内部声源的介入资源构成，体现由“我们”到“我”的变化过程；（b）链表示介入范畴所协商的态度意义，属于由及物性过程引发的积极可靠性（+7）；（c）链由相关鉴赏范畴组成；（d）链包括可引发某一态度意义的级差范畴。

需要注意，尽管判断链（b）的评价对象不一致，前三个评价成分的评价对象为“我们”，be pardoned和make all allowance的评价对象为听话者“你们”，最后offer的评价对象为说话者“我”，但无论是“你们”还是“我”都包含在“我们”之中，它们之间具有整体与部分的关系。这样，整个判断链就会突出“天下兴亡、匹夫有责”的人际意义。（c）链serious（+10）—crisis（-10）的评价对象也有变化，由组阁任务变为国家当前所处的形势，评价意义也由积极变为消极。在这一转变过程中，对立资源but（14）发挥了重要作用，具有“超出预期”的修辞效果，使评价对象自然改变的同时又强调后者更需要引起我们的关注。（d）链preliminary（23）—greatest（24）—many（21）—continuous（23）—many（21）分属于不同的级差范畴，在语篇中可旗示（flag）形势的险恶，增强消极反应意义（-10）。

图5箭头表示的互动关系有：

i 态度来源；

ii 原因（消极鉴赏意义为积极行为判断提供依据）；

iii 级差引发相关态度；

iv 过程目标。

由此，图5鉴赏链中的crisis不仅是“我们”进行具体行为的原因，也是说话者运用不同介入资源向大家喊话的原因，因此是整个互动过程的中心。说话者在本段末尾以第一人称单数再次向听话者宣告为解决当前的危急，要奉献出自己的热血、辛劳、眼泪和汗水。显然，说话者这里不仅是要强调热血、辛劳、眼泪和汗水的重要性，更是期盼大家与他一道为国家献出自己的一切。

最后，演讲第四段评价单元的分布密度最大，尤以鉴赏资源突出。这些鉴赏资源依据评价对象和评价意义极性可形成两条鉴赏链。

鉴赏链$_1$：ordeal（-10）—grievous（-10）—struggle（-10）—suffering（-10）monstrous（-10）[tyranny（-12）]—dark（-10）—lamentable（-10）[crime（-12）]

鉴赏链$_2$：victory（5次）（+12）—survival（2次）（+12）—survival（+12）—survival（+12）

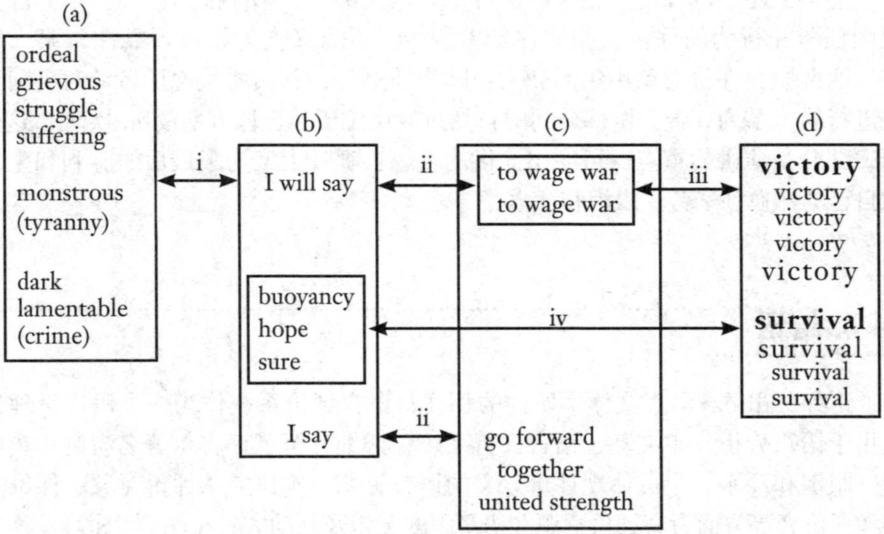

图6 鉴赏链与判断链、情感链在语篇中的互动

这两条衔接链也可用图6的（a）链与（d）链的形式表示。其中，（a）链即鉴赏链$_1$的评价对象与英国当前形势有关，主要体现消极反应性意义（-10）。（d）链即鉴赏链$_2$的评价对象是评价成分本身，与其自身经验意义有关，属于积极估价性（+12）。鉴赏链$_2$中victory重复出现5次，且所指相同；survival重复出现4次，前2次所指相同，指英帝国的生存，后面两个survival分别指英帝国所代表一切的存在与世代奋勇前进的欲望和动力的存在。此外，为突出victory和survival的重要性，说话者先巧妙运用in spite of、however等对立资源构建语篇对话背景，调节并协商由级差资源at all costs、all、long、hard引发的消极鉴赏意义，突出要赢得victory的决心；再用一个否定条件句表明victory对于survival的重要性，即只有胜利才能存在；最后又通过另一个否定条件强调英帝国的存在对于其他存在的重要性。

除这两条鉴赏链外，图6还包含由说话者情感资源构成的情感链（b）和由“我们”的行为构成的判断链（c）。（b）链各成分是语篇中说话者积极情感的体现，包括意愿性、愉悦性和安全性。除情感意义外，I will say和I say还具有宣告意义（16），突出说话者对相关立场和态度的坚定。（c）链则是说话者通过介入资源所表达观点的具体内容，即需要“我们”有所作为。图6箭头所表示的互动关系为：

i　原因（消极鉴赏意义为积极行为判断提供依据）；

ii　态度来源；

iii　目的；

iv　结果（积极估价意义带来积极情感）。

由图6人际意义衔接链之间的交互关系可知，第四段中提到的当前形势的严峻性仍是整个互动过程的中心。围绕这个中心，说话者向大家宣告为夺取最后的胜利要采取相应的行为。对胜利的向往和憧憬使说话人在演讲最后再次向大家呼吁：让我们同心协力、一道前进。

基于上述评价分析，整个演讲可分为两大部分：第一部分为一、二两段，是对组阁任务和行为的评价，整体评价由积极鉴赏意义变为积极可靠性；第二部分为三、四两段，评价对象由组阁变为英国当前形势，其实质是说话者针对英国当前局势进行的一系列宣告。两部分间的自然过渡由位于第三段开头的but实现，这也表明第二部分是演讲的重点，可突出演讲的主题：呼吁大家为了最后的胜利和生存，奉献自己的热血、辛劳、眼泪和汗水。

4. 结语

正如Halliday语言文体学所说的那样，语言评价系统作为一个语言学理论，可应用于语篇分析。本文基于语言评价系统，详细分析了丘吉尔著名演讲《热血、辛劳、眼泪和汗水》中可体现评价意义的语言资源。本研究从评价对象、评价意义范畴和评价者等方面考察评价资源在语篇中的组织及互动方式（图3—图6）。

研究发现，语篇中态度链的形成通常需要评价对象相同或一致。评价对象与话语范围有关，由同一话语范围内的评价对象所构成的经验意义衔接链可为相应人际意义衔接链的形成提供条件（图3）。介入链的形成与介入资源所涉及的态度或观点有关，以态度链的形成为前提（图4、图5）。不同范畴的级差资源可形成衔接链并引发相应的态度意义（图5）。

语篇评价资源的互动方式可包括：（一）原因关系，如消极鉴赏意义为积极行为判断提供依据；（二）过程目标，如积极行为（判断意义）与积极目标（鉴赏意义）；（三）结果关系，如积极鉴赏意义伴随积极情感意义；（四）目的关系，即行为目的；（五）来源，即态度或观点的来源；（六）引发，即旗示态度意义。其中，前四个主要是态度链间的互动方式，后两个涉及介入链、级差链与态度链间的互动。本文较多地关注语篇态度链间的互动，今后可继续深入考察态度链与介入链、级差链间的互动关系。

参考文献

Hood, Susan. 2009. Texturing Interpersonal Meanings in Academic Argument: Pulses and Prosodies of Value. In G. Forey & G. Thompson (eds.) *Text Type and Texture*. London: Equinox, 216-233.

Martin, James R. 2000. Factoring out Exchange: Types of Structure. In M. Coulthard (ed.) *Working with Dialogue*. Tubingen: Niemeyer.

Martin, James R. 2004. Sense and Sensibility: Texturing Evaluation. In J. Foley (ed.) *Language, Education and Discourse: Functional Approaches*. London: Continuum.

Martin, James R. & P. R. R. White. 2005. *The Language of Evaluation: Appraisal in English*. London: Macmillan.

Peng, X. W. 2009. Appraisal Textuality in Discourse: Case Observation from the Motivation Perspective. In G. W. Huang (ed.) *Studies in Functional Linguistics and Discourse Analysis (I)*. Beijing: Higher Education Press.

Peng, X. W. 2010. Appraisal Textuality in Discourse: A Case Observation from the "Foregrounding" Perspective. In G. W. Huang (ed.) *Studies in Functional Linguistics and Discourse Analysis (II)*. Beijing: Higher Education Press.

张德禄、刘世铸，2006，形式与意义的范畴化——兼评《评价语言：英语的评价系统》，《外语教学与研究（外国语文双月刊）》（6）：423-427。

Markedness and Its Function in Meaning Construal
— From the Perspective of Systemic-Functional Grammar

张建社

江西师范大学

1. Introduction

"The principle of markedness is a central part of structural theories of language and of the linguistic-based approaches to literature, semiotics, art, and culture that derive from these theories" (Battistella, 1990: 16). Conceived in the Prague School linguistic theories of Roman Jakobson and Nikolai Trubetzkoy, the notion of markedness attempts to make a deeper research of polar oppositions that constitute language. Originally employed to example the polarities at the level of phonology, it has gone beyond to analyze lexical, grammatical, and semantic oppositions of language in the present-day linguistic field.

Bearing a very close relationship to the Prague School, Systemic-Functional Grammar, one of the most influential linguistic theories in the twentieth century, places great emphasis on the semantic strata of language. In this paper, the combination of SFG and Markedness Theory is proposed to analyze the story, the Prince of Butterflies, written by Bruce Coville.

Bruce Coville is the extraordinarily popular author of dozens of books, including the best-selling *My Teacher Is an Alien and Jennifer Murdley's Toad*, winner of a California Young Reader's Medal. *The Prince of Butterflies*, a sometimes moving but ultimately puzzling picture book, is constructed a bit like a film drama that rolls a documentary-style addendum at the end. One afternoon, a flock of migrating monarch butterflies surrounds 11-year-old John Farrington. The green field where the flock had stopped on its path south has been bulldozed for a development. They beg John quite clearly to show them the way to a new resting place, and they transform him into a butterfly so that he can lead them there. Both the experience of flying and the privilege of saving the monarchs elate the boy. In the story's second section, John grows up and becomes an activist who helps pass legislation to preserve monarch habitats "The Butterfly Road" bill. In the end, John Farrington is surrounded by another flock of his beloved monarchs, which, for one last time, transform his aged body into a butterfly's. The shifts between fantasy and accurate details give the story sophisticated, screenplay-style impact, which gives us an invitation to treat well the nature in which we live.

2. Theoretical background

2.1 Halliday's Systemic-Functional Grammar

Language is the product of the social acts, and as a tool of communication it carries various functions. We use language to talk about our experience of the world both inside and outside our minds, to describe events and states and the participants and circumstances involved in them, and the like, which is the experiential metafunction of language. We also use language to establish and maintain appropriate social links with other people, to express our attitudes or emotions, to influence their attitudes or behavior, and so on, which is the interpersonal metafunction. Moreover, we use language to organize our messages in a way that makes them fit smoothly into the unfolding language event, and so on, which is the textual metafunction. There is the fourth metafunction, logical metafunction, which shows the logical relationships of the clause complex in language itself.

All these metafunctions are simultaneously realized in a clause on the stratum of lexicogrammar: the experiential is mainly realized by transitivity; the interpersonal by mood, and the textual by thematic structure. (Halliday, 1994/2000, 2004/2008; Eggins, 1994; Thompson, 1996/2000; Hu, 1989, 2005; Martin, 2010)

Transitivity functions to construe "who is doing what to whom when where why and how" (Eggins, 1994: 77) into six process types and to identify participants and circumstances involved in the process. These process types are material, mental, relational, behavioral, verbal and existential. Material, mental and relational are the three main types of process in the English transitivity. Material process represents experience as going on in the external world, involving physical actions such as running, throwing, scratching and so on. Opposite to it, mental process describes experience as going on in the world of consciousness and imagination, for example, thinking, imagining, linking, wanting, seeing, etc. Relational process is of classifying and identifying. Between material and mental is behavioral process that represents outer manifestations of inner workings, the acting out of processes of consciousness and physiological states; between material and relational is verbal process in which symbolic relationships are constructed in human consciousness and enacted in the form of language; and finally between relational and material is existential process which essentially express the mere existence of an entity without predicating anything else of it.

In interpersonal terms, the mood is the core of the exchange, carrying "the burden of the Subject and the Finite". The Subject "expresses the entity that the speaker wants to make responsible for the validity of the proposition being advanced in the clause," and the Finite makes the Subject "possible to negotiate about the validity of the proposition." (Thompson, 1996/2000: 45) The basic function of the Finite is to orient the listener towards the kind of validity (positive or negative) being claimed for the proposition, by relating it either to the here-and-now reality of the speech event or to the speaker's attitude.

Thematisation relates to the "structuring of the clause itself" or "the order in which elements appear in the clause" (ibid: 118). In textual meaning a clause contains two parts: Theme which is the "starting point for the message" or "the ground from which the clause is taking off" (Halliday, 1994/2000: 38) and Rheme, which is "the part in which the Theme is developed" (ibid: 37). Theme must include a constituent that plays a role in transitivity: a participant, process or circumstance. It is the "topical" Theme.

2.2 The theory of markedness

"One of the hallmarks of human language is the existence of polar oppositions among the signs of any linguistic system" (Battistella, 1990: 1). Such oppositions are manifest at any level of our language: phonologically, vocalic and consonantal, nasal and oral, etc; lexically, male and female, beauty and ugliness, truth and falsity, etc; grammatically, singular and plural, positive and negative, present and past; semantically, generality and specification, etc. Trubetzkoy believes that oppositions could be isolated or proportional, and also bilateral or multilateral. He classified them into three types: privative, equipollent, and gradual. Privative oppositions are those between the presence and absence of a feature (i.e. between A and not A); equipollent oppositions are defined as ones in which the terms of a polarity assert the presence of contrary features rather than the presence or absence of a single feature. Gradual oppositions are referred to as ones in which opposed terms contain various degrees of the same property, e.g. the opposition between "cold" and "hot". Trubetzkoy continues that markedness only applies to oppositions whose logical character is privative. However, Jakobson argues that all oppositions are binary and privative, and that even gradual and equipollent oppositions can be analyzed into a fundamental binarism. Thus here we take privative oppositions as the starting point in our later analysis.

In his first grammatical paper, "Structure of the Russian Verb", Jakobson began his study of markedness by means of the analysis of polar oppositions into underlying binary relations. In the paper "The Concept of Mark" (with Krystyna Pomorska) Jakobson argues that "on the phonological level, markedness is determined by distinctive features that are either simultaneously or temporally contiguous; on the grammatical level, the distinction between marked and unmarked terms lies in the area of the general meaning of each of the juxtaposed forms." (Jakobson, 1995: 134-140) Later extending this into semantics, he observes that "every single constituent of any linguistic system is built on an opposition of two logical contradictories: the presence of an attribute (markedness) in contraposition to its absence (unmarkedness)" (Jakobson, 1972: 76; see Battistella, 1990: 16).

Simply put, at the semantic level of language, markedness is a relation between a very specific linguistic sign (the marked term) and a very general sign (the unmarked term). In this sense, marked and unmarked elements are not strictly opposite. Of course, semantic components are usually realized by linguistic lexicogrammar. In languages containing an opposition between the past tense and the present tense, the former is always marked while the latter unmarked. The past tense signals past time in which narrated event precedes the speech event in time whereas the present tense envelops past time, present time and future time, designating a narrated event taking place at the same time as the speech event, a constant action unlimited in time, and an act preceding the speech event. However, markedness relations are not fixed, but contingent and contextually determined. For example, we normally typewrite roman type, and then italics are marked. But in a text printed in italics, a word in roman type stands out as marked.

Battistella (1990: 65-67) puts forward several criteria to help us to diagnose markedness values in a language. The first criterion is that the unmarked term has a broader, subsuming meaning. The second one is that the unmarked category frequently serves as the prototype, or best example of an opposition. Third is that the unmarked is in broader distribution or use. A fourth criterion is that the unmarked sometimes shows a large number of subcategorial distinctions. The fifth is that the unmarked semantic category is often signaled by formal simplicity. The last one is cross-linguistic optimality, i.e. the unmarked term is probably universal cross-linguistically. All these criteria provide a very powerful tool to determine the evaluation of opposition. However, the point should be kept in the mind that markedness depends on context, and that what is marked in one context may be unmarked in another.

2.3 Integration of markedness and SFG

SFG is a sociologically oriented functional linguistic approach, providing an extremely powerful means to analyze the text objectively. Markedness is on the one hand universal across all languages, and on the other hand particular within one language. It also plays a very important role in text construction by making some elements salient or prominent. Hence in the next section we will combine these two into the analysis of the narrative text, *The Prince of Butterflies*.

3. Text analysis

3.1 Markedness and transitivity analysis[1]

Transitivity is the overall grammatical resource for construing our experience of goings-on in terms of configurations of a process, participants and circumstances. "Such configurations are determined by two major systems, those of PROCESS TYPE and CIRCUMSTANTIATION" (Martin, 2010: 100).

3.1.1 Process Type

From Table 1 below[2], there are 196 clauses in total[3], of which 184 have verbs. In the story, most of the clauses are constructed into Material process, which ranks the first, accounting for 57.07%. Mental and Relational processes take 16.85% and 15.76% respectively. Behavioural accounts for 2.72%, verbal 6.52% and existential only 1.08%.

Table 1 Process type realized in the text

Process / Statistics	184 verbal clauses with 12 verbless ones					
	Material	Mental	Relational	Behavioural	Verbal	Existential
Number	105	31	29	5	12	2
Percentage	57.07	16.85	15.76	2.72	6.52	1.08

According to Halliday (1994/2000: 107), Material, mental and relational are the three main types of process in the English transitivity system. Material construes "what we experience as going on 'out there', in the world around us" whereas mental construes "what we experience as going on inside ourselves, in the world of consciousness and imagination" (Halliday, 1994/2000: 106). Relational clauses are constructed to construe "attribution and identification" (Martin, 2010: 104). All these process types are closely employed to function in different text types. In the descriptive

1 In this paper ergative analysis is not taken into account.

2 All the tables are created based on the author's analysis.

3 Embedded clauses functioning postmodifiers are left out of the author's analysis.

text, relational plays a larger role while material does function very importantly in the narrative text (Li, 2005: 16-17). Relational clauses attempt to construe a static quality or attribute pertaining to the participants, which is in line with the purpose of the descriptive text to provide the reader with some information of the entity. Material clauses take a high percentage of occurrences in the narrative text to narrate what happens in the physical world. However, no matter what kind of text, all these major processes, along with three minor types: behavioural, verbal and existential, combine to create a resourceful meaningful text.

The story is presented in two sections; the first one describes the disappearing habitat of monarch butterflies and the assistance given to them by John Farrington from his 11th birthday to his age of 17, and the latter recounts his contribution to make the "The Butterfly Road" bill passed. In this narrative text, material clauses are used to describe what goes on around John and what he does to the monarch butterflies. This is the main plot of the story. Since the material process type takes the largest share in narrating stories, it is the unmarked type in story narration. Other process types are marked. It is with certainty that the unmarked clauses convey basic information of doings and happenings whereas the marked ones make something salient.

Mental process helps to describe surprise, excitement, and sometimes contradictory emotions flowing in John's mind; relational clauses here are supplementary to attribute to John some qualities which are not prototypical for such a small boy, e.g. "This sitting still was not easy for John." and on describing butterflies' beauty, e.g. "It was the most beautiful thing he had ever seen." "Delicate creatures, fragile and... frightened."

It is very interesting that verbal clauses are mainly used to construe the dialogues between the butterflies and John. The first dialogue happened when the butterflies surrounded John asking for his help: they whispered, "We've lost the path, lost our home. Please help us!" In this way the information is conveyed that the butterfly habitat is disappearing, and that if we do not do something, they will be extinct. John responded that he remembered there was still a meadow left, and promised to lead them to go there. Then something magical happened: John was converted into a beautiful butterfly and could fly. Later he asked to be turned back for fear that his parents would miss him, but after he was turned back, he very often remembered the feeling to be a butterfly. Behavioural clauses are scattered in the text: when he found a huge flock of butterflies he "swallowed nervously"; when he told the butterflies his recalling a meadow, they "rustled with excitement and relief"; when he was a butterfly, he was "luxuriating in the feel of the sun on his wings". These clauses stand out, carrying the message that human and nature should live in harmony. The whole text has only two existential clauses. Both have "green" as the Existent; one is the indicative, telling us that "once there was so much green"; the other the interrogative, questioning where the green went. These two clauses indicate that if we do not protect the environment around us, we will find no green, no clear water, no fresh air and the like.

3.1.2 Circumstantiation

Circumstantiation is "the resource for 'augmenting' the configuration of 'process + participants' by means of elements that are less directly involved in the process, circumstances" (Martin, 2010: 101). It can be classified into Extent, Location, Manner, Cause, Accompaniment, Contingency, Matter, Role and Angle.

Circumstances also play a very important role in the construal of the text by essentially encoding the background against which the process takes place. In this text, there are so many circumstantial elements.

In the narrative, we have to construe the goings-on in the real world and to record the thoughts in the mental world. When we do that, we have to attach a great number of circumstantial backgrounds: where, when, how, and why something happened. In this text, Location that indicates place and time accounts for the largest part, 54.63% (See Table 2 below). Thus, it is the unmarked circumstantial element; Extent, Manner and Cause are less unmarked. Others are marked. The unmarked element lays down the foundation of the whole text, locating place, time, manner, cause, while the marked helps to put something into the prominent position.

Table 2 Circumstances in the text

Circ.	There are 119 circumstantial elements without a Matter one.							
	Extent	Location	Manner	Cause	Contingency	Accompaniment	Role	Angle
Number	11	65	23	14	2	2	1	1
Percentage	9.24	54.63	19.33	11.76	1.68	1.68	0.84	0.84

There are only two Contingency elements: one is at the very beginning of the text, "in this case" and the other at the almost end, "whatever the reason". These two wordings draw our attention to what is happening. "In this case" in the clause "But in this case he was willing to make an exception" indicates that as a eleven-year-old boy John was very rambunctious by nature, preferring running and shouting, but when he saw such a beautiful flock of monarch butterflies even he would like to stay motionless not to disturb the attractive pattern. Although circumstances are typically realized by adverbial groups or prepositional phrases, the verbless clause "whatever the reason" serves as the contingency element to make prominent the fact that the butterflies never came back to John when he turned seventeen. Because of this, he felt most painful and wept in his bed at night. Only two Accompaniment elements are found as comitative. "With the butterflies" John, turned into one of them, spent the most brilliant morning in his life, "crawling along slender green stems, unrolling his long tube of a tongue to sip sweet nectar, luxuriating in the feel of the sun on his wings". With the butterflies he could do all such butterfly things. When he realized that he needed to be converted back to a boy, he asked them to do it. However the butterflies whispered, "Stay with us" to invite him to continue all the wonderful things. There is one Role element and one Angle element. The role element "to a caterpillar" helps to focus John's shift back to human from the butterfly; the Angle element helps to emphasize the fact that although John was thrown out of the program of collecting butterflies "he continued to work on his own", i.e. used his own way to protect the butterfly.

3.2 Markedness and mood analysis[4]

Mood is "the key interpersonal system of the clause, and is the grammatical resource for realizing an interactive move in dialogue" (Martin, 2010: 56). In an interactive event involving speaker, or writer, and audience, there are four primary speech roles: giving information, demanding information, giving goods-&-services and demanding goods-&-services, which correspond respectively to four speech functions: statement, question, offer and command. Congruently, statements are realized by declarative clauses, questions by interrogative clauses, and commands by imperative clauses. Offers are "not associated with a specific mood choice though they are strongly with modality" (Thompson, 1996/2000: 40) (See Table 3).

Table 3 Speech function choices and mood realizations

(a combined one; Halliday, 1994/2000: 69; Martin, 2010: 57)

Commodity exchanged / Role in exchange	(a) goods-&-services	(b) information
(i) giving	'offer' ↘ (various)	'statement' ↘ 'declarative' *The spy will* come in.
(ii) demanding	'command' ↘ 'imperative' *Come in!*	'question' ↘ 'interrogative' 'wh-' *Who will* come in? 'yes/no' *Will the spy* come in?

4 Mood is the major part to realize the interpersonal metafunction, and then modality is left out in this paper.

In the narrative text, the function of statement is unmarked, narrating the plot of the story of the little boy and the butterflies, and other functions are marked, letting some turning points stand out. From Table 4, the clauses with Mood structure accounts for 81.63%, while the ones with no Mood takes 18.37%. For the clauses with Mood structure, there are 66.33% clauses of complete Mood structure in the declarative form, 5.61% clauses of complete Mood structure in the interrogative form, and 9.69% elliptical clauses with 4.59% having only Subject and 5.10% having only Finite. All the elliptical clauses with part of Mood are in the declarative form. For the clauses without Mood, 2.04% are in the imperative form, and others are not. Those that are not in the imperative form are basically in the elliptical declarative form, only 3 clauses in the interrogative.

Table 4 Speech functions realized in the text (196 clauses in total)

Mood / Statistics	Mood structure				No mood	
	Complete		Elliptical		Imperative	others
	statement	question	only Subject	only Finite		
Number	130	11	9	10	4	32
Percentage	66.33	5.61	4.59	5.10	2.04	16.33
Total	81.63				18.37	

There are 11 complete interrogative clauses. The first one, "where does it go", implies that the green place the butterflies rested had gone, and the next two "what shall we do" and "where can we go now" bring us into the butterfly position in which without habitat they will die. Then John thought to himself in the following three questions "what can I do? Is there another green place? Somewhere not too far away[5]?" that he must do something to help those butterflies. After he experienced as a butterfly and led them to the green, he realized that he had to turn back to be a human, thus asking, "Can you turn me back?" When he was seventeen, the flock stopped coming, and then he suffered and wondered why. Four imperatives are uttered by the butterflies who asked John to help them out and later invited him to join them. In other clauses with no Mood, two extremely stand out. The clause "And then..." serves as a transitive point to remind the reader of the attention shift from John's enjoying the beauty of the butterfly pattern to the dialogue that will happen between the boy and the butterflies. The other "How?" serving as a paragraph implies that John knew that it was not possible for him to lead those butterflies to the place simple because he couldn't fly. However, after that, something unusual happened that they turned him into a very beautiful butterfly with orange and back wings.

5 This is not in the complete interrogative form, but it occurs in John's mind with the preceding two, so it is analyzed here.

3.3 Markedness and thematic analysis[6]

Theme is "concerned with the organization of information within individual clauses and, through this, with the organization of the larger text". (Martin, 2010: 21) According to Halliday (1994: 43-44; 2004: 73-4), the unmarked Theme of a declarative clause is conflated with Subject; the item most often functioning as unmarked Theme is the first person pronoun I; then the other personal pronouns you, we, he, she, it, they; next the impersonal pronouns it and there; and next nominal groups and nominalizations. A Theme that is any experiential element preceding Subject is marked in the declarative clause. In a WH-interrogative the unmarked Theme is constituted solely by the WH-element, i.e. the group or phrase in which the WH-word occurs and in a yes/no interrogative the unmarked Theme includes two parts in the order of "Finite + Subject". In imperatives with you implicit, positively, the Predicator is the unmarked Theme and, negatively, "don't + Predicator" is the unmarked Theme; in imperative beginning with "let's", "let's" or "don't let's" is clearly the unmarked Theme. In exclamatives, the unmarked Theme is any nominal group or adverbial group functioning as exclamatives (WH-) element. Some other element coming first constitutes a marked Theme, which "either expresses some kind of setting for the clause or expresses a feature of contrast." (Halliday, 1994: 45-8; Halliday, 2004: 75-8)

Table 5 Thematic realizations in the text

Theme / Statistics	Unmarked (178; 90.82%)						Marked (18; 9.18%)	
	Present (138; 70.41%)			Elliptical (40; 20.41%)			Time	Other
	John	Butterfly	Other	John	Butterfly	Other		
Number	68	41	29	26	8	6	13	5
Percentage	34.69	20.92	14.80	13.27	4.08	3.06	6.63	2.55

From the analysis presented in Table 5, we conclude that up to 90.82% Themes are unmarked, of which 70.41% are manifest in the text and 20.41% are elliptical or understood. In addition, 47.96% unmarked Theme choices are realized by the nominal group with "John" or something including him, and 25% unmarked Themes are "the butterfly/ butterflies" or something the like. Marked theme choice only account for 9.18%.

The unmarked Theme choices keep shifting between "John" and "butterflies" (these two taking 72.96% of the total Themes), unfolding the story of the butterflies' losing their habitat and being forced into difficulties, and of John's helping them find

6 In this part, information structure is not included.

a new meadow and finally urging the Congress to pass "The Butterfly Road" bill. However, when the Theme is marked, it "gains a greater textual prominence". (Martin, 2010: 24). It is the marked Theme 'two days after John Farrington's eleventh birthday' that begins the story. It indicates the time when something unusual happened. The next marked Theme is "in this case" indicating that sitting still was very difficult by he made it. When the text goes on, we can find there is a pair of sentences beginning with marked Themes "under it" and "above it". These two form a rather strong contrast, presenting the butterflies' appeal to the new meadow. The marked Theme "twice more" occur twice successively, putting into prominence the times John help those butterflies. It implies that the butterflies lost their living place two more times, and that it is John who led them to safety. By the marked Theme "thirty years later" is meant that John eventually did a great favor to the butterfly (also to himself and our whole human beings) after so many years' continuous effort. At the end of the story, when John was left alone "a few minutes after the nurse left", he was turned into a butterfly and flew away with a cloud of butterflies of his kind.

4. Conclusion

Markedness makes itself manifest everything at any level of language: phonological, lexical, grammatical, and semantic. Language performs simultaneously three metafunctions: ideational, interpersonal and textual, which is realized respectively in a clause on the stratum of lexicogrammar: Transitivity, Mood and Theme. Thus, semantically, markedness happens along with these grammatical systems. From the analysis above, experientially any of three major process types are unmarked respectively by taking the large share in different text types. For example, in the narrative text, the material process is construed in very high proportion, describing what happens in the physical world around us, and other processes are marked to put what they construe prominent. Interpersonally, any of four primary speech functions function very well in different texts; in the narrative, in order to offer the information of the story plot, the unmarked statement function is employed that is realized in the declarative form. Others are marked with the question function eliciting the information in the question-answer sequence, and with the command function construed as the imperative to persuade or order someone to do something. Textually, the unmarked Theme and marked one are distinctive. By maintaining the same unmarked Theme, the text can be unfolded in a successful succession; by selecting marked Theme, we can signal or change "the framework for the interpretation of the following clause (or clauses)" (Thompson, 1996: 141).

In this paper, there are still a lot of things left out of our analysis. First, the logical metafunction is not taken into account. Secondly, when we analyze the experiential metafunction, we still leave ergative interpretation aside. Thirdly, modality in the interpersonal system is untouched, which does not mean that it is not important. Fourthly, the information structure is not included here mostly because it is closely associated with tonic group.

However, in a word, markedness really plays a very important role in meaning construal of the text in a thoroughly convincible way.

References

Andrews, E. 1990. *Markedness Theory: The Union of Asymmetry and Semiosis in Language*. Durham & London: Duke University Press.

Battistella, E. L. 1990. *Markedness: The Evaluative Superstructure of Language*. New York: State University of New York Press.

Coville, B. 2002. *The Prince of Butterflies*. Orlando: Voyager Books.

Eggins, S. 1994. *An Introduction to Systemic Functional Linguistics*. London: Pinter.

Halliday, M. A. K. 1978/2001. *Language as Social Semiotic: The Social Interpretation of Language and Meaning*. London: Arnold/ Beijing: Foreign Language Teaching and Research Press.

Halliday, M. A. K. 1994/2000. *An Introduction to Functional Grammar* (2nd edition). London: Arnold / Beijing: Foreign Language Teaching and Research Press.

Halliday, M. A. K. 2004/2008. *An Introduction to Functional Grammar* (3rd edition). London: Arnold / Beijing: Foreign Language Teaching and Research Press.

Jakobson, R. 1995. The Concept of Mark. In L. R. Waugh & M. Monville-Burston (eds.) *On Language*. Cambridge, Massachusetts: Harvard University Press.

Martin, J. R, C. M. M. C. Matthiessen & C. Painter. 2010. *Deploying Functional Grammar*. Beijing: The Commercial Press.

Martin, J. R. 2010. *SFL Theory* (Volume 1 in the Collected Works of J. R. Martin). Z.H. Wang (ed.). Shanghai: Shanghai Jiaotong University Press.

Thompson, G. 1996/2000. *Introducing Functional Grammar*. London: Arnold/ Beijing: Foreign Language Teaching and Research Press.

胡壮麟，2000,《功能主义纵横谈》。北京：外语教学与研究出版社。

胡壮麟、朱永生、张德禄，1989,《系统功能语法概论》。长沙：湖南教育出版社。

胡壮麟、朱永生、张德禄、李战子，2005,《系统功能语言学概论》。北京：北京大学出版社。

李国庆，2005, 试论及物性系统结构和语篇体裁，《外语教学》(6): 16-17。

沈家煊, 1997, 类型学中的标记模式,《外语教学与研究》(1): 1-10。
徐盛桓, 1982, 主位和述位,《外语教学与研究》(1): 1-9。
徐盛桓, 1985, 再论主位和述位,《外语教学与研究》(1): 19-25。
朱永生, 2001,《系统功能语言学多维思考》。上海: 上海外语教育出版社。